The Hamwic Glass

The Hamwic Glass

by J R Hunter and M P Heyworth

with contributions by
W Fletcher, J Henderson, D C W Sanderson,
S E Warren and D Whithorn

CBA Research Report 116
Council for British Archaeology

1998

Published 1998 by the Council for British Archaeology
Bowes Morrell House, 111 Walmgate, York YO1 9WA

British Library Cataloguing in Publication Data
A catalogue for this book is available from the British Library

ISSN 0141 7819

ISBN 1 872414 87 7

Typeset from authors' disks by Calderdale Typesetting Limited, Ripponden, West Yorkshire

Printed by Pennine Printing Services Limited, Ripponden, West Yorkshire

Front: Fragment of vessel glass with red streaking and applied reticella rod containing opaque yellow spirals
Back: Collection of coloured glass fragments

Contents

List of plates

List of figures

List of tables

Authors

Professor J R Hunter
Dept of Ancient History & Archaeology
University of Birmingham
Edgbaston
Birmingham
B15 2TT

Dr M P Heyworth
c/o Council for British Archaeology
Bowes Morrell House
111 Walmgate
York
YO1 9WA

Summary

This report deals with over 1,700 fragments of 8th and 9th century AD glass recovered from excavations at Hamwic (Saxon Southampton) undertaken since 1946. The corpus contains fragments of known vessel types (32%), decorated pieces which cannot be assigned to vessel types (19%) and non-diagnostic fragments which offer little discussive potential (45%). Other items (4%) include window fragments, beads, wasters and non-durable material. Known forms consist mostly of types belonging to the palm cup/funnel beaker vessel series and these are classified typologically according to rims. A small number of tall beakers, small jars and flasks are also represented.

In view of the fragmentary nature of the material vessel quantification analysis, a method new to glass studies, was introduced into the study. Although a number of experimental difficulties were encountered in comparing various methods of approach, the overall results suggest interesting anomalies in the corpus as a whole. Investigation was also extended to decorative techniques, in particular to colouring/decolouring properties. Spectrophotometry has been used in an attempt to understand more clearly the compositional distinction between the light blue and light green glasses which constitute approximately 90% of the total assemblage. Other analytical investigation, using x-ray fluorescence, neutron activation and inductively coupled plasma spectrometry techniques, was applied to selected samples from both Hamwic and other relevant European sites, including nearby Winchester. The overview suggests compositional distinctions indicative of raw material variation, with subsequent inferences for production location.

The interpretation of the material as a whole takes into account the observations derived from these investigations and suggests that the Hamwic glass results from a number of activities. Some fragments appear to represent cullet, probably for bead-making, others may represent complete vessels used within the town; a part of the material, represented by decorated or thick items, is thought to have been the residue from a selection process which required lightly-tinted glass as cullet for a secondary (but unlocated) glassworking process in the immediate vicinity.

Sommaire

Ce rapport traite de plus de 1700 fragments de verre du 8ème et du 9ème siècle récupérés au cours des fouilles de Hamwic (le Southampton saxon) entreprises depuis 1946. Le corpus contient des fragments de types de contenants connus (32%), de morceaux décorés qui ne peuvent pas être attribués à des types de contenants et de fragments non diagnostiques au sujet desquels on ne peut pas dire grand chose (45%). Parmi les autres articles se trouvent des fragments de fenêtre, des perles, des déchets de fabrication et du matériel non durable. Les formes connues sont principalement celles des types faisant partie de la série de contenants englobant les coupelles et les gobelets coniques, et elles sont classées par type selon leurs bords. Est également représenté un petit nombre de hauts gobelets, de petites jarres et de flacons.

Compte tenu de la nature fragmentaire du matériel, une analyse quantitative des contenants, une nouvelle méthode pour les études portant sur le verre, fut introduite dans l'étude. Bien que la comparaison de diverses façons de s'y prendre ait donné lieu à un certain nombre de difficultés expérimentales, les résultats ont généralement suggéré d'intéressantes anomalies dans le corpus dans son ensemble. L'enquête porta également sur les techniques décoratives, en particulier au niveau des propriétés de coloration/décoloration. La spectrophotométrie a été utilisée afin d'essayer de mieux comprendre la différence constitutionnelle entre le verre bleu clair et le verre vert clair qui représentent environ 90% de tout l'assemblage. D'autres enquêtes analytiques, utilisant les techniques d'analyse par la fluorescence aux rayons X, d'analyse par activation des neutrons et de spectrométrie au plasma par couplage inductif, furent employées pour sélectionner des échantillons en provenance et de Hamwic et d'autres sites européens pertinents, y compris celui de Winchester, à proximité. La vue d'ensemble suggère des différences constitutionnelles indiquant des variations de matières premières et on en tire par conséquent certaines conclusions concernant le site de production.

L'interprétation du matériel dans son ensemble prend en compte les observations tirées de ces enquêtes et suggère que le verre de Hamwic est le résultat de plusieurs activités. Certains fragments semblent représenter du calcin, probablement pour la fabrication de perles, d'autres peuvent représenter des contenants entiers utilisés dans la ville ; on pense qu'une partie du matériel, représentée par des articles épais ou décorés, est le résidu d'un processus de sélection qui nécessitait du verre de couleur claire comme calcin pour un processus de fabrication du verre secondaire à proximité (dont on ne connaît pas le site).

Übersicht

Dieser Bericht befaßt sich mit über 1700 Dieser Bericht befaßt sich mit über 1700 Glasfragmenten aus dem 8. und 9. Jahrhundert, die seit 1946 bei Ausgrabungen in Hamwick (sächsisches Southampton) entdeckt wurden. 32% des Korpus sind Fragmente bekannter Gefäßtypen, 19% sind verzierte Glasstücke, die man nicht in Gefäßtypen einteilen kann und 45% der Glasstücke sind nicht zu diagnostizieren und würden nur wenig Potential für eine Diskussion darstellen. 4% anderer Stücke sind Fensterglasfragmente, Glasperlen, Weißblech und nichtdauerhaftes Material. Die Mehrzahl der bakannten Formen gehören zu den Palmenschalen/Trichter - Bechern und sind typologisch nach Glasrändern eingeordnet. Eine kleine Anzahl von großen Bechern, kleinen Gläsern und Flaschen sind auch darin enthalten.

Da die Gefäßmaterialien nur in Glasstücken bestehen, ist die Analyse der Quantifizierung schwierig. Deshalb hat man ein neues Verfahren bei Glasuntersuchungen eingeführt. Obwohl es anfangs eine Anzahl von Experimentalschwierigkeiten bei dem Vergleich mit verschiedenen Verfahren gab, lassen die Resultate im allgemeinen annehmen, daß die Anomalien der Sammlung im großen und ganzen interessant sind. Diese neue Art von Untersuchung wurde auch bei den Verzierverfahren angewendet, besonders an Färbungs - und Entfärbungseigenschaften. Die Spektrophotometrie wurde eingesetzt in einem Versuch den Unterschied zur Zusammensetzung zwischen den hellblauen und dunkelgrünen Gläsern, die zu 80% in der Gesamtassemblage auftreten, besser zu verstehen Andere Untersuchungen, wie Röntgenfluoreszenz-, Neutronenaktivierung -, zusammen mit Induktionsplasmaspektrometrie - Verfahren wurden an ausgewählten Materialien in Hamwic und anderen relevanten Geländen in Europa angewendet. Dazu gehört auch das in der Nähe liegende Winchester. Der Überblick läßt darauf schließen, daß es Unterschiede zwischen der Zusammensetzung verschiedenen Rohmaterials gab, mit der Schlußfolgerung, daß es auch verschiedene Herstellungsorte gegeben haben mußte.

Die Interpretation des Materials im ganzen berechnet auch die Beobachtungen dieser Untersuchungen und läßt darauf schließen, daß die in Hamwic gefundenen Glasgegenstände auf eine Anzahl von Aktivitäten hinweisen. Einige Fragmente dürften Glasbrüche sein, die in der Herstellung von Glasperlen verwendet wurden, andere wiederum könnten eine Reihe von Glasgefäßen dargestellt haben, die in der Stadt gebraucht wurden. Andere Materialfragmente waren verziert oder dick und scheinen Überreste eines Selektivverfahrens gewesen zu sein, wozu man leichtgefärbte Glasbrüche für eine zweite Glasverarbeitung in der unmittelbaren Umgebung, dessen Ort aber unbekannt ist, benötigte.

1. The Background

Previous excavations at Melbourne Street, Southampton, have already highlighted the potential contribution of Middle Saxon Hamwic to early glass studies (Hunter 1980). This additional and larger corpus of material (1,735 fragments compared with *c* 100 fragments from Melbourne Street), recovered from excavations variously undertaken since 1946, now serves to extend a growing awareness of glass forms, techniques, and vessel availability in the Middle Saxon period in both England and the continent.

Chronologically, the corpus pertains to a critical phase in English glass history when the furnished burials of the pagan era were no longer practised, and for which the historical and archaeological evidence of production is especially perplexing. The Christian period immediately following the 7th century has hitherto yielded only a relatively small quantity of material (for example Harden 1978, 7–10), although new material is now emerging from settlement excavations, particularly within modern urban centres, for example Ipswich (Evison forthcoming) and Fishergate, York (Hunter and Jackson 1993). Other useful assemblages derive from proto-industrial activity in both pagan and early Christian times (for example Alcock 1963, 53; Hunter 1982) and are characteristic of sites within the Atlantic region where traditional contact with continental Gaul is now well attested. The material here is normally interpreted as evidence of bead-making resulting from trade in cullet. In both settlement and proto-industrial contexts the glasses are characteristically fragmentary and incomplete.

Only outside Britain, and particularly in Scandinavia, where Christianity was initially less successful in taking root, can complete vessel forms still be identified from burial contexts of the 8th and 9th centuries. These provide a backbone typology, but one heavily dependent on individual cemeteries, notably that at Birka, Sweden (Arbman 1943), a site with strong mercantile connections. This typology has been generally supported by findings from more recent excavations, including those from trading or proto-industrial sites such as Helgö (Lundström 1981), Kaupang (Hougen 1969) or Dorestad (Isings 1980). The necessary comparison between English and Scandinavian material has tended to assume that vessel seriations of the period were common to most parts of north-western Europe and has thus presupposed a common origin for all the material. The interpretation of the Melbourne Street material has only partially supported this assumption; certain visual typological differences were apparent between the English and Scandinavian sets (Hunter 1980, 71) and these were subsequently emphasised by analytical investigation (Sanderson and Hunter 1982).

Although contemporary glass manufacturing sites have been interpreted within eastern Europe (for example Olczak 1971), few post-Roman production centres have been identified further west, with examples at Torcello (Tabacynska 1965), Cordel (Evison 1990), Dunmisk (Henderson 1988) and possibly at San Vincenzo (Moreland 1985) perhaps being most noteworthy. A number of other sites have tended to yield evidence which confuses **glassmaking** (the primary process) with **glassworking** (a secondary process), particularly in instances where Roman tesserae or Roman vessel fragments appear as part of the assemblage; these have caused a number of difficulties of interpretation. Not least of these has been at Coppergate, York where fragments from Roman glassmaking appear to have been re-used in the context of a 9th century furnace (Bayley 1987; Jackson *et al* 1991). In England, apart from a tantalising published reference to possible furnace remains at Glastonbury, Somerset (Radford 1958, 167) for which the more informative primary archive data is now being examined (Bayley 1991), and a furnace possibly used for glass melting recently excavated at Barking Abbey, east London (Heyworth 1992), evidence for manufacturing centres has been interpreted from the distribution characteristics of specific vessel forms. Evison (1982), for example, has suggested differing production centres for certain styles of claw beaker, and more work by Näsman (1986, 81–5) has postulated a British manufacturing origin for several forms found in Scandinavia. Analytical work by Hunter and Sanderson (1982) has also demonstrated the probability of diverse manufacture for the Snartemo/Kempston vessel types; the same idea of diversity has since been suggested by the compositional analysis of a small group of glasses from Borg, Norway (Henderson and Holand, 1992). The overview now suggests that glass production may have been more widespread than had been originally appreciated and has prompted more rigid definitions and criteria by which process-related glass remains should be judged (Lundström 1981, 16–26).

The backcloth is one which, in England, also sees the introduction of short-term ecclesiastical glazing taking place in the late 7th and 8th centuries AD. With the possible exception of Barking Abbey (Heyworth 1992), none of the excavated centres where glazing occurred such as Jarrow and Monkwearmouth (Cramp 1970; 1975), or Repton, St Wystan (M Biddle pers comm) has so far yielded furnace remains, one possibility being that ready-made glass was brought to the site for cutting.

Recent analysis of contemporary window material from Whithorn has so far been unable to clarify the situation (Hold 1991), although the site also yielded tesserae. According to Bede (HA, 5), the glazing at Jarrow and Monkwearmouth was carried out by imported continental craftsmen – a fact largely at odds with the notion of a more widely spread production pattern. More significant perhaps are the Winchester sites where glazing may have been carried out continually from the 7th or 8th centuries through to the Middle Ages (Biddle and Hunter 1990), and where 'permanent', controlled furnace sites, as yet unlocated, might be expected. However, a pit was recently excavated at the Brooks site in Winchester containing a large collection of early medieval glass, predominantly window glass, presumably brought together for recycling in a local glassworking operation (Heyworth 1992). In this respect the geographical proximity of Winchester to Hamwic is of particular relevance.

Above all else, the research carried out over recent years has begun to indicate that glass in this period was a much more common artefact than had originally been thought. However, its fragmentary state requires a new approach to information recovery and the archaeologist can no longer rely on standard reference sets of complete forms. During the last twenty years medieval archaeology has gradually moved away from an emphasis on artefact form and design towards more conceptual approaches to society as a whole within which artefacts, technologies and distribution systems can be better interpreted; (noteworthy early examples include Hinton 1983 and Hodges 1982). Such changes have also been evident in glass-production studies, for example by Callmer (1982). It can be no coincidence that this occurred in tandem with a discernable shift of excavation emphasis from burial to settlement contexts, notably to those of major urban centres to which both Ipswich (Wade 1988) and *Quentovic* (Hill *et al* 1990) are important recent additions. Before this evolution of the discipline glass studies had reached a point of virtual *impasse*, partly brought about by the difficulties of applying modern systematic approaches to burial material derived by the methodologies of the 19th and early 20th centuries. Another factor is also relevant, namely the scholarship of the late Dr Donald Harden whose fundamental classification of pagan typologies and chronology (1956), despite minor updating (1978), has required little revision.

Glass from settlement sites poses new problems of interpretation, one aspect worthy of preliminary mention being the assumption that individual vessel fragments (particularly on known trading sites) represent original complete forms at the place of excavation. Broken glass had many uses, not only for working into beads, best illustrated at Ribe,

Denmark (Näsman 1979; Jensen 1991) and more recently at Åhus, Sweden (U Näsman pers comm), but also in the manufacture and repair of jewellery (for example Bimson 1978; review by Evison 1983, 8–9) and there is much evidence to suggest that cullet was a marketable commodity. Although Hamwic's trading status and range of contacts were such that complete items could have been imported, it is equally likely that items which were already broken could also have been introduced.

The Middle-Saxon dating of the Hamwic material provides an enviable opportunity to apply current methods of investigation to items recovered by modern excavation techniques. The text below commences with a general typological overview of the material recovered, followed by a series of complementary approaches including vessel quantification analysis (a method innovative to glass studies), the investigation of colouring phenomena and compositional analysis, and with a concluding section which examines the implications of the archaeological context and the significance of the assemblage. Sites mentioned in the text are shown in Figure 1.

The work has been carried out at the University of Bradford and the authors are grateful to Wendy Fletcher, Julian Henderson, David Sanderson, Stanley Warren and David Whithorn whose various contributions lie absorbed within the following discussion. Leo Biek, Justine Bayley and Vera Evison also provided valuable comment during the preparation of the text. Martin Biddle kindly made available the Winchester and Repton material for study. The writers are grateful to Jean Brown for the colour photography. Part of the analytical investigation was funded by the Science and Engineering Research Council.

Authors' note

Research for this project was carried out by the authors from 1983, the final text being submitted in 1986. At that time the Hamwic material represented one of the few glass assemblages of the period in Europe. It still remains by far the largest, and one of the most important, but in the lengthy period of time caused by publication delay much other material has been recovered from excavations. Wherever possible these new findings have been taken into account and the text has been heavily amended as a result. Final textual revisions were made in 1995, but rather than include extensive discussion that these new findings ideally necessitate, the authors have found it preferable to present the material to colleagues without unnecessary further delay. The authors would like to express their regret and apologies that such an important corpus of material has taken so long to appear in print.

Figure 1   Location of sites mentioned in the text

2. The Material

A total of 1,735 find units were recorded (excluding a small number of post-medieval contaminants) from 32 sites excavated since 1946 (Fig 2). Six of these sites (SOUs 23, 24, 26, 30, 31, and 169) represent the area known as *Six Dials* and together account for approximately 54% of the material. One of these sites, SOU 169, yielded the largest number of sherds from any one site, amounting to *c* 27% of the entire assemblage.

For ease of discussion the items are classified into a series of broadly based groups, the general distribution of which is shown on Table 1 in relation to the individual sites of recovery. These groups contain fragments of known or inferred vessel type (32%), fragments of non-diagnostic vessel type but exhibiting specific decorative or technical qualities (19%) and fragments denoted as non-diagnostic offering minimal discussive potential (45%). The remaining 4% comprises window fragments, beads, wasters or working material and non-durable pieces. This grouping therefore takes vessel **type** as a primary classification factor; general representations of these types are illustrated in Fig 3. Decoration is taken as a secondary element for discussion, and material attributes (ie non-durable glass) as the final factor. A number of other approaches would have been possible, but it was felt that this method most satisfactorily took into account the character of the material and enabled it to be discussed within the context of other contemporary vessels and assemblages.

The known vessel types consist predominantly of palm cups and funnel beakers which have been argued previously to belong to a common seriation (Ypey 1963) supported by earlier finds from Melbourne Street (Hunter 1980, 68–70). The distribution of complete palm cups in late pagan England has been documented by Harden (1956, 164–5) and comparable forms are well attested in contemporary Scandinavian contexts, for example at Vendel (Stolpe and Arne 1927, pl VII, 6). A reference collection for funnel beakers is best provided from the Birka gravefield, and the increased attention given to settlement excavation such as at Helgö, Sweden (Holmqvist 1964, 256-7) and at Dorestad, Holland (Isings 1980) has now presented additional comparable material, albeit in fragmentary form. The most recent compilation of the type (*trattbägare*) has been produced by Näsman (1990, fig 7) and shows a distribution centred on Scandinavia but with examples in both England (Hamwic and York) and Eastern Europe.

The forms here were identified with a high degree of confidence from characteristic rim and base pieces. In common with many other blown vessels, the palm cup/funnel beaker vessel series exhibits relatively sturdy rim and base areas, especially in comparison to the mid-body region, which in the case of the developed funnel beaker, is normally less than *c* 1mm thick. Rims and bases are therefore likely to have survived to a greater extent than body fragments and consequently provide a more reliable criterion for an estimation of the original number of vessels represented (see section 3).

Non-palm cup/funnel beaker forms were also identified (notably tall beaker and squat jar types) although these constitute a relatively minor proportion of the material as a whole, as does a quantity of small decorated items whose size excludes them from any accurate association with specific types. The greater majority of the palm cup/funnel beaker fragments are either of light blue or light green glass (the distinction between the two being a significant discriminating factor even by the subjective standards of colour measurement) and the term 'decorated' is used here to denote strongly coloured fragments which do not conform to this arbitrary norm. The value of this distinction is debatable, but, given the light blue and light green colour dominance in the material, it is useful for working purposes, particularly in the light of research into the distribution and chronology of coloured glasses (Evison 1983). The analytical investigation of colour with respect to these light blue and light green pieces is pursued below (pp 38–41). Throughout this report any reference to glass colour refers to a translucent colour unless specifically stated otherwise.

Vessel fragments not falling into any of these categories were denoted as non-diagnostic fragments although a small number exhibit a profile largely in keeping with the general palm cup/funnel beaker vessel series. With only a few exceptions these non-diagnostic fragments are of light blue or light green glass, and it might be argued that the greater majority probably belong to palm cup/funnel beaker vessel types, bearing in mind the absence of similarly coloured items among the non-palm cup/funnel beaker vessel forms identified.

2.1 Palm cup/funnel beaker vessel series

These fragments were sub-divided into four categories according to rim forms and bases. Three styles of rim were interpreted on the basis of information already gained from the Melbourne Street material, where it was noted that specific variants might be attributed to stages within the overall

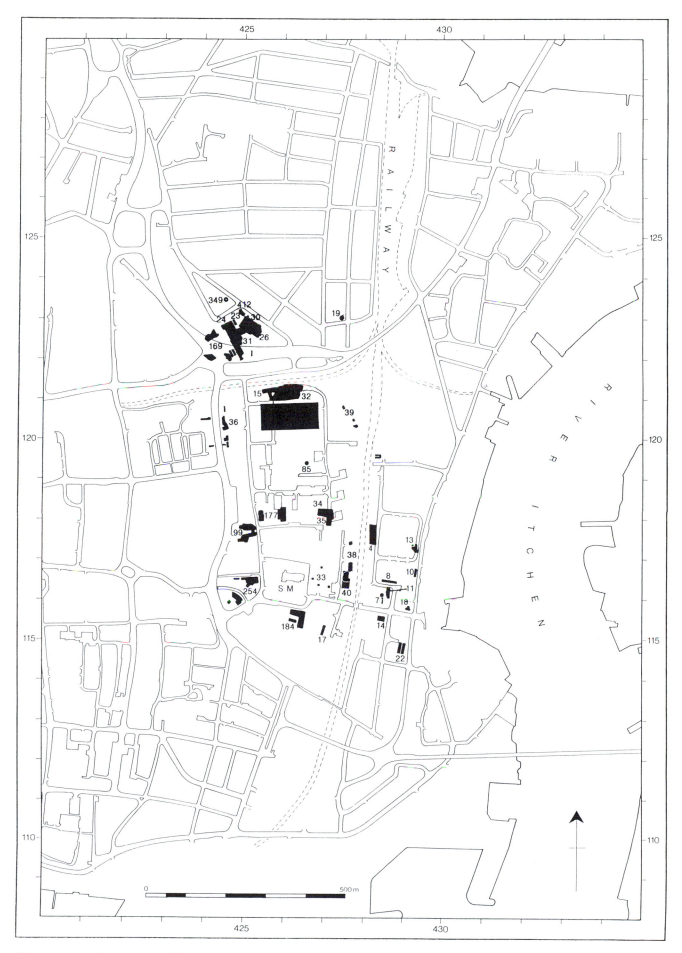

Figure 2   Location of Hamwic sites (SOU numbers) within modern Southampton

Table 1   General distribution of glass fragments from Hamwic sites

Site	P/F	OVT	DND	Ww	Bd	Wt	ND	NoD	TOT
SOU 7	2	2	2	0	0	0	0	0	6
SOU 8	2	0	3	0	0	0	0	0	5
SOU 10	0	0	0	0	0	0	1	0	1
SOU 11	19	1	12	0	0	0	21	0	53
SOU 13	1	0	1	2	0	0	3	0	7
SOU 14	23	6	33	0	5	0	49	0	116
SOU 15	24	8	12	0	2	0	31	0	77
SOU 17	0	0	1	0	0	0	2	0	3
SOU 18	0	0	1	0	0	0	0	0	1
SOU 19	2	0	0	0	0	0	0	0	2
SOU 22	0	0	3	0	1	0	0	0	4
SOU 23	4	5	5	0	0	0	12	0	26
SOU 24	51	14	43	3	4	3	101	0	219
SOU 26	17	3	5	0	2	0	15	0	42
SOU 30	5	5	7	1	1	0	19	0	38
SOU 31	39	5	25	1	4	1	57	0	132
SOU 32	24	3	5	0	1	1	14	0	48
SOU 33	8	0	8	0	0	1	5	0	22
SOU 34	11	0	2	0	1	0	6	0	20
SOU 35	5	1	0	0	0	0	3	0	9
SOU 36	54	4	28	2	5	0	34	1	128
SOU 38	12	1	13	0	0	0	19	0	45
SOU 39	15	3	7	0	0	0	9	0	34
SOU 40	1	1	0	0	0	0	0	0	2
SOU 85	1	0	0	0	0	0	0	0	1
SOU 99	7	1	7	0	0	0	7	2	24
SOU 169	100	16	55	0	8	11	282	3	475
SOU 177	31	4	16	0	1	0	34	0	86
SOU 184	3	0	5	1	0	0	2	0	11
SOU 254	2	1	11	2	1	0	56	5	78
SOU 349	2	2	8	0	0	0	4	0	16
SOU 412	0	0	1	0	0	0	0	0	1
1946–51	1	1	1	0	0	0	0	0	3
TOTAL	**466**	**87**	**320**	**12**	**36**	**17**	**786**	**11**	**1735**
	27%	5%	18.5%	0.7%	2%	1%	45.3%	0.5%	100%

P/F   =   Palm cup/funnel beaker vessel series   Wt   =   Waster
OVT   =   Other Vessel Types   ND   =   Non-diagnostic
DND   =   Decorated, non-diagnostic   NoD   =   Non-durable
Ww   =   Window   TOT   =   Total
Bd   =   Bead

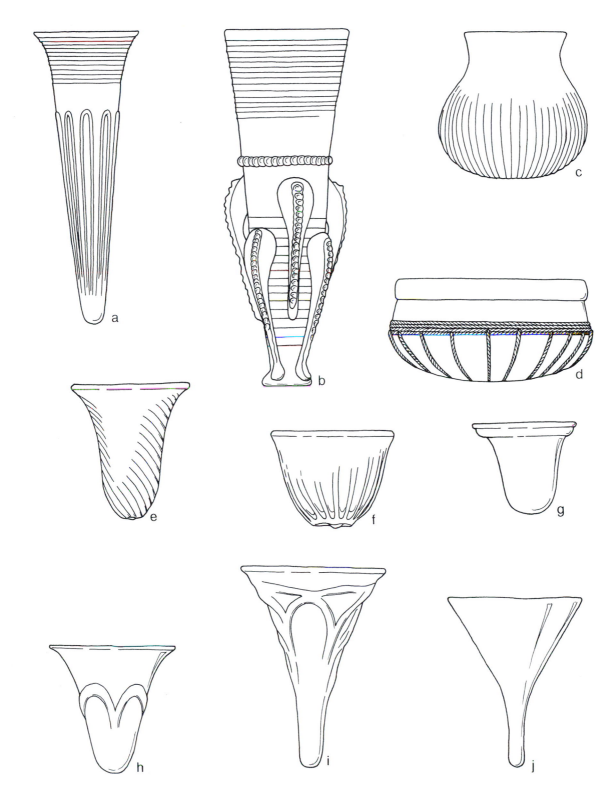

Figure 3 *Generalised glass types alluded to in the text (after Ypey 1963 and Näsman 1990): (a) tall beaker (b) claw beaker (c) squat jar (d) bowl (Valsgärde type) (e–g) palm cup types (h–j) developing funnel beaker types (scale 1:2.5)*

sequence. The model identified the thick folded (or rolled) examples containing a cavity (hereafter denoted as tubular rims) as deriving directly from palm cups and belonging to the earlier part of the sequence; the finer, rounded rims were considered to belong to the later part. This is generally supported by the stratigraphy, though with considerable overlap. The third category, an interpreted stage exhibiting a tubular rim without cavity, was viewed as being intermediate, and allowed a more accurate measurement of individual numbers to be undertaken. The distinction between the tubular rims and those without cavity can be considered significant only if the difference was originally intended. There is no conclusive evidence to suggest that this was the case, particularly since the two rim types are technically similar. However, the three methods of rim formation fall into an overt typological sequence in which the tubular rim without cavity can perhaps be interpreted as representing an intermediate stage between the tubular and rounded forms respectively. This also coincides with a general thinning of the rim throughout the series and in this respect the evolution is certainly feasible. The duration of this inferred development is little more than two centuries – a period beyond the scope of any contextual dating method. An alternate hypothesis, which might envisage tubular, (without cavity) and rounded types as being contemporary versions produced at different sources, is not borne out by compositional analysis (see section 5). Table 2 indicates the distribution of these fragment types within the sites excavated.

The **tubular** rims are the thickest forms represented, typically between 3mm and 5mm, although a small number lay beyond this range giving an overall band of 2mm–6.5mm. The estimated diameters however, are in accord with those of other rim groups with an average value of approximately 100mm. Many are badly formed but the majority have been carefully smoothed on the inside. Without exception the cavity has been created by folding (or rolling) the rim inwards. The illustrations (for example 24 462 (see Plate 3 and Fig 4), 24 465 (see Fig 4), 24 526 (see Plate 4 and Fig 4), 24 580 (see Plate 3 and Fig 4), 169 66 (see Fig 4), 169 826 (see Fig 4), 169 1152 (see Fig 4), 169 2820 (see Fig 4), 169 2840 (see Fig 4)) indicate the general range of variation within the group as a whole.

Only three examples are not of the light blue or light green colour characteristic of the series. These are a blue example (24 509, see Plate 4 and Fig 5), a green example (169 2840, see Fig 4), both of which were of a significantly deeper shade, and a colourless example (15 425). Of the 163 fragments in the group only fifteen are decorated and this is in contrast to the rounded rim group where the proportion is considerably higher. However, the decorative techniques are identical, for example in the use of marvered trailing in opaque yellow (24 597 and 36 22a) or opaque white (36 106), applied trailing (15 407), rims with applied reticella rods (169 1152 (see

Fig 4), 169 2328 (see Fig 5) and 36 301 (see Fig 5)), body twisting (24 465, see Fig 4) and coloured streaking within the metal (24 526 (see Plate 4 and Fig 4), 31 2589 and 169 2243 (see Fig 5)). These decorative methods dismiss any suggestion that the production expertise available was in any way inferior to that which created the more sophisticated styles represented by the other rim groups. Indeed, one example (35 35, see Plate 4 and Fig 5) shows specific innovation with marvered trailing inside the cavity of the rim itself. The interpretation of these forms places them in the earlier part of the palm cup/funnel beaker sequence evolving directly from the types identified by Harden (1978, fig 1, X) with the characteristic thick tubular rim and splayed upper profile.

The **tubular rims without cavity** are less easy to assign but would seem to occur most satisfactorily as the natural subsequent stage in the sequence as a whole in which the rim progressively thins and the body splay becomes more pronounced. Certain uneven rims containing a crude or partial cavity have already been noted from Hamwic (Hunter 1980, 69) and might perhaps be used to indicate the inferred evolution. It would be useful to make some comments on the width of the individual cavities, but the unevenness is often such that measurement proved pointless. It might however be noted that the later complete palm cup examples from pagan burials (Rademacher 1942, 301) contain wide and apparently deliberate cavities and that the general narrowing of the cavity and its eventual exclusion might be seen as a trend within the strictly limited tolerance of the tubular rim form. It is, however, also possible that the tubular rims are a single production phenomenon and the presence or absence of a cavity merely reflects accidental production variation.

Forty-five examples of tubular rims without cavity were recorded, the rim thicknesses generally lying between 2.5mm and 4.5mm with a total range of 2mm–6mm. The estimated diameters are similar to those of the tubular group. Only three of these however are smoothed on the inside (26 696, 169 709 (see Fig 6), and 177 408 (see Fig 6)), perhaps indicating that this operation was less necessary on forms significantly more regular and precise than the larger examples with cavities. Only two depart from the light blue/light green colour norm: a yellow/green example (32 492) with darker streaking in the metal, and a green example (14 303) with opaque yellow marvered trailing (see Plate 4 and Fig 6). Similar opaque yellow marvering was noted on two further pieces (24 500 and 177 408 (see Fig 6)), the latter showing a trail termination. Other decorative forms include two examples of reticella rods applied to the rim (23 18 (see Fig 6) and 32 473) and fragments exhibiting dark or coloured streaking within the metal, for example 177 517 (see Fig 6). A further example of these also exhibits applied trailing (24 598). Simple applied trailing is seen on only a single further example (177 649, see

Table 2   Distribution of palm cup/funnel beaker vessel series fragments from Hamwic sites

Site	Rim Tubular (with cavity)	Rim Tubular (without cavity)	Rim Rounded	Base	Total
SOU 7	1	0	1	0	2
SOU 8	1	0	1	0	2
SOU 10	0	0	0	0	0
SOU 11	10	0	6	3	19
SOU 13	0	0	0	1	1
SOU 14	7	2	12	2	23
SOU 15	8	2	10	4	24
SOU 17	0	0	0	0	0
SOU 18	0	0	0	0	0
SOU 19	1	0	1	0	2
SOU 22	0	0	0	0	0
SOU 23	2	1	0	1	4
SOU 24	24	4	18	5	51
SOU 26	0	3	10	4	17
SOU 30	1	2	2	0	5
SOU 31	15	4	16	4	39
SOU 32	7	5	7	5	24
SOU 33	3	0	4	1	8
SOU 34	2	1	5	3	11
SOU 35	2	0	2	1	5
SOU 36	19	1	28	6	54
SOU 38	4	0	8	0	12
SOU 39	6	3	5	1	15
SOU 40	1	0	0	0	1
SOU 85	1	0	0	0	1
SOU 99	3	0	0	4	7
SOU 169	36	14	41	9	100
SOU 177	4	3	21	3	31
SOU 184	2	0	1	0	3
SOU 254	1	0	1	0	2
SOU 349	2	0	0	0	2
SOU 412	0	0	0	0	0
1946–51	0	0	0	1	1
TOTAL	**163**	**45**	**200**	**58**	**466**
	35%	10%	43%	12%	

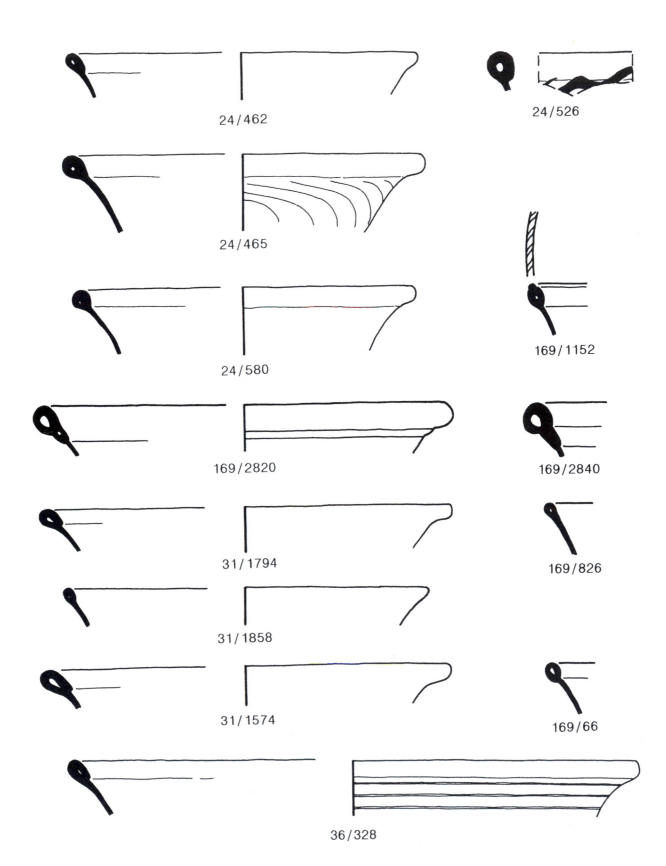

24/462

24/526

24/465

169/1152

24/580

169/2820

169/2840

31/1794

169/826

31/1858

31/1574

169/66

36/328

Figure 4   Palm/Funnel series. Tubular rim types (scale 1:1)

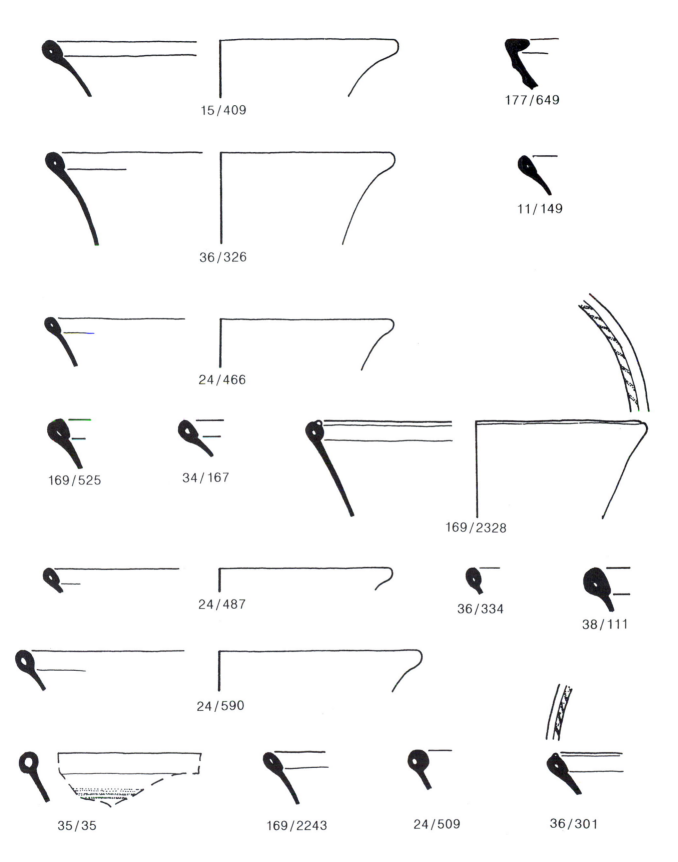

15/409

177/649

11/149

36/326

24/466

169/525

34/167

169/2328

24/487

36/334

38/111

24/590

35/35

169/2243

24/509

36/301

Figure 5   Palm/Funnel series. Tubular rim types (scale 1:1)

12

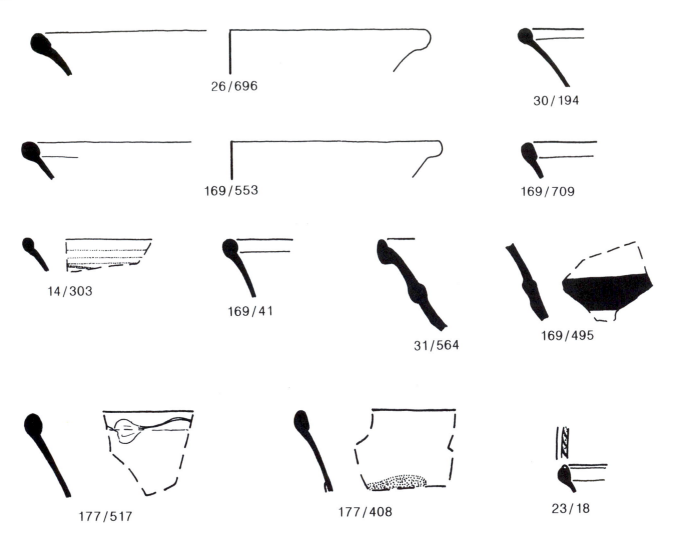

26/696

30/194

169/553

169/709

14/303

169/41

31/564

169/495

177/517

177/408

23/18

Figure 6   *Palm/Funnel series. Tubular rim without cavity types (scale 1:1)*

Fig 5). Two remaining fragments are of particular interest in that the rims had been formed in separate stages using alternate bands of colourless and dark blue glass (31 564 (see Plate 8 and Fig 6) and 169 495 (see Fig 6)) in a manner paralleled at both Helgö (Holmqvist 1964, 256) and Birka (Arbman 1943, pl 190,1). The fragments illustrated from this group (for example 23 18 (see Fig 6), 26 696 (see Fig 6), 30 194 (see Fig 6), 31 564 (see Plate 8 and Fig 6), 169 41 (see Fig 6), 169 553 (see Plate 3 and Fig 6) and 169 709 (see Fig 6)) demonstrate the general range of rim variants and decoration. All are tentatively considered to represent an intermediate stage between the palm cup and funnel beaker forms proper.

The third rim group, interpreted as representing the final stages in the sequence, is defined by a simple **rounded rim** usually of thickness between 2mm and 3mm. Estimated diameters vary between 60mm–150 mm again with an average value of approximately 100mm, and with only nine exceptions of a darker green or yellow/green hue (for example 14 259 (see Plate 2 and Fig 8), 36 236, 36 292, 177 191 (see Plate 4 and Fig 7) and 177 281 (see Plate 4)) all are of characteristic light blue or light green colour typical of the series. Of the 200 examples recorded approximately one third are decorated – a significantly higher proportion than in either of the two other rim groups. These decorated fragments are too numerous to denote here individually; they comprise of fragments exhibiting the application of reticella rods to the lip or to the inside of the rim (31 items, for example 11 166 (see Fig 8) and 24 501 (see Plate 2 and Fig 7)), opaque yellow marvered trailing (fifteen items, for example 169 880, see Plate 4 and Fig 7), opaque white marvered trailing (seven items, for example 15 395, see Fig 7) some of which had been executed on or inside the rim itself, and dark streaking within the metal (eight items, for example 30 57, see Plate 4 and Fig 8). A small number exhibit a combination of techniques, for example applied trailing together with dark streaking (177 498, see Plate 4 and Fig 9)). Other combinations presumably occurred but are not proven from the relatively small proportions of vessels surviving. The remainder of the decorated items, with the exception of a two-stage rim executed in blue glass on a light green vessel (36 195), consist of trailing forms where the trails themselves have weathered beyond colour recognition (for

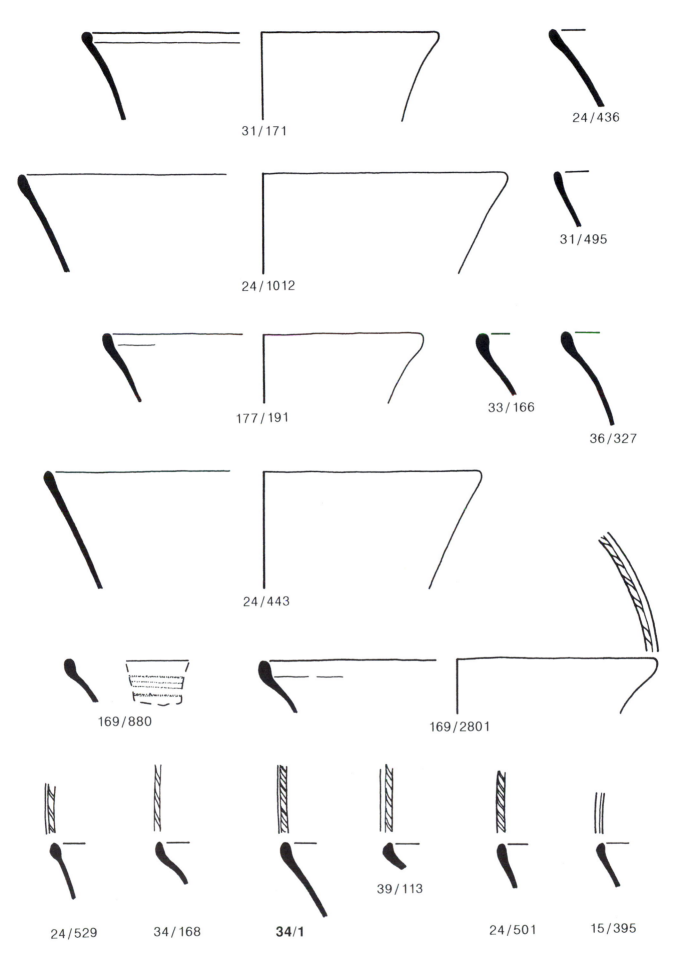

31/171

24/436

24/1012

31/495

177/191

33/166

36/327

24/443

169/880

169/2801

24/529

34/168

34/1

39/113

24/501

15/395

Figure 7   Palm/Funnel series. Rounded rim types with some examples exhibiting reticella rims (scale 1:1)

example 169 3778).

As the rim thicknesses suggest, the forms represented in this group are of a thinner, more elegant type than those discussed previously and many compare well with the interpreted, more developed funnel forms seen for example at Birka (Arbman 1943, pl 191,1). Many of the fragments here also exhibit a pronounced inward turn of the lip which has previously been argued to reflect the ultimate stage of the funnel beaker sequence in the 9th or even 10th centuries (Hunter 1980, 69). The illustrations of this group cover a representative number of variants, notably those of the final phase (for example 24 436 (see Fig 7), 24 529 (see Fig 7), 31 171 (see Fig 7), 169 880 (see Plate 4 and Fig 7) and 169 2801 (see Plate 2 and Fig 7)).

Together the three groups may be used to indicate a gradual development from the thick tubular rim to a more refined rounded form over a period of approximately two centuries, according to analogy with surviving forms outside Britain. The actual sequence was almost certainly less straight-forward and vulnerable to the craftsmanship of manufacture in which accidental variation could easily lie beyond the tight system of measurement employed here. Nevertheless, the evolution from tubular rim to absence of cavity and thence to simple rounded rim is wholly in keeping with observed development which sees the refinement of the original palm cup form of the 7th century into the tall elegant funnel beaker of the 9th century. What is seen is not so much a rigid typological sequence but a trend, the end points of which are more clearly identifiable than those areas that lie between. Reference to Table 2 indicates how these end points are more clearly defined from the fragments, the intermediate forms being less numerous by a factor of three or four.

The **base** area of the palm cup/funnel beaker vessel series is the thickest and most durable part of the vessels and as such base fragments are most likely to survive and be identified in buried contexts. It is perhaps surprising therefore that only 58 fragments were recovered, presumably spanning the range of the series. Of these 58 examples well under half had survived with a full base area showing a base diameter varying between 13mm–25mm, thus identifying a broad range of forms compatible with the interpreted series. The wider diameters (for example 24 426, see Plate 7 and Fig 11) might therefore be seen as belonging to the palm cup end of the sequence and the narrower examples (for example 169 1483, see Fig 11) to the later developed funnel form.

Many bases also exhibit traces of pontil wad and mark and give further indications of the manner of production in which the unfinished vessel was held at the base to allow the rim and body decoration to be carried out. The pontil mark diameter normally varies between 9mm–22mm (with some exceptions to this range), generally the narrower rod being used for the narrower bases. This at least dispels

some doubt that variation in base diameter was a wholly accidental phenomenon and the evidence here could be used to suggest that variation was deliberate, production implements having been devised or utilised accordingly. Interestingly, the normal extent of the base diameter variation is somewhat greater than that of the rims, thus reaffirming the concept that the general trend was towards tallness and finesse rather than towards a specific change of vessel form. This may reflect a changing role, or value, for glass vessels in a social market where elegance was more important than simple functional aspects of vessel form.

All the base fragments are coloured light blue or light green and, with the exception of a few pieces, show the termination of applied or reticella trails (for example 24 703, 32 503 (see Plate 7 and Fig 11), and 169 440 (see Fig 11)), or dark streaking (34 4, see Fig 12). One form (11 154) appears to have a decorative base formed by the pontil wad itself and is considered to belong to the earliest part of the sequence on grounds of size (see Plate 7). The most complete examples are illustrated (for example 23 15 (see Fig 11), 24 421 (see Fig 11), 24 426 (see Plate 7 and Fig 11), 24 585 (see Fig 11), 31 17 (see Fig 11), 32 484 (see Fig 11), 32 503 (see Plate 7 and Fig 11), 169 440 (see Fig 11), 169 1007 (see Plate 7 and Fig 11), 169 1483 (see Fig 11), 169 3325 (see Fig 11) and 177 816 (see Plate 7 and Fig 11)).

2.2 Other vessel types (for general types, see Fig 3)

A relatively small, but significant group of fragments (4%) can be ascribed to other vessel types. The majority of these can be identified with known general types but others show vessel profiles and features that are specific only to the extent that they could not be considered part of the overall palm cup/funnel beaker sequence. The forms represented are to some extent predictable and include tall beakers and flask/jar and bowl forms with interpreted parallels in Melbourne Street, Scandinavia, and late pagan Saxon burials. At least eight **tall beakers** are probably represented, characteristically showing a range of colours including dark opaque (14 265, see Fig 13), brown/yellow (15 412, see Fig 13), red or red/brown (15 460 (see Plate 8 and Fig 13) and 23 29), green (24 546, see Plate 8) and blue (177 286). A further example exhibits vertically applied reticella trails (15 436, see Fig 13). Six examples in the group are decorated with marvered trailing either in opaque white or opaque yellow. The precise forms represented are a matter for conjecture although it might be noted that a number would conform to later claw beaker styles, the problems of which Evison has discussed in some detail (1982 and 1988a). Colours characteristic of claw beakers can be identified among the small pieces catalogued in section 2.3 below. A possible 'claw' (24 570) was also recorded in the material.

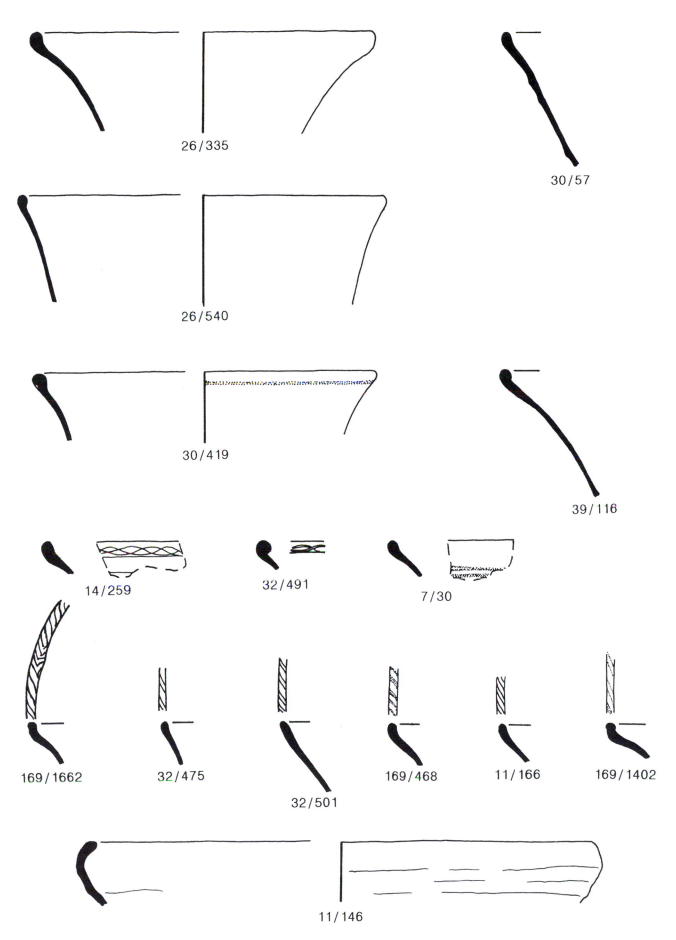

26/335

30/57

26/540

30/419

39/116

14/259

32/491

7/30

169/1662

32/475

32/501

169/468

11/166

169/1402

11/146

Figure 8   Palm/Funnel series. Rounded rim types with some examples exhibiting reticella rims (scale 1:1)

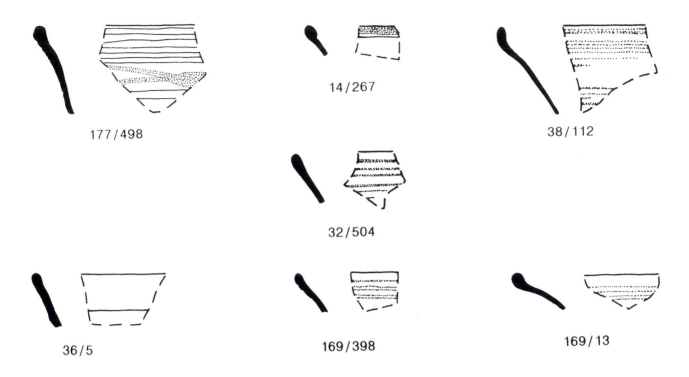

177/498

14/267

38/112

32/504

36/5

169/398

169/13

Figure 9   *Palm/Funnel series. Some decorated examples (scale 1:1)*

More easily identifiable are fragments of small **flasks or jars** (at least 24 examples) characterised by a pushed base, rim form, or contour of body form, and together exhibiting a remarkable range of colouring and decorative qualities. At least thirteen of the pieces belong to a region of the pushed base, a thick durable area of good survival potential, and several of these exhibit the remains or terminals of reticella rod decoration (for example 14 230 (see Fig 14) and 32 502 (see Plate 1 and Fig 15)), two being of an unusual dark red vessel colour (15 462 (see Fig 15) and 26 770 (see Fig 15)). Other decorative forms include applied trailing (15 414, see Fig 14), fluting (7 32), dark streaking (for example 24 428), and marvering. The last of these shows a variety of styles, either simply on a dark red or dark blue vessel (36 112 and 169 2136 (see Plate 8 and Fig 14) respectively), as a series of marvered flashes on a green vessel (169 147 (see Plate 8 and Fig 14) or as a broken trail under the base itself (169 889, see Plate 6 and Fig 15). In all instances the marvering is of an opaque yellow colour. Additional decoration to the base is evident in one example (31 801, see Fig 15) which shows the presence of a brown/yellow wad or boss attached to the pushed area, another which indicates a possible perforation (99 113) and a further fragment, from a dark green vessel (169 770, see Plate 8 and Fig 13), which shows a pushed base with central perforation surrounded by concentric opaque yellow marvered trails on the inside of the vessel itself. The perforation (diameter *c* 6mm) appears to have been deliberate and the function remains a matter for speculation, a lamp perhaps being a plausible interpretation. A similar function might be suggested for a flat fragment of blue glass (24 510, see Plate 5 and Fig 13), also with

a deliberate perforation surrounded by concentric marvered trails but without the obvious turn of the vessel wall. An item similar to these, but undecorated, has since been recovered at Liege, Belgium (Evison 1988b).

In general the suggested vessel profiles conform to styles already established by the 7th century, notably in Kent (Harden 1956, 141 VIII). Later and more sophisticated versions comparable to the Hamwic pieces with reticella rods are known from Hopperstad, Norway (Hougen 1968, 100) as well as from Birka (for example Arbman 1943, pl 189). Estimated rim diameters of between 60mm (169 2136, see Plate 8 and Fig 14) and 80mm (169 147, see Plate 8 and Fig 14) accord with the known typology. It might also be noted that the number of base fragments from the flask/jar types (15) compared with the total number of fragments assigned to this type (24) might be interpreted as a much more realistic indication of minimum numbers than the ratio of similar fragment types from the palm cup/funnel beaker vessel series if the fragments represent the original presence of whole vessels. This issue is pursued below (p 59).

A small number of **bowl** forms could be interpreted from the larger, rounded fragments including those of a plain blue or green colour (31 759 and 169 2582). Decorative methods involved show the use of marvered trailing in opaque yellow (26 542, see Plate 5 and Fig 14) or opaque white (169 1654, see Plate 5 and Fig 15), the latter example being combed. A remarkable fragment (169 1185, see Plate 1 and Fig 14) exhibiting a band of five reticella rods, but with little of the body adhering can be paralleled with the decorative rods on a bowl from Valsgärde, Sweden (Arwidsson 1932, pl XIV) and

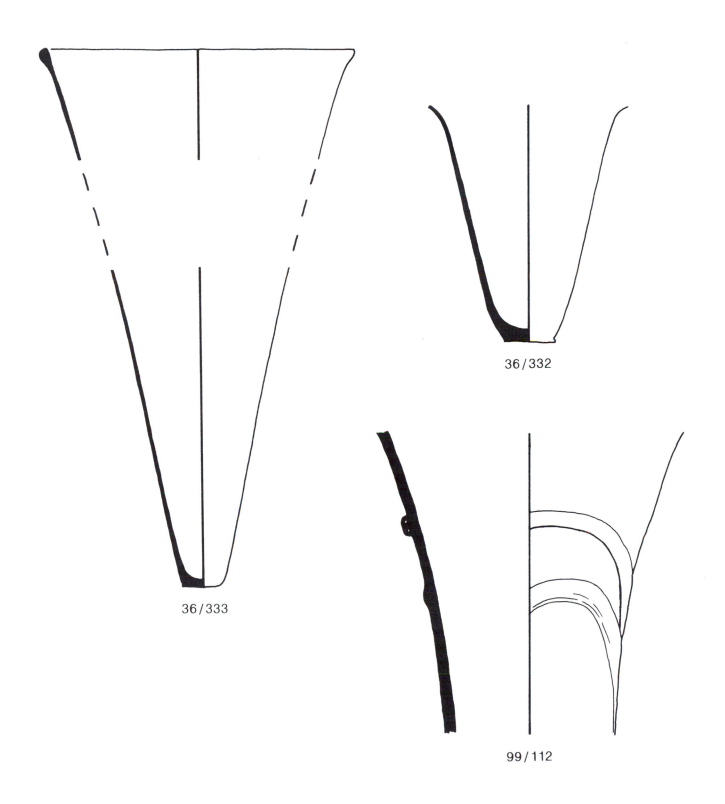

36 / 332

36 / 333

99 / 112

Figure 10   *Palm / Funnel series. Substantially surviving examples (scale 1:1)*

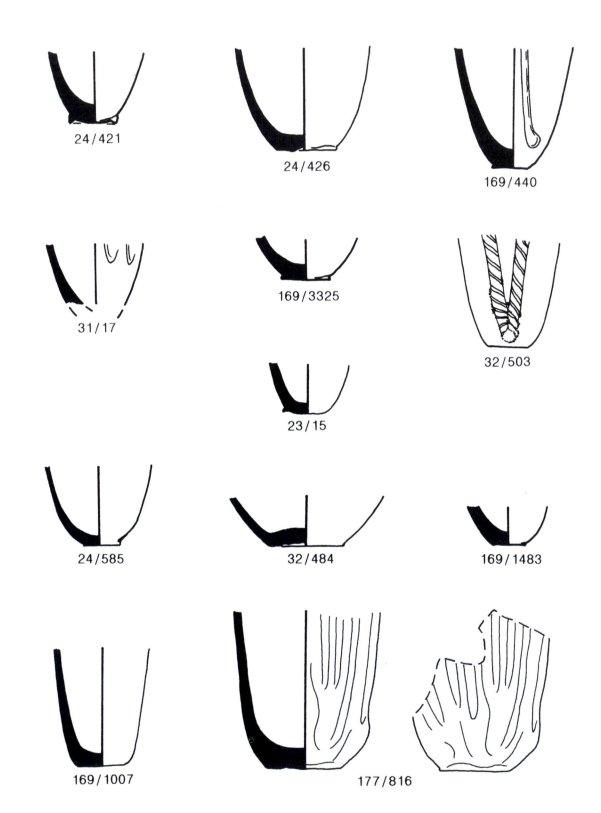

24/421

24/426

169/440

31/17

169/3325

32/503

23/15

24/585

32/484

169/1483

169/1007

177/816

Figure 11   *Palm/Funnel series. Base fragments (scale 1:1)*

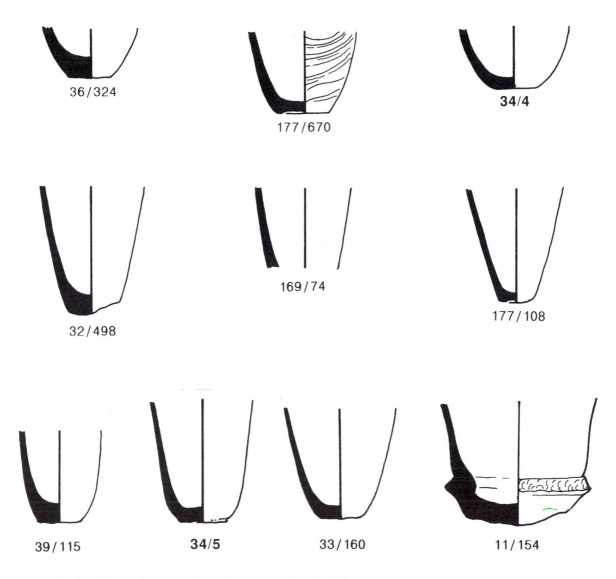

Figure 12   Palm / Funnel series. Base fragments (scale 1:1)

elsewhere, and a tentative association of forms can be made. Other similar pieces are catalogued below as decorative, non-diagnostic items. The same association of forms can be extended to include a number of rim fragments where the rim is folded outwards (as opposed to the inward folding of the palm cup/funnel beaker rims) and where the estimated diameter lies between 110mm–140mm. These include brown/yellow examples (15 446 (see Fig 14) and 30 112 (see Plate 8 and Fig 14)), the latter showing marvered trailing, and a green form (169 3058, see Plate 4 and Fig 14) where the original trailing has been lost.

The remaining forms are less easy to identify and are included here on the basis of profile features that differ significantly from those of the palm cup/funnel beaker vessel series. At least thirteen exhibit a pronounced, almost angular carination in the body not dissimilar to the base profile of earlier bell beaker forms or, more likely, to a rarer type identified by Holmqvist as possibly belonging to bottle types, on the basis of fragments from Helgö (1964, 257 and Figs 123–4). It is interesting to note that an assemblage from Maastricht contains bell beaker fragments as well as both fragments of vessels and decorative elements recorded here (van Lith 1988). Almost all the Hamwic examples were of light blue glass (for example 14 252, 15 413 and 15 424), the exceptions being light green (for example 169 1063, see Fig 13) or colourless (24 524, see Fig 13). Other unassigned forms include a blue example with possible combed decoration (169 176, see Fig 13), a green vessel with opaque white marvered trails below the rim (169 1300, see Fig 14) and two fragments of a brown/yellow vessel with reticella rods (30 269 and 30 374 (see Fig 14)). One piece (24 527) appears to belong to the base of a Roman flask or jar.

2.3 Decorated, non-diagnostic fragments

This group consists of fragments exhibiting specific decorative features (including colour) but which are too small to be interpreted as belonging to known or inferred vessel types. Their main advantage lies in demonstrating the variety of colour and range of decorative techniques available during the period of Middle Saxon occupation.

A number of techniques predominate, notably marvered trailing in opaque yellow (over 50 examples) or opaque white (over fifteen examples). Although the trailing can normally be interpreted as being wound horizontally, a few pieces exhibit variation using curves (for example 38 105, see Plate 5 and Fig 17) or small blobs and bosses (for example 14 264, 30 550 and 39 93). Among the fragments showing opaque white marvering are at least two vessels (33 155 and 169 1615) where the trailing had been combed. Simple applied trails, of the same colour as the vessel, were identified on over 70 examples, normally with the trail applied horizontally but in a number of instances using an arcaded form (for example 31 137 and 169 242), sometimes with additional darker streaking (for example 32 466 and 36 230c). Other trailed effects included apparent random or lattice designs (for example 15 414 (see Fig 14) and 31 1565). In one instance (36 317) the trail is surmounted by opaque white marvering. Applied and marvered trailing also occur separately on the same vessel (for example 177 74).

Even more sophisticated techniques are evident in the use of reticella rods which cover several of the manufacturing variables denoted by Evison (1998a, Fig 12). These occur on over 40 items, with a roughly equal proportion of opaque white and opaque yellow spirals. Other colours are few, one notable example being a rod bearing alternate yellow and red spirals (412 5). Although the majority of the fragments are too small for the form of the decoration to be identified, a few larger examples indicate arcaded application (for example 36 4 (see Fig 16) and 39 98) some employing pairs of rods with different coloured spirals for the inner and outer curves. A few further examples exhibit alternating coloured spirals within the same rod, either singly (for example 177 782), or in a combination of rods (for example 38 108). Several of the trailed or reticella pieces show little trace of associated vessel walling (for example 14 255, 31 1014), giving the impression that the final form of the fragments may have been the result of deliberate breakage. The significance of this is pursued below (p 60).

Although the majority of all the fragments in this section belong to light green or light blue vessels, many, including those with surface decoration, show a wide range of colour variation. Dark streaking or clouding, often as green (for example 169 2564) or as red (for example 24 550), occur with all decorative forms already discussed and is considered (below p 35) to have been a deliberate phenomenon. More homogeneous, richer colours are dark blue (for example 24 471), brown/yellow (for example 169 1356), dark green (for example 169 500) and red (for example 26 263). The red examples occur with varying degrees of opacity, the fragments with the densest colour often showing a layering effect of apparently dark/light red glass in section (though in fact the 'dark' glass is colourless, but appears dark due to total internal reflection of light between the layers). Fragments of this type have hitherto been rare finds in contemporary contexts; such was the relative profusion here that they merit a more detailed technological consideration (below).

The remaining decorative methods evident appear to be confined to manipulation of the vessel prior to annealing. Body twisting is the most common (for example 169 2384) and was presumably achieved at a critical temperature state while the base was held firm. Several of these probably belong to the palm cup/funnel beaker vessel sequence in which the technique has already been observed. Indeed, the majority of the fragments listed in this section show either surface or colouring characteristics already attested on known or inferred forms and are arguably thus related. These forms were identified however by rim and base elements, while the fragments here are by definition body sherds and therefore represent traditionally different decorative fields. In combination, however, they attest to a remarkable luxury of ornamentation and quality in glasswares of this period.

2.4 Non-diagnostic fragments

This section contains almost 800 items (45% of the total) and represents the largest group categorised. By definition it is also the group on which least comment can be made. The fragments are predominantly of either light blue or light green glass (arbitrary colour norms in the classification of the material) and identical in both colour and metal to the majority of the rim and base fragments attributed to the palm cup/funnel beaker vessel series. A small number are of colourless glass. It is perhaps worth noting that nearly all the non palm cup/funnel beaker forms identified are of colours markedly different from the light greens and light blues seen here; this itself is a strong argument in favour of a palm cup/funnel beaker interpretation for many of these non-diagnostic fragments. They are, nonetheless, grouped here in view of the levels of uncertainty involved with such an association. Light blue fragments are more numerous than those of a light green colour (approximate ratio 3:2) and this is in accord with the distribution of colour evident in the palm cup/funnel beaker vessel series itself. The problems of producing coloured vessels in these two shades (deliberately or otherwise) is a matter of considerable technological interest and is examined below (p 36).

2.5 Window glass

Only twelve fragments are recorded in this section, not all of which can be ascribed to a glazing function with a high degree of confidence, although several

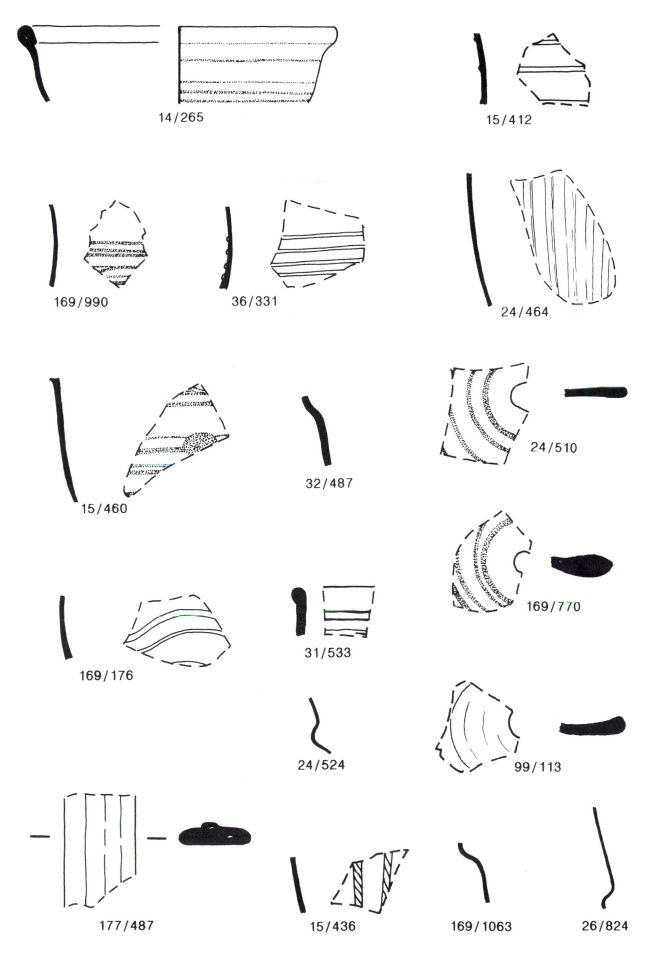

14/265

15/412

169/990

36/331

24/464

15/460

32/487

24/510

169/770

169/176

31/533

99/113

24/524

177/487

15/436

169/1063

26/824

Figure 13   Other vessel types (scale 1:1)

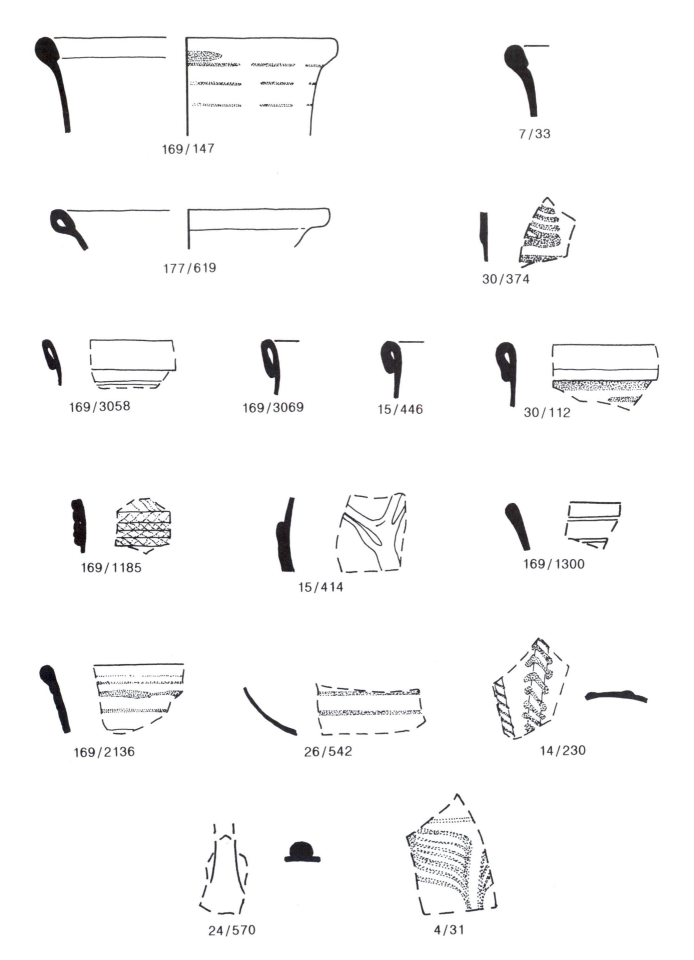

169/147

7/33

177/619

30/374

169/3058

169/3069

15/446

30/112

169/1185

15/414

169/1300

169/2136

26/542

14/230

24/570

4/31

Figure 14   Other vessel types (scale 1:1)

169/889

26/770

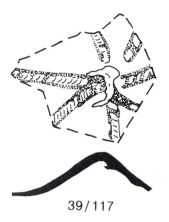

39/117

36/7

15/462

169/1654

36/325

31/801

32/502

14/264

30/550

39/93

Figure 15   Other vessel types. Jar bases. Decorated, 24
non-diagnostic fragments (scale 1:1)

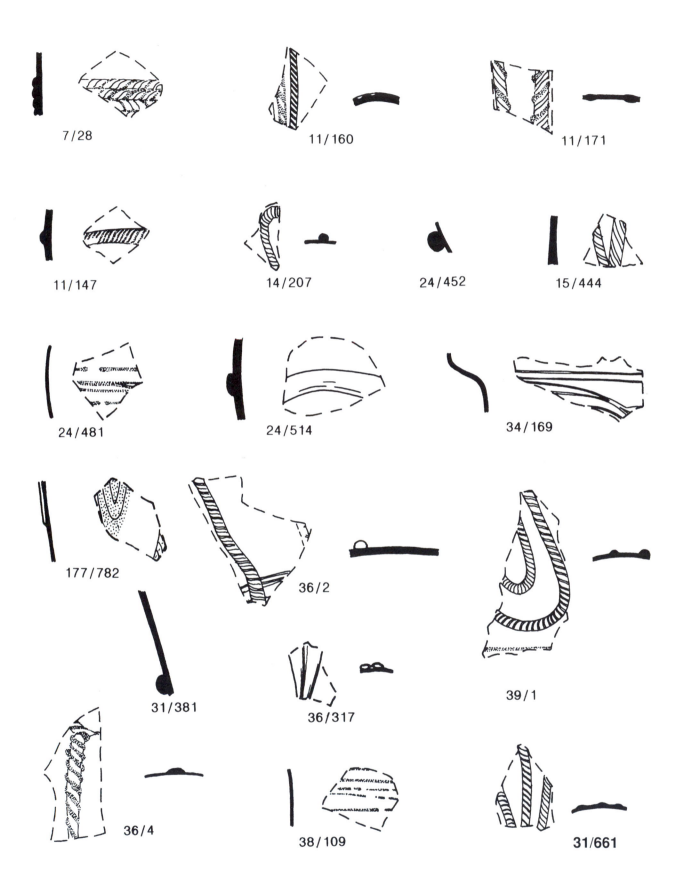

Figure 16   Decorated, non-diagnostic fragments (scale 1:1)

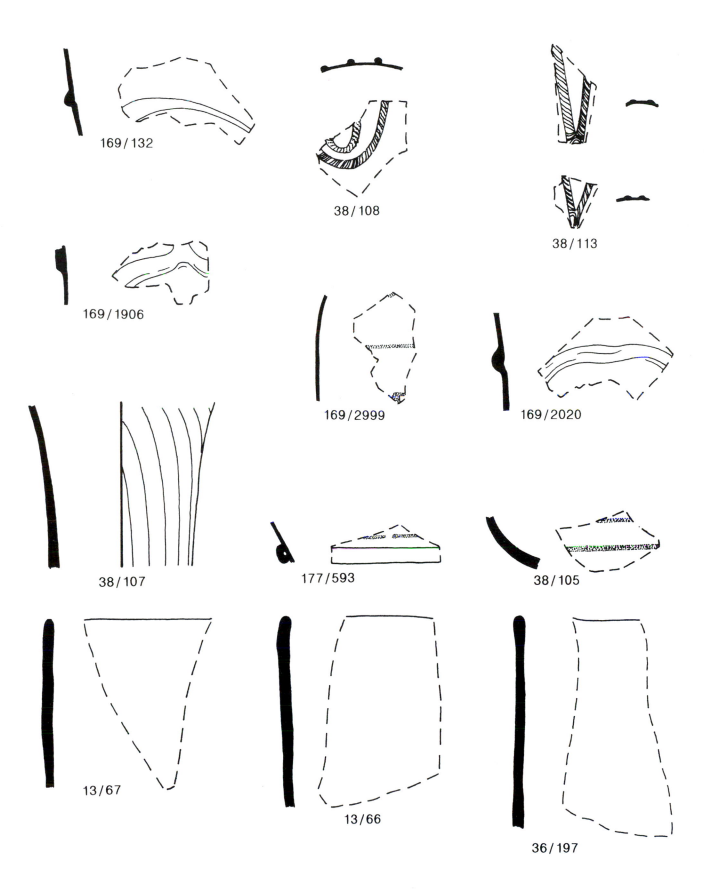

169 / 132

38 / 108

38 / 113

169 / 1906

169 / 2999

169 / 2020

38 / 107

177 / 593

38 / 105

13 / 67

13 / 66

36 / 197

Figure 17   Decorated, non-diagnostic fragments (top), window fragments (bottom) (scale 1:1)

possess a number of relevant attributes such as grozing or opposing matt and gloss surfaces. All are effectively flat and seven show evidence of possible grozing (13 66 (see Fig 17), 13 67 (see Fig 17), 24 576, 24 620, 31 1736, 36 194 and 184 65). Four of these also exhibit flame-rounded edges (13 66 (see Fig 17), 13 67 (see Fig 17), 184 65 and 36 194) but quarry forms are only broadly evident in a curved example (31 1736) and in a piece exhibiting a geometric shape (24 620). All are dull light blue or light green with the exception of a brown/yellow fragment (24 620), and none is of the more richly decorated types known from elsewhere (for example, as reviewed by Harden 1978, 7–10). Two, however, (30 538 and 184 65) appear to be of Roman origin and may represent the utilisation of fragments excavated or discovered during the Middle Saxon period. Window glass would appear to be an incongruous find in the town at this time, the known structures having been timber-supported (Andrews 1997) and unlikely to have been glazed. The presence of so few and scattered fragments within the excavated areas might be regarded as an indicator of cullet rather than *in situ* windows.

2.6 Beads

A number of beads are recorded showing a variety of forms and decorative effects. Approximately one-half of the total are small annular types, with diameters often less than 3mm, and interpreted as spacers. These were produced in a range of colours, typically opaque blue, opaque red, or opaque green (for example 169 2729, see Fig 18), with two examples showing a hexagonal form (for example 15 453, see Fig 18). Larger forms also include both annular types (for example 31 2627) and hexagonal types (for example 15 453, see Fig 18), one example of the latter exhibiting tapered ends (24 492, see Fig 18). Tubular forms are also evident, with one example being faceted with chamfered edges (31 2310). Only five beads show surface decoration; an annular example with reticella rods (15 411, see Fig 18), a similar form with small opaque yellow bosses around the perimeter (24 427, see Fig 18), two cylindrical types with marvered zig-zag trailing (24 645 (see Fig 18) and 177 406 (see Fig 18)) and a segmented form exhibiting opaque green and opaque yellow marvered blobs (14 297, see Fig 18). The last of these is one of a small number indicative of poor quality and finish, almost to the extent of being a reject. Evidence for possible bead making at Hamwic was postulated previously on the basis of a twisted rod from Melbourne Street (Hunter 1980, 71) and the few inferior examples here offer a mod-

icum of support. Additionally, it might be noted that the colours of all the beads recovered can, without exception, be paralleled among the vessel fragments discussed above – an association which might add some weight to a bead-making interpretation.

2.7 Wasters

Seventeen examples of glassy or similar deposits were identified which might be used to indicate the presence of working processes in the vicinity of the sites excavated. A number suggest that glass melting had occurred, notably droplets or globules (for example 24 518 and 24 460) and a partially formed trail (24 592). Further fragments, however, (mostly from SOU 169) indicate the presence of more sophisticated glass-related processes, several showing green vitreous deposits on either stone or a hard fired pottery (for example 169 1428 and 169 2594). At least two of these were from pottery base areas which additionally exhibited other deposits and concretions suggesting that the objects may originally have been forms of crucible. Similar remains from York have since been interpreted as belonging to the primary glassmaking process (Bayley 1987) and have been investigated within a wider framework of (Roman) glassy residues and working materials (Jackson *et al* 1990). The fragments are thus of considerable interest and are discussed further below (p 61).

2.8 Non-durable fragments

Glass of the Roman and early post-Roman periods was normally a durable product, defined as high soda-lime-silica glass in contrast to the less durable 'forest' glasses of the medieval period which relied on a variety of organic potassium-rich alkalis as a raw material component. The distinction between the two types is evident not only analytically (Sanderson and Hunter 1980, fig 7) but also often visually in that the later wares have a tendency towards severe weathering and internal decomposition. Investigation into window glass has shown that less durable glasses may have been used in Winchester as early as the late 9th or early 10th century (Biddle and Hunter 1990, 362) and might therefore be expected within the contexts at Hamwic. Only eleven fragments were recovered (for example 99 117 and 169 212), none of which showed specific typological qualities, but their presence at least reaffirms the likely availability of this compositional type within the period of occupation.

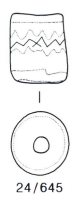
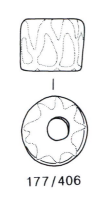
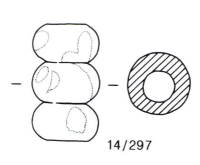
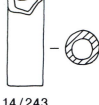

24/645

177/406

14/297

14/243

15/453

32/1259

24/492

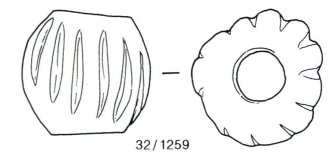

32/1260

32/1261

24/427

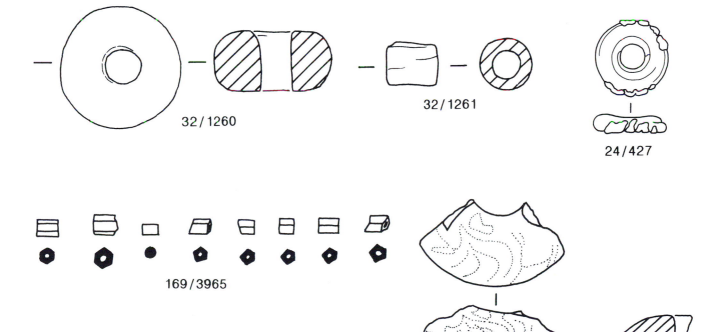

169/3965

169/2729

15/411

Figure 18   Beads and spacers (scale 1:1)

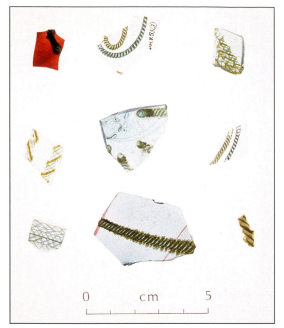

Plate 1

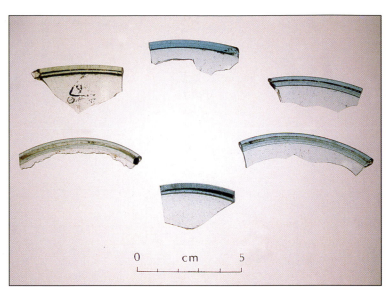

Plate 3

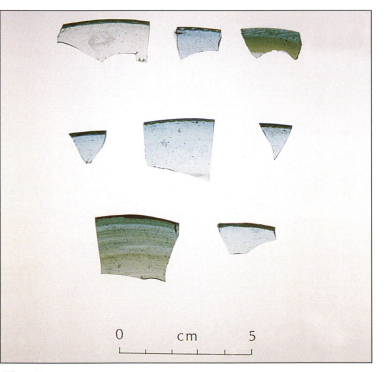

Plate 2

Plate 4

1. Reticella fragments, from left to right: (top) <u>14</u> 304, <u>38</u> 108, <u>7</u> 28; (middle) <u>11</u> 171, <u>32</u> 502, <u>38</u> 108; (bottom) <u>169</u> 1185, <u>24</u> 555, <u>24</u> 552

2. Reticella rim fragments, from left to right: (top) <u>169</u> 2801, <u>24</u> 501, <u>14</u> 259; (middle) <u>169</u> 1402, <u>14</u> 287, <u>169</u> 468; (bottom) <u>169</u> 1662, <u>36</u> 330

3. Tubular rims, from left to right: (top) <u>36</u> 326, <u>169</u> 553, <u>24</u> 466; (bottom) <u>24</u> 487, <u>24</u> 580, <u>24</u> 462

4. Decorated rims, from left to right: (top) <u>14</u> 303, <u>169</u> 13, <u>177</u> 649, <u>177</u> 281; (second row) <u>24</u> 447, <u>169</u> 398, <u>35</u> 35, <u>169</u> 525; (third row) <u>30</u> 419, <u>7</u> 33, <u>36</u> 5, <u>24</u> 526; (fourth row) <u>169</u> 880, <u>169</u> 3058, <u>24</u> 509, <u>30</u> 57; (bottom) <u>177</u> 191, <u>177</u> 619, <u>177</u> 498

5. Decorated body fragments, from left to right: (top) <u>36</u> 331, <u>169</u> 1390, <u>6</u> 24, <u>38</u> 105; (second row) <u>99</u> 96, <u>169</u> 1654, <u>24</u> 510; (third row) <u>26</u> 542, <u>169</u> 132, <u>24</u> 481; (fourth row) <u>169</u> 990, <u>24</u> 554, <u>24</u> 547, <u>8</u> 11; (bottom) <u>36</u> 1, <u>24</u> 420, <u>24</u> 582

6. Pushed bases, from left to right: <u>39</u> 117, <u>36</u> 7, <u>169</u> 889

7. Palm/funnel bases, from left to right: (top) <u>177</u> 670, <u>169</u> 1007; (middle) <u>32</u> 503, <u>177</u> 816, <u>36</u> 333; (bottom) <u>24</u> 426, <u>11</u> 154, <u>32</u> 498

8. Decorated fragments, including rims, from left to right: (top) <u>30</u> 112, <u>169</u> 2136, <u>31</u> 564; (second row) <u>31</u> 533, <u>24</u> 546, <u>26</u> 198; (third row) <u>11</u> 158, <u>169</u> 770, <u>26</u> 600; (bottom) <u>11</u> 163, <u>15</u> 460, <u>169</u> 2999

Plate 5

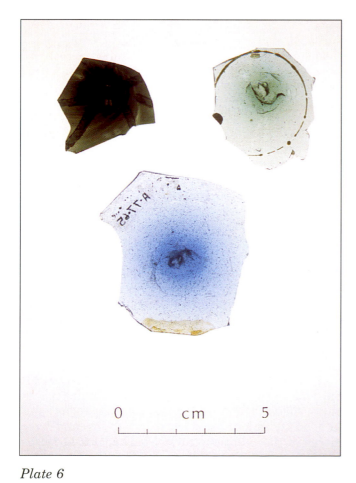

Plate 6

Plate 7

Plate 8

3. Vessel quantification analysis

Glass from settlement sites is invariably fragmentary and normally cannot be reconstructed into whole vessels. There is therefore a need for a method of quantification in order to be able to compare the numbers of each type of vessel. This would allow the proportions of the types in a total fragment population to be compared within a site or groups of sites. It has the advantage of offering greater scope for interpreting the function and distribution of the material, issues which are of particular importance at Hamwic where working processes might be inferred from the nature of the fragments. Various methods of quantification, with a range of advantages and disadvantages, have previously been applied to ceramic studies (see for example Hulthen 1974; Millet 1979; Orton 1975; 1980), but glass has been a largely untested material and offers a number of idiosyncratic problems. The exercise here was carried out using the *Six Dials* material on the basis of the importance of its archaeological context and in view of the close geographical proximity of the individual sites represented.

Quantification of glass fragments can follow a number of directions, the simplest and most rapid being those of fragment count and fragment weight. Neither requires sophisticated equipment but both suffer from obvious shortcomings. In the former method the number of fragments can be increased by breakage, a factor which is partly dependent on the size and finesse of the vessel, causing smaller, thicker vessels to be under-represented in the count. Inaccuracies of this method are argued from experimentation (see for example Chase 1985). Weight, on the other hand, is unaffected by breakage patterns but bulky, thick-walled forms are likely to be over-represented, with the converse true for finer, thin-walled forms. A combination of the count and weight methods might be used to determine average fragment weight but this is of limited value for interpreting the material as a whole.

Ceramic studies have identified adjusted weight or surface area as viable approaches (for example Hulthen 1974) on the basis that the weight of a sherd is dependent on its surface area, thickness and density. The adjusted weight method divides the weight by the thickness and thus removes the influence of the thickness variable. Vessels with a high density tend to be over-represented, but in the case of glass of this period density-variation is minimal with the exception of highly coloured glasses some of which contain high levels of lead oxide.

Calculation of the <u>maximum number of vessels</u> or of the <u>minimum number of vessels</u> is more subjectively based, giving rise to further problems of accuracy. In the former, owing to the friable nature of

glass, breakage is potentially a significant cause of inaccuracy and the method can be misleading unless the site under study was completely excavated. In ceramic studies the minimum number method has tended to be calculated using the average rim circumference of particular vessel types (see for example Fulford 1973, 23–4) or by an exercise of grouping fragments according to rim form, rim diameter, base characteristics and colour. The latter approach becomes extremely laborious for a large group of material and has the additional disadvantage of over-representing types which are of rare occurrence. It does, however, utilise most fragments irrespective of size, though non-diagnostic body sherds have to be excluded from the analysis.

The concept of <u>vessel equivalents</u>, formulated by measuring rim or base length as a percentage of average rim or base circumference of specific vessel types, is a further method which relies on knowledge of typical rim/base seriations. In the case of the Hamwic material these cannot be specified with any confidence; moreover the base diameters of the palm cup/funnel beaker vessel types are difficult to measure accurately. The use of body fragments might be included in the calculations, but only if the surface areas of specific types could be used as standards. Again this is not the case at Hamwic.

The problems therefore are two-fold: firstly in establishing the most accurate and useful quantification methods according to previous ceramic studies, and secondly in applying those methods to a material with a different technological background and physical matrix, the typological variables of which contain a number of unknowns. Orton's statistical assessment of the theory underlying these various approaches led him to argue that the vessel equivalents method was the most suitable for ceramics, followed by sherd weight, with sherd count a close third (Orton 1975). Others (for example Millet 1979) have since suggested a different ranking as the result of practical application and the outcome has tended to suggest that methods vary in their suitability according to fabric type, vessel forms and the extent to which objective controls can be applied. Accordingly, it was concluded that the application of quantitative analysis to glass could be carried out only by independent experimentation (Fletcher and Heyworth 1987).

Of the *Six Dials* material 805 of the 932 individual find units recorded were made available for this study. All were of durable soda-lime-silica glass and in good condition. They consisted of rim and base pieces of the palm cup/funnel beaker vessel series together with simple body fragments. The palm cup/funnel beaker vessel series has relatively sturdy rim and base portions but the mid-body of these blown forms (according to position in the series) is often less than *c* 1mm in thickness. Division of the rim forms into three types has been argued above on the grounds of both typological and technological criteria; the tubular rims are thickest (average 3mm–5mm), followed by tubular rims without cavity (average 2.5mm–4.5mm), and rounded rims (average 2mm–3mm). These three rims forms were identified as valid discriminants for quantification purposes and the material was subjected to tests using the four methods of count, weight, adjusted weight and surface area. An attempt was also made to estimate the minimum number of vessels in each category, using the subjective exercise of grouping the fragments ostensibly belonging to the same vessel according to rim form, base form and colour.

The majority of the find units consists of only one sherd. In a few cases a find consists of more than one sherd and where these appeared most likely to come from the same vessel they were counted as a single unit for the purposes of the study. The separation into fragments may have occurred during, or since, excavation. All the find units were weighed to an accuracy of 0.1g using a digital mass balance. Where the find unit contained more than one sherd the total weight was recorded. Measurements of the dimensions of the fragments were also made, although this was a somewhat subjective assessment when dealing with irregular shapes. A micrometer was used to determine thickness mea-

surements and the adjusted weight was calculated for each find unit using the formula given by Hulthen (1974, 3):

$$\frac{Weight\ (g)\ x\ Standard\ Thickness\ (cm)}{Wall\ Thickness\ (cm)} = Adjusted\ Weight\ (g)$$

A standard thickness of 0.2cm was chosen for the fragments on the basis that this represented the most realistic value for vessel walling across the range of palm cup/funnel beaker vessel types. The surface area of each find unit was calculated according to the formula given by Hulthen (1974, 2):

$$\frac{Weight\ (g)}{Wall\ Thickness\ (cm)\ x\ Density\ (g/cc)} = Surface\ Area\ (cm^2)$$

In calculating surface areas the parameter of density was removed from the formula on the basis that all the glass fragments in the analysis were of similar density. The value of the surface area must therefore be considered fictive, being directly proportional to the actual surface area.

The fragments were divided into categories according to type: tubular rims, tubular rims without cavity, rounded rims, bases and body sherds. As density had been ignored during the measurement of surface area the calculation was therefore similar to that for adjusted weight but without a standardisation factor. The two methods therefore produce

Table 3   Comparison of quantification methods on the *Six Dials* material

	Count	Weight	Adjusted weight	Surface area
	(no)	(g)	(g)	(cm²)
Tubular Rims	74	135.6	64.7	323.6
	9.2%	23.2%	11.4%	11.4%
Tubular Rims	30	35.1	20.9	104.5
(without cavity)	3.7%	6.0%	3.7%	3.7%
Rounded Rims	86	110.7	98.8	494.0
	10.7%	19.0%	17.5%	17.5%
Bases	20	65.3	37.6	188.1
	2.5%	11.2%	6.7%	6.7%
Body fragments	595	236.6	343.3	1716.3
	73.9%	40.6%	60.7%	60.7%
TOTAL	**805**	**583.3**	**565.3**	**2826.6**
	100.0%	100.0%	100.0%	100.0%

the same percentage values. Table 3 illustrates the results from the methods used.

Taking into account the biases of the methods employed, these figures can be used to reveal information about the different types of glass fragment within the material as a whole, for example in a comparison between the count and adjusted weight methods. Here incorrect estimation of the adjusted weight is considered unlikely on the basis that the vessel types all lie broadly within the same size range. Any bias therefore is likely to be a consequence of the count system. Where the count gives a higher percentage than that given by the adjusted weight, then the total surface area of that type is deemed to be broken up into a greater number of items. If the count gives a lower percentage, the type is broken into a smaller number of items. In comparing figures between weight and adjusted weight, variation between percentages will be due to an over- or under-estimation of weight according to the thicknesses of the individual fragments and types. Tubular rims, for example, are comparatively thicker than body fragments.

The results shown in Table 3 provide a useful preliminary insight to the distribution of the material. As expected, body fragments predominate, but analysis of the different rim groups indicates a consistent minority role played by the tubular rim without cavity (intermediate) form. The number of base fragments would appear to be much lower than the total number of rim fragments. This is likely to be a reflection of the fact that bases do not break up as readily as rims.

Some form of control can be exercised on the data by using the minimum numbers system on rim and base fragments. For example, within a type category, if the percentage by count is higher than that by minimum numbers then it suggests that the fragments in that type are most likely to have belonged to the same vessel. If the converse occurs, the fragments are less likely to have belonged to the same vessel. This is particularly important at Hamwic in attempting to define whether glass was originally present on the site in the form of whole vessels or whether it was introduced as cullet for reworking purposes. Quantification by estimation of minimum numbers of vessels is subjective and will lead to an over-estimation if fragments from the same vessel have not been recognised as such and have been counted as separate vessels. The method can also lead to an under-estimation if fragments from different vessels have been grouped together and counted as single vessels. Owing to the caution normally exercised with subjective measurements the method is more likely to lead to an over-estimation. The results of the analysis are shown on Table 4 in comparison to the earlier methods employed. Body fragments have been removed from the calculations.

The interpretation of bias is difficult, as every single comparison has more than one factor as the possible cause. However, for the base types the minimum number is the same as the count as the base fragments are never from the same vessel, and thus the figure can be used to identify the specific disparities interpreted above from the other methods. Given that the minimum number of bases is argued to be an accurate reflection of base distribution, it would appear that very few original, complete vessels are represented in the material. However, this interpretation is difficult to support from the rim items owing to possible biases caused by breakage pattern.

Tubular rims are over-estimated by weighing on the grounds of thickness while tubular rims without cavity and rounded rims are narrower and tend to be under-estimated by the same method. The method of adjusted weight appears to over-estimate rounded rims and under-estimate tubular rims and tubular rims without cavity. It seems that the method of calculating the adjusted weights is being biased by the different parts of the vessel. However, any modification to the figures resulting from these inherent biases seems unlikely to have any funda-

Table 4   Comparison of count, weight, adjusted weight and minimum numbers methods on the *Six Dials* rim and base fragments

	Count	Weight	Adjusted weight	Minimum numbers
Tubular Rims	35.4%	39.2%	29.2%	30.7%
Tubular Rims (without cavity)	14.4%	10.1%	9.5%	15.3%
Rounded Rims	41.1%	32.1%	45.0%	40.1%
Bases	9.1%	18.6%	16.3%	13.9%

Table 5   Comparison of quantification according to colour on the *Six Dials* material

	Count	Weight	Adjusted weight	Surface area
	(no)	(g)	(g)	(cm²)
Light Blue	453	367.1	340.6	1703.2
	56.3%	63.0%	60.3%	60.3%
Light Green	261	186.2	191.0	954.9
	32.4%	31.9%	33.8%	33.8%
Blue	17	5.4	6.3	31.3
	2.1%	0.9%	1.1%	1.1%
Green	20	12.2	12.0	60.1
	2.5%	2.1%	2.1%	2.1%
Red	6	1.1	2.2	11.2
	0.8%	0.2%	0.4%	0.4%
Yellow-brown	4	1.2	2.4	12.1
	0.5%	0.2%	0.4%	0.4%
Opaque	18	6.7	6.2	30.8
	2.2%	1.1%	1.1%	1.1%
Colourless	26	3.3	4.6	23.1
	3.2%	0.6%	0.8%	0.8%
TOTAL	**805**	**583.2**	**565.3**	**2826.7**
	100.0%	100.0%	100.0%	100.0%

mental effect on the overall relative percentage distribution of types.

Despite inevitable problems of interpretation the exercise has considerable potential for other glass assemblages and on those grounds alone is a useful innovation. Further analysis extended the scope of the study to the use of different methods of quantification in order to compare groups of glass of similar colour from *Six Dials*. Each colour group incorporated a number of rim, base and body sherds, thus removing many of the problems associated with vessel typology and measurement in this type of study. As a result, the data (Table 5) indicate a much greater consistency among the methods used.

The colour table which is inclusive of non-diagnostic body fragments emphasises the dominance of light blue and light green glass in the material (range c 89%–95%). Rim and base fragments identified with the palm cup/funnel beaker vessel series are almost invariably in these colours, while other vessel types tend to be of other, stronger colours.

Recent work by Tyers and Orton (1991) has begun to develop a new statistical approach to the study of vessel fragments using the measurement of estimated vessel equivalents (EVES). As they are mostly working with ceramics the EVES are transformed into pottery information equivalents (PIES). This approach allows information about, for example, the context, fabric and form of a ceramic assemblage to be represented as two-way tables of PIES (Orton and Tyers 1991). It is possible to apply standard statistical techniques for categorical data to the PIES which are real numbers that can be treated as integers. Comparisons between assemblages are then possible so that the significance of observed differences between assemblages can be assessed.

The new approach based on PIES which is currently being developed has been applied to the ceramics found in late Roman pit assemblages at Portchester Castle (Orton and Tyers 1991). However, the groupings of the forms recovered do not appear to be valid when compared with the archaeological evidence and further work is now underway on a variety of assemblages to gain a better understanding of the application of the technique. The technique should be equally applicable to glass vessels and this will no doubt be done in due course.

4. Colour

Research into the colouring characteristics of post-Roman glasses, notably beads, has been a relatively recent area of enquiry stimulated by excavation of settlement and working sites (see for example Callmer 1977, Biek and Bayley 1979; Lundström 1981, figs 4 and 5; Biek *et al* 1986; Sanderson and Hutchings 1987). Recovered vessel glass items are normally fragmentary, colour being one of the few descriptive criteria applicable. A number of these sites, like Hamwic, belong to the post-pagan era from which complete types are rare, and colour is therefore of importance in making any technological assessment of prevailing manufacturing standards. Glasses of the pagan period are, with some exceptions, not highly coloured, but by the 7th century brightly coloured glasses are more commonplace and may attest to superior production and quality controls. Coloured vessels of the 7th and 8th centuries have been examined in some depth (Evison 1983) and the study has pointed out the presence of latent decorative and colouring techniques, notably on glass beads, throughout the pagan period. The emergence of these techniques on vessel types from the late 6th century was perhaps due to the evolution of wealthier, more formalised markets, but on manufacturing grounds the phenomenon is best viewed as little more than a resurgence of glass-making traditions the roots of which belonged within the late Roman Empire.

Colour and coloured decoration are characteristic aspects of putative beadmaking assemblages such as Helgö (Lundström 1976), Ribe (Näsman 1979) or at the Brough of Birsay, Orkney (Hunter 1982), but are equally prevalent on 7th–9th century sites where colour variety may not have been a collection criterion. These include Ipswich, Repton, Eketorp (Näsman 1986), *Quentovic* (Heyworth 1988) and early ecclesiastical establishments such as Barking, and Jarrow and Monkwearmouth (Cramp 1970; 1975) where the glazing places considerable emphasis on colouring effect. All attest to a positive trend towards clarity and the use of bichrome or polychrome decoration. The Melbourne Street material from Hamwic also conforms to this pattern and further emphasises the renewed skills practised by contemporary craftsmen. These same skills are evidenced in this new material from Hamwic and the two sets might be considered complementary in terms of the decorative attributes and techniques exhibited.

According to the colour quantification data (Table 5) approximately 10% of the new material under study can be defined as deliberately 'coloured' glass on the grounds that the colours depart from the norms of light blue and light green which appear to typify the palm cup/funnel beaker vessel series. A number can be identified with known forms, but the majority are unassigned. All are considered to be 'decorative' on the basis of self-colouring. Also included within this definition are fragments exhibiting coloured streaking within the matrix of the vessel wall. The effect is considered here to have been due to colouring attempts (see below) and a decorative technique in its own right. Other decorative features utilise colour in a more subtle way, notably with opaque yellow or opaque white marvered trailing or with the application of reticella rods containing coloured threads. Streaking, trailing and reticella rods are extensively recorded on palm cup/funnel beaker forms but only a small number of pieces from that series are 'coloured' vessels as defined above (see for example dark green pieces 30 57 (see Plate 4 and Fig 8) and 177 191 (see Plate 4 and Fig 7)).

From the many coloured glasses represented it seems clear that the glassmakers responsible exercised considerable expertise and understanding of glass colourants, particularly for dark blue, red and green vessels. Their expertise was almost certainly the result of traditional formulae originally derived from innovation rather than a fundamental knowledge of the materials involved, and is evidenced by reference to known early medieval manuals such as those of Eraclius and Theophilus. Colour in glass was derived by the addition (deliberate or otherwise) of certain elements to the basic silica/alkali constituents, but could equally be affected by the redox conditions of the furnace in which the batch was melted. Absence of control over these variables may have contributed to many of the duller, less consistently coloured glasses of the pagan period (Hunter 1985), but the ability of the glassmaker to influence or counter them here and to produce glass to these standards, reflects highly on the expertise of the day.

The dominant vessel colours recorded are of brown/yellow, green, blue and red glass. Several of the brown/yellow items seem to belong to the squat jar vessel, a type noted previously as being of idiosyncratic colour range with purple and dark green examples at Melbourne Street (Hunter 1980, 70). The colour here (for example 15 446 (see Fig 14) and 177 619 (see Plate 4 and Fig 14)) may have been brought about by the presence of sulphur, possibly from furnace gases, in conjunction with iron, under oxidising conditions. Green (for example the tall beaker 24 546, see Plate 8) is a natural product of iron impurity in the sand constituent and can occur as a dark, almost opaque colour (for example 177 243) depending on the concentration present.

Another, more vivid green glass (for example 15 410) would have been more likely to have been the result of a copper presence with lead under oxidising conditions. Normally copper is also the colourant in many light blue glasses (for example 36 112), although iron in a reduced state is equally or even more common. A darker blue glass colour will almost certainly be due to cobalt, with copper also usually present. At least one funnel beaker type (31 564, see Plate 8 and Fig 6) exhibits a multi-stage rim formed by alternate bands of dark blue and light green glass. Similarly formed rims are known from Helgö and two have been analysed in order to determine colouring elements (Hunter and Sanderson 1983, 162). One showed the addition of copper, tin and lead and the other copper and zinc, thus suggesting that filings of bronze and brass respectively were utilised as colouring agents.

4.1 Red glass

One of the more unusual colours identified is that of red glass, fragments of which were recovered showing varying depths of colour and degrees of opacity. Several examples appear to belong to the squat jar type (for example 169 2136, see Plate 8 and Fig 14) although the exact number of vessels represented is open to conjecture. Red glass is sufficiently rare in this period to have merited previous discussion from both art-historical and technological standpoints, the former in relation to the re-emergence of coloured glasses from the 7th century (Evison 1983, 8) and the latter in terms of production dynamics (Biek and Bayley 1979, 11–12). The rarity of the types is unquestionable, although it remains to be seen whether, like the emergence of reticella fragments, the known distribution is a consequence of excavation strategy giving a false reflection of actual occurrence.

Until lately red glass has been recovered from contexts consistent with speculated glassworking sites such as at the Brough of Birsay, Orkney (Hunter 1982) and Helgö (Holmqvist and Arrhenius 1964, Fig 113), and it has also been identified as inlaid settings at Esslingen (Haevernick 1979, 165–7). On glassworking sites it occurred within assemblages of predominantly brightly coloured glasses and its presence here within an equally colourful group is predictable. Other (unpublished) fragments have since been recovered from Repton, St Wystan, where an industrial context seems unlikely and where the small assemblage of vessels appears to represent the highest quality available at the time. Dating is arduous and to some extent can be tied to that of the reticella technique, both types occurring together on the same vessel at Helgö, at Repton and at Hamwic (for example 31 661 and 26 770 (see Fig 15)), although the origins of the technique are clearly earlier with examples noted from inlaid settings of the earlier 7th century (Evison 1983, 9).

The production of translucent red glass was a considerable technological achievement requiring skilful handling of redox conditions, timing control and selection of raw materials. The essential compositional element was copper, usually with lead present, and the dynamics of the process have been detailed by Bayley (1995). A translucent red glass was possible with both metals in total solution, but normally cuprous oxide would be precipitated to produce a bright red, but opaque product in which the opacity was determined by the particle size of the 'copper' precipitate. Partial, incidental oxidation at the solidifying stage, however, could cause this bright red to change to duller brownish or dark red (for example 22 3) or even black (for example 169 2136, see Plate 8 and Fig 14) according to the degree of care.

The majority of the Hamwic fragments conform to this latter phenomenon, the effects of which are clearly visible in section as narrow layered bands of bright red, dark red, brown and colourless glass which appears black due to total internal reflection, with the two surfaces being visually red but created from aspects of all the colours represented. A few of the examples suggest higher levels of control but without the clarity seen in vessels of other colours. In the Repton fragments difficulties appear to have been tolerated and possibly utilised. Seen by reflected light these glasses appear black in colour, but in transmitted light the rich red is evident, possibly suggesting, if the effect is considered to have been deliberate, that the vessels may have been used as ornamental lamps. The same arguments are unlikely to apply to the Hamwic pieces some of which can be associated with known drinking types. On the basis that the chief characteristic of early glass was its finesse and quality, particularly in relation to its more serviceable and more easily obtainable competitors of horn, wood and ceramics, it seems unlikely that the opaque layered effect was intentional. The pieces might be better viewed as being of reject status, and as such their presence might be argued to indicate secondary glassworking activity. However, this view must be qualified since there is also present red clouded or streaked glass, argued below to have been a deliberate attempt to produce a coloured glass and caused by similar, but more easily resolved, technological and manipulative factors.

4.2 Streaked glass

Streaked glass is a fairly common occurrence in this present Hamwic material but was noted only on a single example from Melbourne Street (Hunter 1980, 70). The fundamental cause is the presence within the glass fabric of metallic elements (presumably copper) which have not achieved a state of total solution. This could be brought about by contamination from working implements, by the addition of colourants during the melting process but at temperatures below that required for total homogeneity, or, as Evison (1983, 19) has pointed out, by the rolling of a gathering in coloured glass powder or metallic particles before regathering and blowing. In all cases the technique is carried out before the glass is blown and the effect is one within the material itself rather than on the surface. The most common 'pure' colour recorded was red (for example 24 481, see Plate 5 and Fig 16) although a number of pieces exhibit dark, almost black streaking, some of which was almost certainly unintentional and caused by impurities during manipulation. Outside Hamwic the main parallels lie in the richly coloured window glass from Jarrow and Monkwearmouth (Cramp 1970; 1975) where the effect was used as a major decorative attribute. Other individual fragments have been recorded from Repton, Northampton (Hunter 1979, 253), and Whithorn (Hold 1991); the effect has also been noted by Evison on the late 7th century claw beakers from Valsgärde, Sweden (Evison 1983, 15). At *Quentovic* a fragment of a crucible containing light green glass with extensive red streaking was recovered (Heyworth 1988). The Hamwic pieces include a number of examples not assigned to known vessel types as well as others belonging to the spectrum of the palm cup/funnel beaker vessel series, where streaking appears to have been used as a random decorative feature on an otherwise pale vessel colour.

Compositionally these fragments containing red streaks can usually be distinguished from the other lightly tinted fragments on the basis of much higher iron, potash, lead and copper contents. This suggests that different raw materials were used in their production, or that other minerals were added separately to the glass batch. The red streaks are caused by the existence of discrete coloured particles in the glass. These are probably crystals of cuprous oxide and/or metallic copper which are held in suspension in the glass. The crystals are present due to precipitation of the copper out of solution when the glass melt has become supersaturated at the heat treatment temperature (Paul 1982, 265). This type of coloured glass is known as copper ruby glass, and usually has a copper content of about 0.5%.

In the production of a copper ruby glass a batch containing copper, together with a reducing agent, is melted under reducing conditions. Initially, the melt shows the blue colour characteristic of cupric (Cu^{++}) ions, but as the melting proceeds, and the furnace atmosphere becomes more reducing, the colour changes to become almost colourless (cuprous Cu^+ ions). By subsequent heat treatment commonly known as 'striking', at a temperature somewhere between the annealing and the softening temperatures, the ruby colour is developed (Paul 1982, 261). In the streaked glass the presence of lead, at levels over 0.8% in some samples, may have facilitated the initial solution of the copper and the subsequent precipitation of the crystals by lowering the temperature necessary for the striking to take place (Guido *et al* 1984, 251). The relatively high iron level, over 1.2% in some samples, may have assisted in the process by acting as a reducing agent, although these levels are not sufficient on their own. The apparent lack of a suitable reducing agent in the glass composition is therefore significant, and may indicate the use of carbon in the glassmaking process, probably as plant material.

It seems unlikely that the ancient glassmakers were attempting to produce a streaked glass, and the deliberate addition of copper to the glass batch probably indicates that they were attempting to produce a coloured glass. As copper ruby glasses are colourless when first made it is possible they were hoping to produce a colourless glass but it seems improbable that they would add copper to a glass to achieve this. If they intended to produce a colourless glass then it is more likely that they would have added a decolouriser such as manganese to the base glass. Copper in glass is usually associated with a blue colour, although in the presence of lead it produces a turquoise-green colour, and it may be that this is what was intended. However, the presence of higher than usual levels of lead and iron, combined with the presence of carbon, caused the glass to 'strike' unexpectedly, though this is unlikely without the presence of a stronger reducing agent. Another possibility is that they were attempting to produce a red glass. Modern experiments to produce an opaque red glass have shown it to be a difficult process. Attempts by Professor Cable often resulted in red streaks in the glass, which developed either during initial cooling, or on reheating in an attempt to 'strike' the colour (Brighton and Newton 1986, 219). It is possible that ancient glassmakers reduced the level of copper in an attempt to produce a paler red colour and it reached a level where it would 'strike' in some areas of the glass while adjacent areas would remain relatively colourless. However, the lack of any known examples of pure (ie not streaked) red copper ruby glasses of similar date suggest this alternative may be unlikely.

To an extent, given their lack of understanding of the chemistry of the glassmaking process, ancient glassmakers would have been at the mercy of the raw materials available to them and the impurities they contained (Newton 1978, 59). However, following an ancient tradition, there was clearly a deliberate attempt in the production of some early medieval glass to produce a blue glass by the addition of copper to the glass batch. The lead could have been added to make the glass colour a more turquoise-green. As the glass was to be coloured there would have been few problems with impurities in the raw materials and a lower grade sand may have been used which contained more iron. The attempt to produce a coloured glass would have relied on control over the thermodynamics of the redox system and, in the case of these glasses, the control was perhaps not adequate to produce an evenly coloured glass. Examined together this evidence does show considerable knowledge and skill on the part of the early medieval glassmakers who were clearly able to manipulate furnace atmosphere and melting conditions sufficiently to alter the colour of glasses independently of their composition. However, the complexities of glass chemistry, combined with a limited understanding of the raw materials with which they were dealing, meant that not all technical obstacles could be overcome.

4.3 Trailing

Colour is also intrinsic to trailing, typically in either opaque white or opaque yellow, and is commonly marvered as horizontal decoration on many recorded vessel forms. In the case of the palm cup/funnel beaker vessel series it occurs not only around the body of the vessels, but also in some instances around the lip (for example 14 204) or even within the sealed inner cavity of a tubular rim (35 35, see Plate 4 and Fig 5). The same decorative form was also observed around and below the base of a squat jar (169 889, see Plate 6 and Fig 15) and is also seen in broken lines (for example 169 147, see Fig 14) or as small bosses (for example 14 264). In a few putative bowl types the marvering has been combed into festoons (for example 33 155). Opaque white trails are formed using tin oxide, whereas opaque yellow trails can be formed either by lead-tin oxide or by a lead antimony oxide, or even by a combination of both. In each colour the tin acts as the opacifying agent and its relatively late occurrence for this purpose in glassmaking traditions has been the cause of some interest (see for example Turner and Rooksby 1961, 2; Biek 1982, 308–310; Biek and Bayley 1979, 9). Tin has been used as the opacifier for both the Hamwic opaque white and opaque yellow trails (see Appendix 3). The use of antimony is of longer tradition, and Sayre (1963) has interpreted a broad chronology for its deliberate addition from analytical evidence. There are a number of problems in assessing the importance of antimony in glasses, not the least of which lies in determining the level of concentration at which the presence might be deemed an intentional measure. Antimony has also been identified as a common impurity in glasses of this period (Sanderson and Hunter 1982, 406) and might equally be used as an indicator of difference between raw material groups.

The understanding of raw material compositions has not yet progressed sufficiently to enable an accurate distinction between levels which might be considered deliberate and those which represent impurities. Other work (Biek and Bayley 1979, 15) has also pointed out that antimony can produce both opaque white and opaque yellow glass according to whether lead is present. Antimony's role in early glassmaking is still not fully understood, thus making it difficult to formulate any accurate observations regarding its significance or chronological distribution. The use of coloured marvering here appears to represent a popular decorative convention and this was also evident on the Melbourne Street material. In Scandinavia, opaque yellow marvering tends not to appear much before the 8th century, and this is also the dominant marvered colour here. This trend also receives support in the Whithorn assemblage (Hold 1991) where some sixty examples of earlier (*ie* pre-8th century) marvering are exclusively white.

Similarly coloured trails were also used in the production of reticella rods and have been the subject of analytical investigation (Appendix 3). These were wound around a narrow glass rod and applied to the vessel surface giving the impression that the trails were threaded or spiralled within the rod itself. The technique is highly sophisticated and recent excavation of Scandinavian workshops at Ribe and Åhus where the methods were used has shown the extent to which production had been mastered (Callmer 1982, 150; Jensen 1991, 37–9). In the Hamwic material the trails are almost without exception either of opaque yellow or of opaque white, although in some vessels (for example 177 782) the individual rods contained both colours, each being wound in a different direction. On the palm cup/funnel beaker vessel series the rods are normally deployed on the lip of the rim (for example 32 473) with some showing a junction within the circumference (for example 169 1662, see Plate 2 and Fig 8). A few pieces (for example 24 703) show vertical application. A few unassigned fragments exhibit arcaded rods and these might tentatively be considered to belong to palm cup/funnel beaker vessel types by analogy with plain arcaded trails known to belong to that series. One example of arcaded rods was formed with inner and outer curves (38 108, see Plate 1 and Fig 17) each containing a different coloured trail. Reticella rods are also evident on the pushed bases of small jars (for example 32 502, see Plate 1 and Fig 15) and a further example, probably from a bowl of the Valsgärde type, shows the use of rods set in bands (169 1185, see Plate 1 and Fig 14). In most cases the colour of the rod is similar to that of the vessel to which it was applied, and this extends even to the use of a red rod (with opaque white spirals) on a red vessel (31 661). The execution of reticella rods is variable; some can be defined as exquisite with fine, precisely wound trails (for example 14 207, see Fig 16), whereas on other examples the rods are much cruder and may have been applied as a secondary process to an existing cooled rod before being applied to the vessel itself. Evison (1988a, 243) sees this as a likely cause of the threads becoming merged within the vessel wall (for example 15 462 (see Fig 15) and 30 374 (see Fig 14)).

The recovery rate of reticella fragments was relatively low until the 1950s when the excavations at Helgö, Sweden produced quantities of this type of decorated fragment. The rare nature of the material prompted Holmqvist (1964, 250–6) to list the total distribution and comment on the quality and geographical spread of the technique. At that time the main sites in Scandinavia were limited to putative industrial sites such as Ribe and Helgö itself, with a small corpus of complete items being recorded from individual burial contexts such as at Hopperstad, Norway (Hougen 1968, fig 7) and Valsgärde (Arwidsson 1932, pl XIV). British sites were few and were represented by isolated fragments such as at Whitby, North Yorkshire (Harden 1956, 152).

Lately, in tandem with a prevailing emphasis on settlement archaeology, reticella fragments have become increasingly common on both sides of the North Sea. A working centre where the technique was used for bead decoration has been identified at Åhus (U Näsman pers comm) with possible further centres at Barking (Heyworth 1992) and San Vincenzo (Moreland 1985). Fragments have been recorded within assemblages at Ipswich, Repton, London, Eketorp and *Quentovic*, the most recent compilation and discussion being by Evison (1988a) who identifies a small but growing number of English examples. Since then, however, a reticella bowl of the Valsgärde type has been recovered from Anglian York (Hunter and Jackson 1993). Strangely, the fewest examples have been found in what has been argued to have been the continental production areas for glasses of this period, and this has invited comment on the prevailing distribution patterns on the occasion of each new discovery. The most recently updated distribution (Näsman 1986, 176–80) has even suggested a British production origin. However, examples from Esslingen in West Germany (Haevernick 1979) have somewhat countered an otherwise north-western bias and further demonstrate the popularity of this decorative form. The quality of material from Hamwic, apart from showing the variety of reticella skills, is an emphatic reminder of how excavation deployment can turn a 'rare' decorative technique into one of widely used application.

4.4 Light blue/green glasses

Approximately 90% of the Hamwic material is of translucent, lightly tinted glass which visually ranges between light blue and light green, the distinction between the two usually being more apparent under conditions of reflected light. In common with the Melbourne Street material, nearly all the palm cup/funnel beaker examples fall into a light blue or light green category. A similar effect has been noted for the Scandinavian material (Hunter 1980, 72) and might also be inferred from palm cup/funnel beaker vessel types discovered at Dorestad (Isings 1980, 227–8), although the colour descriptions of the latter are ambiguous. This phenomenon was considered a potential area of investigation and was seen to be a significant discriminating factor possibly reflecting differences in raw material, furnace conditions or production centres. Preliminary visual classification of the Melbourne Street colours using standards under controlled conditions demonstrated a specific distribution of items within a light green colour range but a more broadly based distribution within a light blue range (Hunter 1980, fig 11,7). It is conceivable that both types reflect attempts to create pure colourless glass, the tinted blues and greens being the closest colours obtainable from the methods used.

In order to investigate this problem a further 195 fragments were analysed for colour and composition in an attempt to identify the underlying causes of the phenomenon. By doing so it was hoped that it might be possible to identify whether the light blues and light greens were the products of attempting to produce colourless glass, or whether they were the results of deliberate colouring or even accidental colouring. The determination of colour, for which archaeological glass poses considerable problems, was carried out by spectrophotometry using the Communitée International d'Éclairage (CIE 1970) units of dominant wavelength (λd) measured in nanometres (nm). Quantitative analysis of composition was performed by energy dispersive X-ray fluorescence (EDXRF). Notes on the experimental methods are contained in Appendix 1.

The shape of the reflectance spectrum given by the spectrophotometer indicates the element or elements responsible for the colour: for example the curve for cobalt blue is particularly distinctive. However, most of the samples selected here were seen to owe their colouration to iron modified by manganese and possibly also by copper. The overall blue/green colour would indicate that a reducing atmosphere furnace was being used. The results indicate a continuum of colour in the blue/green range but with two large groups with colour means of 496nm (light blue) and 561nm (light green) respectively (Fig 19). The strength of the light green tint is far less than for the light blue and this might suggest that the light green glass was a deliberate attempt at decolouring light blue glass.

Glass can be coloured in a number of ways, but in the case of lightly tinted glasses it is the presence of transition metal ions in the batch that contributes most to the colour. Many of these transition metals can exist in more than one valency state in the glass, the obvious and highly relevant example being iron which can exist in the ferrous and ferric states. Since both forms can exist at the same time in a glass the balance between them can be affected by control of the oxidising/reducing atmosphere.

Colour can be fundamentally altered by the furnace in which the glass is melted through the effect on the ultimate oxidation state of the glass. Changes in the fuel:air ratio will obviously have a major effect on furnace atmosphere, as will changes in fuel. Other technological factors which must be considered are the melting times and temperatures which both influence the final result. It is known from documentary sources that early glassmakers

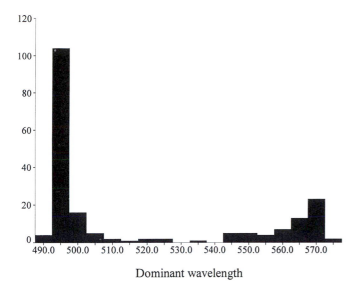

Figure 19   Histogram showing dominant wavelengths for two colour groups within the Hamwic lightly tinted glass (quoted in namometres). Light blue glass has a mean of 496mm and light green glass has a mean of 561mm.

were aware of the significance of these factors and Theophilus, in particular, describes glass changing colour in the pot as it was being heated over several hours (Dodwell 1961)

It is known too that the light tint in first millennium AD glasses is primarily caused by the presence of iron in the glass batch, which usually occurs as an impurity in the sand component of the ingredients used in glass production (Sanderson and Hutchings 1987). Iron plays a very important part in the colour of these glasses, but its effect varies with the balance between the ferric and ferrous states mentioned earlier. Ferrous iron by itself produces a blue colour while ferric iron produces a weaker yellow, the ratio of saturation being approximately ten to one. As the redox changes so the proportions of ferrous iron will change and alter the dominant wavelength. Since the ferrous iron is a stronger colour, the change in ferric iron is of less significance. The contribution of the different states of iron on the glass colour can be determined by spectrophotometry due to the different absorption band structure for each valency state.

A further complication in the colour of lightly tinted glass is the redox equilibrium between iron and manganese which is also frequently present as an impurity in the glass batch but can also be deliberately, and separately, added to the batch. Manganese acts as a decolourant by oxidising the ferrous ions in the glass. As both iron and manganese would be present as unrecognised impurities of components in a glass batch, the resulting ratio of iron:manganese would have been an important factor in the final tint of the glass. Consequently, even if unrecognised, it would have influenced the choice of components for use in glass production.

Initial compositional analysis showed that the lightly tinted glasses from Hamwic subjectively labelled light green contained, on average, less iron oxide and more manganese oxide than the light blue glasses (Fig 20). The EDXRF analysis undertaken with the colour measurement work showed that the iron:manganese ratio (calculated from oxide weight percent figures) for the two colour groups is of the order of 2.1:1 for light blue glass and 1.1:1 for light green glass (Fig 21). This compositional difference between the two glasses accounts for the difference in colour as an excess of iron over manganese in a reducing furnace would give a blue colour, whereas a similar furnace atmosphere with an iron:manganese ratio of near unity would allow the manganese to decolourise the normal iron blue colour into a paler light green colour.

The other feature of the EDXRF analyses is the different level of iron in the two colour groups. There is more manganese in the light green glasses, but there is also less iron. In the light blue the mean levels are 1.39% Fe_2O_3 and 0.65% MnO, whereas in the light green glasses the mean levels are 1.16% Fe_2O_3 and 0.97% MnO. These differences are small in percentage terms and it is possible that a different sand source was used for the production of the two groups which had differing proportions of iron and manganese as impurities, rather than suggesting the ancient glassmakers could control their glass batches to this extent. However, there are some light green fragments which have a typical light blue composition and vice versa. These colours cannot therefore be explained simply by variations in composition, and are more likely to reflect different furnace atmospheres in use when the batch was melted. A light blue glass batch may be turned light green in a more oxidising atmosphere and vice versa. It is again difficult to surmise whether these variations in furnace atmosphere were accidental or the result of deliberate control.

An experimental programme of glass melting was set up in an attempt to gain a greater understanding of the control needed to manipulate the colour of lightly tinted glasses. This involved melting glass to investigate the variations in colour of lightly tinted glass using different compositions and production conditions. It was undertaken in association with Professor Cable of the Department of Ceramics, Glass and Polymers at the University of Sheffield. Sample glass discs were produced, in a variety of conditions, of similar composition to the Hamwic light blue and light green colours. An initial batch of glass was produced under oxidising conditions. The samples were removed from the furnace at one, two, three, four and six hours after final batch charging. In general their colour was roughly constant, *ie* there was little colour variation under these conditions within the time allowed. There was some variation in colour between samples with different ratios of iron:manganese; the lower the ratio, ie the greater the proportion of manganese to iron, the more yellow the glass. These colours closely match

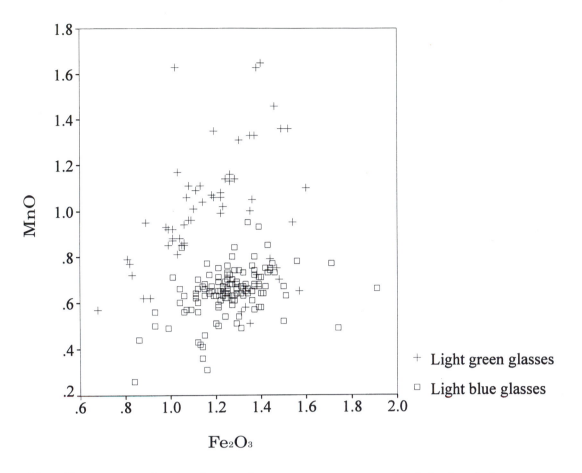

Figure 20   Scattergram showing iron and manganese contents of lightly tinted glasses

the range of light green tinted glasses from the first millennium AD.

A second batch of samples were produced under reducing conditions for a similar length of time. A blue 'streaked' colour, caused by the Fe^{2+} ions, was clearly visible in many of the iron-rich samples. These samples showed a gradual change in colour with time to a general blue colour. The colours produced suggested that with further reduction of the iron, ie longer melting times, the colours would match the range of light blue tinted glasses from the first millennium AD. The duration of the glass melt in the early medieval period would probably have been extended in order to reduce the number of bubbles in the glass and to produce a higher quality glass with the components of the batch well mixed.

In an attempt to improve the reducing atmosphere another batch of samples were produced with two grammes of carbon added to the batch. The colours of these glasses were much darker, due to the higher concentration of Fe^{2+} ions, but they were of the same hue which is dependent on the iron:manganese ratio. The colour still did not match the first millennium AD glasses so a final batch was melted with four grammes of carbon added. These glasses were the closest match to the light blue glasses from Hamwic. The experiment indicates that, although the iron:manganese ratio influences the colour of the glass, it is the presence/absence

and quantity of a reducing agent, such as carbon, during melting which may have the greatest influence on the final colour.

The extremes of colour produced by variations in the redox conditions in the furnace were visually compared. The glass made of 'Hamwic light blue' composition was initially light green in colour and gradually altered from light green to a mix of light green with light blue streaking as the furnace atmosphere became more reducing. However, the colour of the glass made of 'Hamwic light green' composition changed very little in colour. It appears that a light green glass is relatively easy to produce, and it is not very dependent on iron:manganese ratio although a low value favours its production, as does an oxidising atmosphere. Light blue glass is more difficult to produce. A high iron:manganese ratio aids its production but the essential ingredient is a strongly reducing agent, such as carbon, in a reducing atmosphere furnace. The iron:manganese ratio only seems to affect the length of working time for light blue glass – a high ratio gives a much longer working life, a low value can give light blue glass but the glass must be worked much quicker before the colour changes to light green.

Despite this, the abundance of the two colours at Hamwic is in a 3:1 ratio in favour of light blue glass. It is possible that small traces of copper and cobalt in an oxidising atmosphere would have aided the blue colour formation, but the levels of these ele-

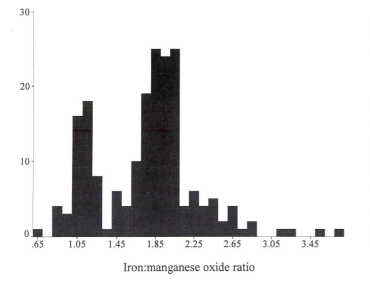

Figure 21   Iron:manganese oxide ratio for lightly tinted glass fragments using EDXRF data

Group of glasses with iron:manganese oxide ratios grouped around 1.1 are predominantly light green, whilst glasses with ratios grouped around 1.9 are mostly light blue

ments in the majority of lightly tinted glasses are barely detectable, so this seems unlikely. Tin, which could aid the reduction of the iron, is sometimes present at trace levels, judging by the EDXRF analyses, but again this seems unlikely to have had a substantial effect.

The experimental results seem to suggest that the ancient glassworkers had a great deal of knowledge and control of the glassmaking process. This is substantiated by previous work which showed that whilst there was considerable variation in the composition of Saxon vessels from Hamwic, with iron oxide values varying from 0.3% to 2.2% in the samples investigated, there was a high degree of consistency in the colour (Sanderson and Hutchings 1987). This implies that glassmakers of the early medieval period were able to compensate for variations in composition by varying furnace conditions, perhaps with the use of added reducing agents such as burnt plant ashes which would have provided a source of carbon. Also, unless special efforts were made to provide a good flow of oxygen into the furnace, smoke and gases resulting from incomplete combustion of the wood or other fuels would have been present. Sadly, little is known of furnace design in the early medieval period in Britain, and any archaeologically preserved remains are unlikely to have sufficient detail surviving of the superstructure.

5. Compositional analysis

A long-term programme of analytical studies has been undertaken on the Hamwic material as part of a wider investigation into the problems of glass and glass manufacture in the Roman and post-Roman periods. Material sampled from Melbourne Street has already been the subject of two technical papers relating to analysis by X-ray fluorescence (XRF) and neutron activation analysis (NAA), with full sets of published data (Sanderson et al 1984; Sanderson and Hunter 1982 respectively). More recent work has applied inductively coupled plasma spectrometry (ICPS) to the material under discussion here (Heyworth et al 1986). The application of standard analytical techniques to ancient glass poses a number of problems which are not amplified; these are discussed fully in the published papers and, in the case of ICPS, in a series of internal reports (Heyworth et al 1984a; 1984b; 1986) and also in Heyworth et al 1991. Notes on the experimental methods are, however, included in Appendix 2. Although the samples selected for analysis derive from both Melbourne Street and the sites under discussion here, it is assumed throughout that the groups are each representative of the total assemblage from the Middle Saxon town.

The purpose of the research was to supplement the inevitably limited typological information available from fragmentary remains by investigation of compositional data. This type of work has previously been successful in identifying major glass types and accounting for some of the characteristics of probable raw materials over broad periods of time (for example Turner 1956; Sayre and Smith 1961). Owing to the complex nature of glass production and thus the potential number of factors that might influence final composition (Hunter and Sanderson 1983, 161), analytical data gives considerable scope for interpretation. The point is particularly important here, bearing in mind that the use of analytical data for the interpretation of compositional differences within specific glass types is a relatively new departure in glass studies.

Earlier work associated with the project (Sanderson and Hunter 1980) has shown that the majority of glass available within north-west Europe from Roman to early medieval times was of the durable soda-lime-silica type, with the alkali source normally attributed to natron. The data from analyses of palm cup/funnel beaker fragments from Hamwic conform to this tradition. Published analyses of this general type of glass show that they have broadly similar compositions and that the most fruitful method of interpreting the major elements is carried out by identification of compositional trends rather than by attempting to determine dis-

crete groups. On present evidence it seems likely that most of the sodium, potassium, magnesium and some of the calcium results from the alkali raw material; while most of the silicon, aluminium, titanium, iron and minor or trace quantities of copper and lead derive from the sand. Calcium, an essential ingredient, might be derived from the selective use of calcareous sands. The presence of manganese causes particular problems (see Geilmann and Bruckbauer 1954) in that it may have been introduced deliberately in order to decolour the natural blue/green tinge of the product caused by the iron. The analysis of major and minor elements normally allows classification into glass types based on the nature of the alkali used, and within this there may be trend information on impurities from sands. Although the addition of elements for colouring or decolouring often has the effect of making this distinction difficult to determine, the choice here of only lightly tinted samples for analysis (with the exception of the ICPS analyses) is considered to have minimised any potential inaccuracies.

5.1 X-ray fluorescence

The XRF analysis for nine relevant major and minor elements was undertaken on a series of samples selected from eleven separate sites spanning the 1st millennium AD. A total of 231 items was examined and these included samples of funnel beakers from Hamwic (25), Dorestad (13) and Helgö (8), three main trading stations of the period. The glass from all eleven sites was seen to be of broadly consistent composition and conformed to an alkali type attributed to natron. Within the range of concentrations, however, it was possible to interpret specific trends, observed both geographically and chronologically, by comparison of the mean values of individual elements (Sanderson et al 1984, 61). Funnel beakers were included in the analysis partly because of their dominance among 8th and 9th century assemblages, and partly to test the traditional view that glasses of the period were of common production origin. These samples from England, Holland and Sweden were considered ideal in view of both the integrity of their archaeological contexts and their widely spaced geographical distribution.

The results of the funnel beaker analyses are shown on Table 6 which lists the means and standard deviations of the relevant elements detected (the full analyses for the individual funnel beakers from Hamwic are listed in Appendix 2). Individual values for each of the 45 fragments analysed were

Table 6   Tabulated mean and standard deviations of individual elements from three funnel beaker groups. Analytical data expressed in oxide weight %. From Sanderson *et al* 1984

Site	Na_2O	MgO	Al_2O_3	SiO_2	K_2O	CaO	TiO_2	MnO	Fe_2O_3
Hamwic									
(25 frags)									
Mean	13.2	0.7	4.25	70.4	1.05	7.91	0.14	0.49	1.11
SD	2.1	0.3	0.66	2.0	0.50	1.07	0.04	0.20	0.34
Dorestad									
(12 frags)									
Mean	14.9	0.9	3.91	64.7	1.13	10.23	0.14	0.74	0.99
S D	1.7	0.4	0.52	6.7	0.52	2.22	0.04	0.17	0.29
Helgö									
(8 frags)									
Mean	16.9	1.2	3.90	65.5	0.99	8.25	0.16	0.93	1.15
S D	2.2	0.4	0.40	2.4	0.25	0.16	0.03	0.18	0.19

also used in a discriminant analysis, and this emphasised the analytical distinctions between the three groups suggested by trends in the concentrations.

The elements mainly responsible for the discrimination are sodium, magnesium, calcium and manganese. The glasses from Dorestad and Helgö, although similar to each other in composition, are analytically distinct and well separated in composition from the glass from Hamwic. Straightforward listing of the mean values in this manner obscures minor variation in each group and it is thus possible that sub-groups exist within each category. Nevertheless there seem to be compositional differences between the three geographically distinct groups, one interpretation of which is that the glass derives from differing production centres.

In the absence of source material from known manufacturing sites it is not possible to make firm attributions of glass to a particular manufacturing centre on the basis of analytical data. Under some circumstances, however, it may be possible to postulate common or different sources, and from this point of view analytical data may be regarded as an important source of information. The XRF results, for example, might be used to argue that particular workshops may have produced glass objects or groups of glass objects which either deliberately or accidentally had characteristic compositions. However, the relatively minor nature of the percentage differences (over and above systematic error) would tend to suggest that these differences were accidental rather than deliberate and were brought about by the use of varying sources of material for the respective groups. Although this could

have been caused by the geographical separation of production centres, it could equally have occurred if a single production centre utilised different sources of a specific material (for example sand) within a locality. In the latter case however, the argument does not easily explain why any batch variation should have such geographical distinctiveness in the locations of the final product.

5.2 Neutron activation analysis

In an attempt to investigate this problem further NAA was carried out on fragments from the same three sites (Sanderson and Hunter 1982), again as part of a larger programme of investigation covering glass of the 1st millennium. This particular method was chosen in order to identify potential impurity elements existing at concentrations below those detectable by XRF. The technique has been widely used in provenance studies of pottery and obsidian for the characterisation of raw material sources (see for example Aspinall *et al* 1972) but its application to glass studies is disadvantaged by problems of interpreting the geochemistry of the natural materials used. Nevertheless, the method was seen to be of some value in discriminating between certain vessel types on the basis of trace level characteristics (Hunter and Sanderson 1982) and was employed here to allow fuller understanding of the analytical data.

Samples were selected from Hamwic (6), Dorestad (7) and Helgö (4), and the data, expressed as parts per million by weight (ppm), are shown in full in Table 7. Major and minor element analysis

44

Table 7   Analytical results of neutron activation analysis. Data expressed in ppm by weight. Minimum detectable levels in parentheses. From Sanderson and Hunter 1982

Site	Sc	Cs	Hf	Co	Ba	Sb	Cr	Ce	Eu	La	Sm	Pa	Np
H	1.0	0.2	1.4	1.5	360	2.9	0.1	0.5	0.4	1.6	0.5	1.0	(0.4)
H	2.2	9.3	2.7	17.0	530	250	0.2	29	0.9	37	5.4	2.8	(1.3)
H	1.8	5.0	2.4	10.0	410	230	0.1	2.0	0.6	1.4	0.3	0.95	(0.4)
H	1.7	5.3	5.3	7.2	390	155	1.8	19	0.6	2.0	1.5	1.5	1.5
H	1.7	9.7	2.5	21	415	255	2.5	17	0.5	9.4	0.8	2.3	(2.0)
H	2.2	6.1	3.0	14.4	440	198	(0.2)	5.8	0.9	9.1	1.5	0.92	(1.8)
D	2.5	12	4.7	23	(250)	2023	0.2	(7)	1	6.7	1.5	1.9	(1.7)
D	2.4	13	2.0	29	60	2675	0.3	14.6	0.64	8.0	1.3	2.3	(3.5)
D	1.9	13	2.5	14	140	2101	0.1	22.4	(2)	8.9	1.5	2.3	(4.3)
D	1.7	11	1.8	27	(300)	1542	0.1	16.1	0.60	5.8	1.6	1.2	(5.0)
D	2.8	11	2.5	23	510	1644	0.1	17	(2.3)	7.4	1.1	1.6	(2.8)
D	2.0	9	1.4	15	310	1492	0.2	10	1.3	5.6	1.7	1.6	(3.5)
D	1.7	7	2.4	12	880	2378	0.1	11	(2)	10.0	1.6	1.1	(5.2)
He	0.9	20	1.4	128	40	15	0.1	3.0	0.1	3.3	0.5	0.7	(0.8)
He	2.3	11	2.2	318	180	271	0.4	3.5	1.8	4.2	0.7	0.7	(1.5)
He	4.2	31	1.6	114	140	170	0.3	2.5	0.6	6.0	1.7	0.9	(1.7)
He	1.9	7.4	2.5	7.4	150	170	(0.2)	3.9	0.5	1.0	0.3	0.8	(1.8)

H = Hamwic   D = Dorestad   He = Helgö

was also undertaken on the same fragments by XRF (Sanderson and Hunter 1982, 406) and this confirmed the expected conformity to high soda-lime-silica glass. The levels of elements detected by NAA show, with some exceptions, a broad consistency within each group. The significance of exceptions of a single element for an individual item is difficult to interpret, but where they occur across a range of elements (for example the first Hamwic piece examined), the item seems likely to be 'misclassified'. In the case of this particular sample the fragment belonged to an earlier palm cup form and the data might be interpreted accordingly.

Among the potential discriminating elements present, antimony (Sb) appears to offer much potential, although its occurrence in glasses of this date is open to a number of problems discussed above. It may be noted here that the variation in antimony content within the constraints of Sayre and Smith's inferred low antimony group (1961, fig 1) raises new questions as to the origins of this element in these glasses. As a result, it might be concluded that the relative differences in antimony content between groups is a consequence of the presence of different raw material sources. On this basis antimony was used as a discriminating factor and plotted against caesium. The results are shown in Figure 22.

The distribution of items plotted shows that fragments from Dorestad and Hamwic are grouped separately, although a single Hamwic piece (noted above) fails to conform to an otherwise tight cluster. By contrast, the Helgö fragments show no such obvious grouping although it could be argued that two of the pieces lie within the Hamwic range. It seems that the antimony contents of the continental material are quite distinct from those of the English or Swedish examples, in so far as these few fragments might be considered representative. These observations do not necessarily confirm the interpretations made from the major and minor element analyses but they can equally be used to provide a similar argument favouring distinct manufacturing centres. This argument is based on raw material differences, but is subject to the interpretation of antimony as a valid characterising element and to the complex geological issues surrounding the study of natural materials.

5.3 Inductively coupled plasma spectrometry

More recent work on the Hamwic material, using the ICPS technique with a much larger range of

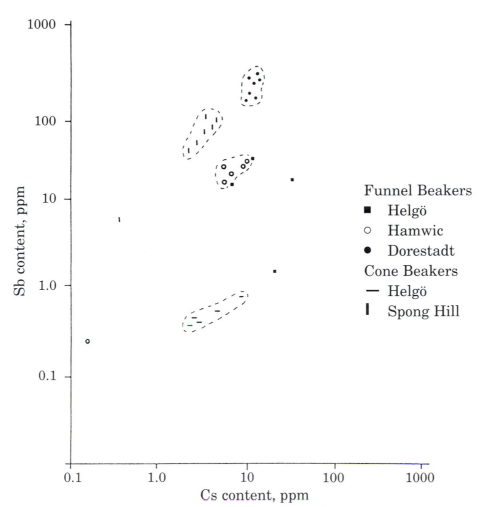

Figure 22   *Scattergram showing antimony (Sb) and caesium (Cs) contents for glass from NW Europe (from Sanderson and Hunter 1982)*

samples to obtain a full range of major, minor and trace elements, has attempted to clarify these problems of compositional disparity as well as other technological aspects of glassmaking. The larger number of samples involved has allowed differences within the Hamwic glass assemblage to be investigated, as well as comparing the glass from Hamwic with that from other early medieval centres in north-west Europe. The full analytical results for the Hamwic glass are listed in Appendix 2.

5.3.1 Palm cup/funnel beaker vessel series

It was argued above (pp 4–14)) that the three rim types for the palm cup/funnel beaker vessel series may represent a technological seriation, with the thickness of the rim gradually becoming thinner through time. A number of fragments of each type of rim were analysed by ICPS and their compositions are compared in Table 8 (using only undecorated lightly tinted examples to ensure there is no variation due to these factors). The compositions of the three rim types are not distinctive and discriminant analysis confirmed that it was not possible to distinguish between the rim types on the basis of their compositions. It is not, therefore, possible to lend any support, on the basis of the compositional evi-

dence, to the hypothesis that the three rim types represent a gradual chronological development. The two tubular rim types were also taken together as a group and compared with the rounded rims, on the basis that the technique involved in the production of the two tubular rim types was similar but different to that of the rounded rims. However, again no discrimination could be seen in the analytical data between the two groups of rim types.

The 50 tubular rim sherds analysed by ICPS included 35 light blue, 13 light green, 1 blue and 1 green fragments. The predominance of lightly tinted rims amongst those sherds analysed reflected the fact that most of the diagnostic palm cup/funnel beaker series fragments were lightly tinted and not strongly coloured. The two tubular rims that were not lightly tinted (blue – <u>24</u> 509, see Plate 4 and Fig 5; green – <u>169</u> 2840, see Fig 4) had similar major oxide compositions to the lightly tinted fragments. The blue tubular rim fragment (<u>24</u> 509, see Plate 4 and Fig 5) had a higher cobalt content of 237ppm and a copper content of 2028ppm with the blue colouration being due to a combination of these two elements. The green tubular rim fragment (169 2840, see Fig 4) had a copper content of 2807ppm and a lead content of 1.60% which imparted a green colour under oxidising conditions. The majority of

Table 8   Summary (mean and standard deviation) of the Hamwic compositional data for the three different rim types of the palm cup/funnel beaker vessel series (including only lightly tinted, undecorated rim fragments)

		Tubular rim with cavity	Tubular rim no cavity	Rounded rim	Overall
Al_2O_3	(%)	2.78 ± 0.35	2.72 ± 0.23	2.62 ± 0.27	2.72 ± 0.31
Fe_2O_3	(%)	1.11 ± 0.31	1.13 ± 0.14	1.04 ± 0.19	1.09 ± 0.24
MgO	(%)	0.80 ± 0.13	0.81 ± 0.06	0.77 ± 0.10	0.79 ± 0.11
CaO	(%)	7.07 ± 0.49	7.15 ± 0.42	6.94 ± 0.48	7.05 ± 0.47
Na_2O	(%)	15.7 ± 1.5	15.9 ± 1.4	16.3 ± 1.8	15.9 ± 1.6
K_2O	(%)	1.13 ± 0.37	1.07 ± 0.31	1.04 ± 0.35	1.09 ± 0.35
TiO_2	(%)	0.14 ± 0.03	0.15 ± 0.02	0.14 ± 0.02	0.14 ± 0.03
P_2O_5	(%)	0.43 ± 0.29	0.39 ± 0.22	0.39 ± 0.25	0.41 ± 0.26
MnO	(%)	0.49 ± 0.17	0.61 ± 0.20	0.55 ± 0.15	0.54 ± 0.17
Pb	(%)	0.55 ± 0.39	0.55 ± 0.28	0.46 ± 0.30	0.52 ± 0.34
Sb	(%)	0.22 ± 0.12	0.21 ± 0.09	0.23 ± 0.10	0.22 ± 0.11
Ce	(ppm)	20 ± 3	20 ± 2	19 ± 3	20 ± 3
Co	(ppm)	16 ± 6	15 ± 3	14 ± 3	15 ± 5
Cr	(ppm)	48 ± 6	49 ± 4	48 ± 6	48 ± 5
Cu	(ppm)	995 ± 822	879 ± 516	978 ± 696	964 ± 718
Ni	(ppm)	32 ± 5	32 ± 3	32 ± 5	32 ± 4
Sr	(ppm)	422 ± 26	429 ± 24	426 ± 24	425 ± 25
V	(ppm)	21 ± 4	23 ± 3	21 ± 3	21 ± 4
Zn	(ppm)	73 ± 43	70 ± 24	67 ± 25	71 ± 34
Zr	(ppm)	71 ± 25	75 ± 15	69 ± 12	71 ± 20
SiO_2	(%)	69.4 ± 1.7	69.1 ± 1.5	69.3 ± 1.7	69.3 ± 1.7
No of analyses		41	20	28	89

the tubular rims analysed were without any form of decoration, although a few fragments were decorated in some way (twisted vessel body – <u>24</u> 465; opaque white reticella rod – <u>169</u> 1152 (see Fig 4) and <u>169</u> 2328 (see Fig 5); marvered trail – <u>36</u> 328 (see Fig 4) and <u>24</u> 597). These fragments could not be discriminated from the undecorated tubular rims on the basis of the analytical data. The two rims that were decorated with marvered trails were similar in composition, although the differences are large enough to suggest that they are unlikely to come from the same vessel.

The 24 tubular rim without cavity fragments analysed by ICPS comprised 15 light blue, 8 light green and 1 green sherds. One green fragment (<u>177</u> 517, see Fig 6), which also has some clouding within the glass, had a distinctive composition from the other tubular rim without cavity sherds. It had a very high copper content of 7395ppm which was responsible for its stronger colour, probably in asso-

ciation with lead (0.54%), and also higher levels of phosphorus oxide (2.73%). The increased level of these oxides corresponded to lower levels of the other oxides, such as calcium (5.99%) and manganese (0.23%) oxides. The increased zinc content in the green fragment suggests that the copper may have been added in the form of leaded brass filings, or some form of waste product containing these metals. A correlation with phosphorus may indicate that the copper originated from a phosphoric ore, though it is also possible that these elements, which are known to be chemically mobile, have been absorbed into the glass from the soil in which the glass was buried. Clouding within the glass is probably due to incomplete mixing of the glass batch, possibly after the colourant was added.

There were four decorated tubular rim without cavity fragments analysed (opaque white reticella rod – <u>14</u> 232; applied trails – <u>24</u> 598, <u>177</u> 649 (see Fig 5); marvered trail – <u>177</u> 408, see Fig 6). Three of

Table 9   Summary (mean and standard deviation) of the compositional data for the lightly tinted bases from palm cup/funnel beaker vessel series compared with lightly tinted rims from similar vessels from Hamwic

		Bases	Rims
Al_2O_3	(%)	2.73 ± 0.24	2.72 ± 0.31
Fe_2O_3	(%)	1.10 ± 0.19	1.09 ± 0.24
MgO	(%)	0.80 ± 0.07	0.79 ± 0.11
CaO	(%)	7.12 ± 0-44	7.05 ± 0.47
Na_2O	(%)	16.1 ± 1.4	15.9 ± 1.6
K_2O	(%)	1.05 ± 0.42	1.09 ± 0.35
TiO_2	(%)	0.14 ± 0.01	0.14 ± 0.03
P_2O_5	(%)	0.49 ± 0.23	0.41 ± 0.26
MnO	(%)	0.53 ± 0.11	0.54 ± 0.17
Pb	(%)	0.61 ± 0.26	0.52 ± 0.34
Sb	(%)	0.24 ± 0.11	0.22 ± 0.11
Ce	(ppm)	20 ± 2	20 ± 3
Co	(ppm)	17 ± 5	15 ± 5
Cr	(ppm)	48 ± 4	48 ± 5
Cu	(ppm)	1189 ± 716	964 ± 718
Ni	(ppm)	33 ± 3	32 ± 4
Sr	(ppm)	429 ± 16	425 ± 25
V	(ppm)	21 ± 2	21 ± 4
Zn	(ppm)	84 ± 32	71 ± 34
Zr	(ppm)	72 ± 15	71 ± 20
SiO_2	(%)	68.9 ± 1.4	69.3 ± 1.7
No of cases		26	89

these decorated fragments could not be discriminated from the other tubular rims without cavity on the basis of the analytical data, although 177 649 (see Fig 5) was significantly different. However, the levels of all the major and minor oxides analysed for this fragment are lower than the other fragments, while the silica figure is correspondingly higher, which suggests that it is a feature of the analysis and not a real difference in composition.

The 56 rounded rim sherds analysed by ICPS comprised 32 light blue, 20 light green and 4 green fragments. Nearly half of these rim fragments were decorated in some way. The green coloured fragments (30 57 (see Plate 4 and Fig 8), 36 330 (see Plate 2), 36 327 (see Fig 7), 177 281 (see Plate 4)) were distinguishable from the lightly tinted fragments, having higher levels of iron, which is likely to be a cause of the green colour, probably in combination with copper and lead which are both found at higher levels in three of the samples. Decoration on the rounded rim fragments included streaking in the metal (four light blue sherds, one green sherd),

applied trails (one light green sherd, one green sherd), marvered trails (six light blue sherds, one light green sherd) and opaque white reticella rods, sometimes applied to the lip of the rim (twelve light blue sherds, three light green sherds, one green sherd). It was not possible, on the basis of the compositional data, to distinguish between the plain, undecorated rounded rims and the rounded rims decorated with either marvered trails or applied opaque white reticella rods. This suggests that they were both produced from similar raw materials and argues against the separate production of decorated and undecorated vessels.

Of the 26 bases from vessels of the palm cup/funnel beaker vessel series that were analysed by ICPS none was strongly coloured, with 17 being decorated, with one being the base of a twisted vessel (31 17, see Fig 11) and 3 having applied trails (169 440 (see Fig 11), 24 703, 177 816 (see Plate 7 and Fig 11)). The majority of the vessel bases were relatively thick, but with a small diameter and probably come from funnel beakers forms. The bases of these

Table 10   Correlation coefficients for the oxides and elements in the lightly tinted, undecorated palm cup/funnel beakers series fragments and non-diagnostic vessel fragments from Hamwic

	Al$_2$O$_3$	Fe$_2$O$_3$	MgO	CaO	Na$_2$O	K$_2$O	TiO$_2$	P$_2$O$_5$
Fe$_2$O$_3$	0.795							
MgO	0.640	0.815						
CaO	0.717	0.705	0.718					
Na$_2$O	-0.640	-0.564	-0.360	-0.550				
K$_2$O	0.811	0.780	0.745	0.747	-0.645			
TiO$_2$	0.499	0.712	0.621	0.329	-0.228	0.443		
P$_2$O$_5$	0.315	0.487	0.482	0.316	-0.247	0.342	0.091	
MnO	-0.515	-0.126	0.052	-0.306	0.524	-0.381	0.358	-0.180
Pb	0.183	0.368	0.359	0.274	-0.110	0.201	-0.033	0.709
Sb	-0.349	-0.104	-0.010	-0.235	0.529	-0.291	-0.155	0.287
SiO$_2$	-0.199	-0.400	-0.573	-0.347	-0.422	-0.248	-0.299	-0.466
Ce	0.587	0.747	0.626	0.678	-0.537	0.604	0.575	0.273
Co	0.260	0.420	0.431	0.340	-0.218	0.301	0.051	0.658
Cr	0.138	0.317	0.324	0.202	- 0.004	0.151	0.428	0.115
Cu	0.109	0.288	0.309	0.118	-0.004	0.113	-0.030	0.945
Ni	0.177	0.526	0.543	0.361	-0.196	0.318	0.261	0.583
Sr	-0.268	-0.118	0.196	-0.026	0.642	-0.200	0.043	0.101
V	0.137	0.532	0.550	0.205	0.112	0.188	0.825	0.072
Zn	0.223	0.419	0.366	0.301	-0.156	0.281	0.071	0.849
Zr	0.478	0.599	0.453	0.300	-0.096	0.351	0.782	-0.026

	MnO	Pb	Sb	SiO$_2$	Ce	Co	Cr	Cu
Pb	-0.128							
Sb	0.233	0.421						
SiO$_2$	- 0.270	- 0.514	- 0.522					
Ce	-0.102	0.153	-0.074	-0.196				
Co	-0.175	0.751	0.249	-0.406	0.198			
Cr	0.216	0.111	0.040	-0.277	0.392	0.122		
Cu	-0.077	0.714	0.456	-0.513	0.075	0.652	0.085	
Ni	0.089	0.495	0.337	-0.415	0.510	0.506	0.374	0.501
Sr	0.600	0.127	0.358	-0.652	-0.293	0.085	0.082	0.223
V	0.702	0.063	0.186	-0.499	0.476	0.068	0.422	0.044
Zn	-0.098	0.572	0.199	-0.445	0.220	0.552	0.110	0.829
Zr	0.211	-0.134	-0.013	-0.308	0.521	-0.090	0.224	-0.101

	Ni	Sr	V	Zn
Sr	0.112			
V	0.382	0.369		
Zn	0.506	0.138	0.106	
Zr	0.183	- 0.003	0.665	- 0.004

Iron, aluminium, magnesium, calcium, potassium and titanium oxide are all positively correlated with each other, but negatively correlated with soda.

The maximum positive correlation is scored at +1.000, the maximum negative correlation is scored at –1.000. Zero indicates neigher a positive nor negative correlation.

beakers are likely to survive better because of their relative thickness. The compositions of the bases were variable and there were no distinct groups in the data. As expected, the compositions of the bases matched closely those of the rim fragments from the palm cup/funnel beaker series (see Table 9).

As the majority of the diagnostic palm cup/funnel beaker vessel series fragments were lightly tinted and undecorated, with the exception of the rounded rim type which had a higher proportion of decorat-ed rims, all the lightly tinted undecorated frag-ments (rims, bases and plain, undiagnostic frag-ments) were investigated together in an attempt to identify any compositional groups. Although there was inevitably some compositional variation, this was insufficient to suggest significant differences in raw materials or necessarily indicate multiple pro-duction centres. It is more likely that the different levels of the various oxides in the glass reflect the imprecise nature of glass recipes where the quantities of the raw materials and cullet added to the glass batches would not be exactly reproduced for each batch. On the basis of this evidence it would seem reasonable to suggest that the lightly tinted palm cup/funnel beaker vessels were made of glass produced of similar raw materials, possibly in the same production centre.

The correlation coefficients for the various oxides and elements analysed in these lightly tinted palm cup/funnel beaker vessel glass fragments (see Table 10) show a number of interesting correlations that may reflect which oxides/elements entered the glass batch together. Iron, aluminium, magnesium, calcium, potassium and titanium oxide are all positively correlated with each other, but negatively correlated with soda. This suggests that the majority of the minor oxides entered the glass batch as impurities in the sand source with the silica, and that the alkali source used was relatively pure soda. Copper, cobalt and lead are all positively correlated with each other and, interestingly, with phosphorus oxide which is normally assumed to enter the glass as an impurity in plant ash. These oxides/elements are not strongly correlated with the alkali source or with the other oxides assumed to enter the glass via the sand component. It is therefore possible that they were added to the glass separately but as they were not being added at levels sufficient for colouring purposes there are no obvious reasons for this, which again suggests that they entered the glass accidentally via the use of cullet.

5.3.2 Other vessel types

The other groups of vessel glass analysed from Hamwic are less likely to come from the palm cup/funnel beaker vessel series, either because they are diagnostic of another vessel type or are strongly coloured and/or decorated, unlike the majority of the palm cup/funnel beaker vessel series.

The other vessel types that have been identified from Hamwic include squat flasks or jars, bowls and tall beakers – see above pp 14–19. The four tall beaker fragments analysed by ICPS included a light blue vessel (<u>24</u> 464, see Fig 13), a blue vessel (<u>24</u> 362), a green vessel (<u>24</u> 546, see Plate 8) and a dark opaque vessel (<u>14</u> 265, see Fig 13). The compositions of these fragments are highly variable which suggests that they may have come from different sources. One fragment analysed had a pronounced and unusual carination in the vessel wall (<u>24</u> 449) – see above p 19. However, in composition this fragment, which was light blue in colour, could not be distinguished from the other vessel types analysed.

The remainder of the other vessel types analysed by ICPS were bowl or jar forms, which were found in a variety of colours at Hamwic, often highly decorated. The compositions of these fragments were variable and no discernible groups could be recognised within these forms, though some fragments which were visually similar had compositions sug-

gesting they originated from the same vessel. These included <u>14</u> 228 and <u>14</u> 230 (see Fig 14), which are both decorated with applied reticella rods containing opaque yellow spirals, <u>169</u> 3069 (see Fig 14) and <u>169</u> 3058 (see Plate 4 and Fig 14), which are both tubular rim fragments with traces of lost marvered trailing, and <u>7</u> 32, a vessel body fragment, and <u>7</u> 33, a rim fragment (see Plate 4 and Fig 14).

Some of the other vessel types were in lightly tinted colours and were only distinguished from vessels of the palm cup/funnel beaker series on the basis of the different curvature of the vessel wall or the shape of the rim. A comparison of the compositional data for the lightly tinted bowl/jar forms and the palm cup/funnel beaker forms (see Table 11) suggests that there is no significant difference between the two vessel groups. On the basis of the compositional data it is not possible to suggest that these vessel types came from different sources. This confirms the statistical analysis of the lightly tinted palm cup/funnel beaker vessel fragments which suggests that all the early medieval lightly tinted glass circulating in Hamwic was made of similar materials and does not lend any support to theories of diverse production centres within early medieval Europe supplying the town.

The five blue coloured fragments of other vessel types analysed, mostly bowl/jar fragments but also a fragment of a tall beaker (<u>24</u> 632) and a flat fragment with a circular hole, possibly part of a lamp (<u>24</u> 510, see Plate 5 and Fig 13), were mostly coloured by cobalt, possibly in combination with copper in some cases. The composition of the possible lamp fragment was not significantly distinctive from the other blue coloured fragments, though the soda content of 18.0% was particularly high.

The seven green coloured bowl/jar fragments analysed all had high iron contents and low manganese contents which led to the stronger green colour. Two fragments (<u>26</u> 770 (see Fig 15), <u>169</u> 2136 (see Plate 8 and Fig 14)) were red due to particularly high lead and copper contents under reducing conditions. All these fragments had similar major/minor oxide levels and, from the compositional data, could not be discriminated from other coloured fragments, except on the basis of the elements responsible for their individual colours.

Two fragments from possible Roman forms were analysed by ICPS. One of these fragments (<u>24</u> 527), a light blue, flat base from a Roman flask or jar form, was analysed twice. It was possible to distinguish this fragment from the majority of the other early medieval vessel fragments by the low levels of lead and antimony. The other fragment of possible Roman type (<u>177</u> 487, see Fig 13) was part of a vessel handle decorated with a marvered opaque white glass strip down the length of the handle. The analysis of this fragment showed that it possessed very high levels of soda (20.3%) and other oxides such as calcium, phosphorus and manganese.

Table 11   Summary of the compositional data for the lightly tinted bowl/jar forms compared to the palm cup/funnel beaker series fragments from Hamwic

		Palm/funnel series	Bowl/jar forms
Al_2O_3	(%)	2.72 ± 0.30	2.90 ± 0.10
Fe_2O_3	(%)	1.09 ± 0.23	1.12 ± 0.21
MgO	(%)	0.79 ± 0.10	0.80 ± 0.13
CaO	(%)	7.06 ± 0.47	6.84 ± 0.67
Na_2O	(%)	16.0 ± 1.5	15.3 ± 0-7
K_2O	(%)	1.08 ± 0.37	1.12 ± 0.17
TiO_2	(%)	0.14 ± 0.02	0.14 ± 0.02
P_2O_5	(%)	0.42 ± 0.26	0.49 ± 0-09
MnO	(%)	0.54 ± 0.16	0.37 + 0.10
Pb	(%)	0.53 ± 0.32	0.75 + 0.22
Sb	(%)	0.22 + 0.11	0.17 ± 0.01
Ce	(ppm)	20 ± 3	19 ± 3
Co	(ppm)	15 ± 5	17 + 2
Cr	(ppm)	48 ± 5	46 ± 9
Cu	(ppm)	1008 ± 729	1083 ± 260
Ni	(ppm)	32 ± 4	31 ± 5
Sr	(ppm)	426 ± 23	404 ± 35
V	(ppm)	21 ± 3	19 ± 2
Zn	(ppm)	73 ± 35	84 ± 42
Zr	(ppm)	71 ± 19	64 i 7
SiO_2	(%)	69.2 ± 1.6	69.8 ± 1.2
No of analyses		111	6

5.3.3 Decorated, non-diagnostic vessel fragments

A large number of vessel fragments were found at Hamwic which were not diagnostic of any particular vessel type, but were either strongly coloured or decorated in some way. The 40 decorated, non-diagnostic vessel fragments that were analysed were mostly lightly tinted in colour but some were strongly coloured. The majority of the diagnostic palm cup/funnel beaker vessel series were also lightly tinted, and many were decorated, particularly those with rounded rims; it is probable that the majority of the lightly tinted, decorated, non-diagnostic vessel body fragments belong to that series. The decoration on the fragments analysed includes streaking in the metal (14 fragments), twisting in the vessel body (1 fragment), applied reticella rods containing opaque white glass spirals (three fragments), opaque yellow glass spirals (2 fragments), or both opaque white and opaque yellow glass spirals (5 fragments), and marvered trails (three frag-

ments), though most were decorated with applied rods (24 fragments).

The strongly coloured decorated, non-diagnostic vessel body fragments included two green fragments (99 96 (see Plate 5), 36 329) which both had high iron and copper contents. There were also three red fragments (99 52, 11 158 (see Plate 8), 22 3) with very high lead contents of nearly 5%, and copper contents over 5000ppm, and a dark opaque fragment (24 502) with a particularly high iron content (1.88%).

The majority of the decorated, non-diagnostic vessel fragments analysed were lightly tinted and decorated with applied trails of the same colour as the vessel body. Even within these fragments there was some variation in composition; cluster analysis showed no clear compositional groups, although some outliers were highlighted (eg 169 1906 with a high manganese oxide content of 1.0%, see Fig 17).

The spread of compositions did not allow any meaningful comparison with the compositions of the diagnostic vessels of the palm cup/funnel beaker series or with the other vessel types identified. It is clear from the analyses of the early medieval vessel fragments from Hamwic that a large number of analyses emphasises the variation in composition, within the overall soda-lime-silica type, of the glasses of the same colour and same vessel type. Consequently, it is very difficult, on the basis of compositional data, to make any meaningful statements concerning the possible sources of the vessel fragments identified, other than to reiterate the broad similarity of the glass compositions which suggests a single source for all the vessel glass.

5.3.4 Non-diagnostic vessel body fragments

The non-diagnostic vessel body fragments, by definition neither strongly coloured nor decorated, are mostly assumed to come from vessels of the palm cup/funnel beaker series. The 24 fragments analysed by ICPS were nearly all light blue in colour, except for a single light green fragment (15 390) and a single colourless fragment (99 53). Both the light green and colourless fragments have very low iron oxide contents in comparison to the light blue fragments, with the light green fragment also having a much higher manganese oxide level. There were no obvious compositional groups within the non-diagnostic fragments analysed, although four fragments, including the light green and colourless ones, did have rather different compositions to the

remainder. One of these fragments, a light blue sherd (14 273) had very low levels of minor oxides such as iron, magnesium, phosphorus and antimony, whilst another (15 389) had much higher levels of iron, magnesium, calcium and potassium oxides and correspondingly lower soda content than the other fragments. This suggests that these fragments were made of different raw materials to the remainder.

5.3.5 Window glass

Two fragments of window glass from Hamwic were analysed by ICPS. Both fragments had cut edges, but one was light blue in colour (184 65) whilst the other (36 197, see Fig 17) was blue. The deeper blue fragment had a higher copper content (1979ppm) and a slightly increased cobalt content (67ppm), a combination of these two elements being responsible for the colour. It was not possible to discriminate between the composition of the two window fragments and the vessel fragments of the same colours.

5.4 Overview

The ICPS technique has also been used to analyse both late Roman and early medieval glass from a range of sites in England and north-west Europe. More work is needed on this data before any final

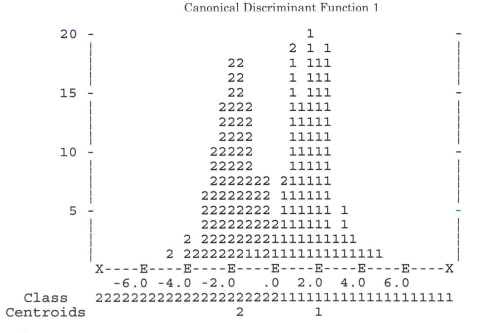

1 – Hamwic vessels

2 – Winchester vessels

Figure 23   Discriminant analysis showing the distinction between the compositions of the late Roman vessel glass from Winchester and the early medieval vessel glass from Hamwic

Table 12   Summary of the compositional data for the vessel glass from Hamwic (lightly tinted, early medieval palm cup/funnel beaker series fragments) and Winchester (late Roman vessel forms)

		Hamwic	Winchester
Al_2O_3	(%)	2.72 ± 0.30	2.52 ± 0.26
Fe_2O_3	(%)	1.09 ± 0.23	1.04 ± 0.44
MgO	(%)	0-79 ± 0.10	0.84 ± 0.34
CaO	(%)	7.06 ± 0.47	6.62 ± 0.81
Na_2O	(%)	16.0 ± 1.5	17.7 ± 1.6
K_2O	(%)	1.08 ± 0.37	0.64 ± 0.26
TiO_2	(%)	0.14 ± 0.02	0.21 ± 0.15
P_2O_5	(%)	0.42 ± 0.26	0.09 ± 0.16
MnO	(%)	0-54 ± 0.16	1.08 ± 0.62
Pb	(%)	0.53 ± 0.32	0.08 ± 0.19
Sb	(%)	0.22 ± 0.11	0.06 ± 0.12
Ce	(ppm)	20 ± 3	16 ± 3
Co	(ppm)	15 ± 5	11 ± 2
Cr	(ppm)	48 ± 5	60 ± 11
Cu	(ppm)	1008 ± 729	154 ± 347
Ni	(ppm)	32 ± 4	28 ± 5
Sr	(ppm)	426 ± 23	458 ± 56
V	(ppm)	21 ± 3	28 ± 16
Zn	(ppm)	73 ± 35	39 ± 23
Zr	(ppm)	71 ± 19	75 ± 57
SiO_2	(%)	69.2 ± 1.6	69.0 ± 2.0
No of analyses		111	102

interpretation can be made, but it is possible to draw out some conclusions from the initial study of the information that has taken place so far.

There is some suggestion from the analyses that it is possible to discriminate between late Roman and early medieval glass vessels. For example, as mentioned above (p 49), two fragments of Roman vessels from Southampton were significantly different to the early medieval vessel fragments. In an effort to see whether these differences could be confirmed for a larger group of data the late Roman vessel glass from Winchester (Price forthcoming) was compared to the early medieval palm cup/funnel beaker vessel fragments from Hamwic. Only lightly tinted glasses were included in the comparison to ensure that the use of colourants, decolourants or opacifiers did not bias the results. Discriminant analysis (Fig 23) showed that it was possible to distinguish between the two groups of glass, with the main discriminator being lead, with a number of the other minor oxides, such as potassium, titanium and phosphorus, being significantly

different between the two groups (see Table 12). These are mostly oxides which are assumed to be impurities in the sand which suggests that it was the sand sources used for glass-making that changed between the late Roman and early medieval periods. It is interesting to note that one of the Roman vessel fragments from Southampton (24 527) was also distinguished from the early medieval vessels from the town in having low levels of lead and antimony, which seems to suggest a widespread compositional feature.

The correlation coefficients for the oxides and elements in the Winchester vessel glass confirm the differences when compared to the correlation coefficients for the early medieval glass from Hamwic (see Table 10). The lead and antimony contents have a stronger correlation in the Winchester glass, and they are not correlated with the iron oxide content. The iron oxide in the Winchester glass is also correlated with the soda figure, which is the opposite to Hamwic where they are negatively correlated. These differences between the late Roman and

Table 13   Summary of the compositional data for the lightly tinted, early medieval vessel fragments from Hamwic and Ipswich compared with the lightly tinted, early medieval vessel fragments from London, Repton and *Quentovic*

		Hamwic & Ipswich	London, Repton & *Quentovic*
Al$_2$O$_3$	(%)	2.72 ± 0.29	2.72 ± 0.18
Fe$_2$O$_3$	(%)	1.08 ± 0.24	0.95 ± 0.15
MgO	(%)	0.80 ± 0.10	0.79 ± 0.06
CaO	(%)	7.09 ± 0.48	6.86 ± 0.24
Na$_2$O	(%)	16.1 ± 1.5	15.8 ± 0.6
K$_2$O	(%)	1.08 ± 0.36	1.31 ± 0.19
TiO$_2$	(%)	0.14 ± 0.02	0.14 ± 0.02
P$_2$O$_5$	(%)	0.42 ± 0.26	0.41 ± 0.18
MnO	(%)	0.52 ± 0.17	0.58 ± 0.14
Pb	(%)	0.51 ± 0.33	0.54 ± 0.30
Sb	(%)	0.21 ± 0.11	0.25 ± 0.15
Ce	(ppm)	20 ± 3	25 ± 2
Co	(ppm)	15 ± 1	16 ± 1
Cr	(ppm)	48 ± 5	36 ± 16
Cu	(ppm)	995 ± 726	4404 ± 2851
Ni	(ppm)	32 ± 4	25 ± 3
Sr	(ppm)	429 ± 25	433 ± 10
V	(ppm)	21 ± 3	23 ± 1
Zn	(ppm)	74 ± 35	99 ± 21
Zr	(ppm)	70 ± 19	50 ± 10
SiO$_2$	(%)	69.2 ± 1.6	68.8 ± 0.8
No of analyses		122	12

early medieval glass, therefore, seem to be part of a widespread pattern which is presumably due to different production centres supplying glass to Europe during and after the Roman period.

Several other north-west European early medieval sites were included in the ICPS analytical programme and it was therefore possible to compare the compositions of fragments of the palm cup/funnel beaker vessel series from a number of the different sites (for details of the other analyses see Heyworth 1991). Attempts to discriminate between the individual sites on the basis of the compositional data were largely unsuccessful. However, discriminant analysis showed that the composition of the glass from Hamwic and Ipswich could be distinguished from the glass found at London, Repton and *Quentovic*. The distinction was largely based on the levels of copper and nickel present (Table 13). Whilst it is not possible to place any significant interpretation on these few analyses, particularly as the number of fragments included from the latter three sites was only twelve in total, it may be an indication of different production sites in the early medieval period, although more work on a greater range of samples is needed before any definite conclusions can be drawn.

The correlation coefficients for each oxide and element contained in the early medieval vessel glasses from the other sites is reasonably consistent with the pattern obtained from the Hamwic analyses. These comparisons indicate that the composition of the early medieval vessel glass, particularly from those vessels that are of related typology such as the palm cup/funnel beaker series, are very similar. It is possible to distinguish some differences between the composition of these vessels, however, the differences are sufficiently small to suggest that they may be the result of the inevitable variation which must have resulted from the use of the same raw material sources over a period of time. These variations are unlikely to have been noticeable to the ancient glassmakers as they would not have affected the working properties or colour of the glass to any great extent. Consequently, it is quite

Table 14 Summary of the compositional data for the early medieval window glass from Winchester, Hamwic and Repton (including fragments of all colours)

		Hamwic	Winchester	Repton
Al₂O₃	(%)	2.69 ± 0.26	2.60 ± 0.29	2.46 ± 0.22
Fe₂O₃	(%)	1.03 ± 0.32	0.92 ± 0.31	0.90 ± 0.20
MgO	(%)	0.70 ± 0.13	0.82 ± 0.30	0.71 ± 0.08
CaO	(%)	7.00 ± 0.06	7.40 ± 0.82	6.85 ± 0.51
Na₂O	(%)	16.4 ± 1.4	17.2 ± 1.4	16.6 ± 2.0
K₂O	(%)	0.93 ± 0.13	1.01 ± 0.64	0.93 ± 0.18
TiO₂	(%)	0.13 ± 0.03	0.11 ± 0.03	0.12 ± 0.01
P₂O₅	(%)	0.33 ± 0.35	0.33 ± 0.27	0.78 ± 0.96
MnO	(%)	0.43 ± 0.04	0.55 ± 0.31	0.54 ± 0.12
Pb	(%)	0.36 ± 0.39	0.27 ± 0.22	0.27 ± 0.27
Sb	(%)	0.35 ± 0.19	0.36 ± 0.33	0.41 ± 0.28
Ce	(ppm)	20 ± 0	18 ± 2	29 ± 7
Co	(ppm)	39 ± 40	92 ± 164	74 ± 92
Cr	(ppm)	47 ± 5	48 ± 4	26 ± 10
Cu	(ppm)	1034 ± 1337	675 ± 809	6320 ± 10000
Ni	(ppm)	34 ± 8	37 ± 17	38 ± 12
Sr	(ppm)	415 ± 18	434 ± 26	433 ± 29
V	(ppm)	20 ± 4	20 ± 4	22 ± 2
Zn	(ppm)	63 ± 39	52 ± 27	158 ± 171
Zr	(ppm)	59 ± 11	53 ± 17	45 ± 6
SiO₂	(%)	69.5 ± 3.2	68.3 ± 1.5	68.5 ± 2.7
No of analyses		2	43	12

possible that the glass used in the manufacture of these vessels was produced at a single location. Unfortunately, it is not yet possible, due to the limited archaeological evidence available for early medieval glassworking in north-west Europe, to suggest whether the vessels were necessarily made at the same site where the glass was produced.

Although the vessel glass compositions were broadly similar, there was a greater compositional distinction between the fragments of window glass. The chief distinction was between the window glass from Winchester and that from Repton (Heyworth and Warren forthcoming), with several compositional sub-groups identifiable within the Winchester window glass (Heyworth and Warren 1990). However, the two fragments of window glass analysed from Hamwic were indistinguishable from those found at Winchester. The main discriminators between the window glass from Repton and Winchester/Hamwic were the trace elements cerium and chromium. A plot of these two variables

showed that the window glass from Winchester and Hamwic clustered tightly together, whilst the window glass from Repton was more variable but clearly different from the other two site groups (see Fig 24). Other oxides/elements which differed, though to a lesser extent, included iron and titanium (see Table 14), which again suggests that the variation between the glasses originates from the use of different sand sources.

In contrast to the analyses of the early medieval vessel glass, the compositional evidence for window glass provides more positive evidence for localised production. The different compositional groups within Winchester which can, in some cases, be linked to specific ecclesiastical buildings, and the distinction with the window glass from Repton suggests that glass was produced specifically for use in these situations. The similarity of the composition of the window glass from Hamwic with that at Winchester may suggest that Hamwic was able to obtain window glass from Winchester, which is only

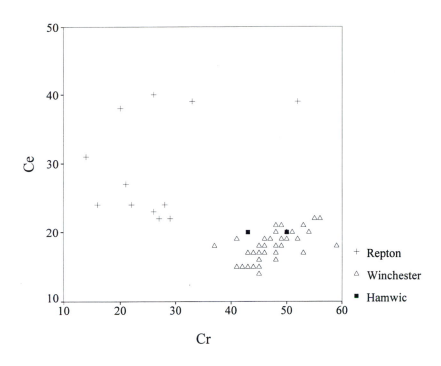

Figure 24   *Scatterplot of cerium against chromium for early medieval window glass fragments from Hamwic, Winchester and Repton*

twelve miles to the north. The frequent discovery of evidence for glassworking at early medieval ecclesiastical establishments suggests that these were the places where glassworking was primarily undertaken in early medieval Europe, presumably under the patronage of the religious orders. However, there has been no evidence for primary glassmaking at any of these sites. If the glassworkers were brought in for each building operation then it is likely that

they had a central base from which they travelled and this is most likely to be the glass production site.

Further analytical work, closely linked to the typological study of vessel and window glass will be required from a wider range of sites before it is possible to begin to make any more conclusive statements concerning the production of glass in the early medieval period.

6. Discussion

This important new collection of fragments from Hamwic is in many respects complementary to the material noted from Melbourne Street, but a number of new modifications and observations can be made. Both sets of fragments were dominated by glass forms of the palm cup/funnel beaker vessel type, the data here suggesting approximately 90% of the material by both weight and count. The evolution of this series seems fairly clear (Ypey 1963, fig 40) and recent finds (for example Isings 1980) exhibit no contradictory features. However, while the end points are easily identifiable, the intermediate stages are inevitably open to some interpretation. A natural division of the rim forms into three, distinct, technologically-defined types is perhaps a useful advance, and one which to some extent overcomes minor differences between individual vessels caused by inevitable variation in the vessel-forming process. The three forms illustrate a trend, the end points of which can be dated by association with complete examples from elsewhere, but only on the assumption that the seriations are directly comparable or that common sources are likely.

The palm cup with tubular rim can be seen from late pagan English burials (for example Harden 1956, pl XVIII m–p), from Scandinavia (for example Vendel, Arwidsson 1942, fig 99; also for general distribution see Näsman 1986, 73–4) and from the immediately adjacent areas of the continent (for example Rademacher 1942, pls 38 and 59) all within 7th or early 8th century contexts. It is a reasonable assumption (given the absence of similar rims on other forms) that these general types are either represented in the material, or are those from which the Hamwic pieces directly evolve. At the later end of the sequence the more elegant funnel beaker with rounded rim is best identified from complete examples in Scandinavia (for example Birka: Arbman 1943, pls 189/1, 190/1–2, 193/3), typically within the 9th century. However a number of fragments from Hamwic which exhibit a pronounced inward turn of the lip are much rarer, and if considered to represent the ultimate stage in the development (as interpreted here) must belong to a slightly later date. Nevertheless, as a group, these palm cup/funnel beaker pieces can be seen to lie predominantly within the 8th and 9th centuries.

It has been noted previously (Hunter 1980, 71) that certain Hamwic palm cup/funnel beaker pieces showed attributes that were either unique or rare among types discovered elsewhere, notably the marvering on the rim and the application of reticella rods to the lips. Further examples are noted here and additional features can be added: these include marvering within the tubular rim, the presence of

reticella trails to the lips of vessels across the full range of the series, and the likely use of arcaded reticella rods on a few examples. Whether these represent an original distinctiveness of the Hamwic assemblage or whether the variants should be statistically probable from the sheer quantity of material excavated is a question that can be answered only by the future discovery of comparable fragments from elsewhere. In this respect it is worth noting that the occurrence here of a palm cup/funnel beaker base exhibiting vertical reticella rods was considered unique to Hamwic until the publication of a vessel exhibiting similar rods (Isings 1980, fig 154:3) served to emphasise the extent to which excavation strategy might be affecting distribution.

The dating of the series by association with similar material from pagan burials has suggested a broad 8th–9th century range, arguably extended into the 10th century by the presence of 'ultimate' forms with inturned lip which appear to be a characteristic of this local group. However, in Hamwic a narrower chronology of deposition has to be inferred, for at the sites dug in this town, especially those of *Six Dials*, there has been found a relative stratigraphy which is fairly closely datable through the existence of a large number of associated artefacts, most notably the coins (Metcalf 1988). It is likely that the chronology should be compressed at Hamwic to a period between the earlier 8th and earlier 9th centuries. The site matrices, however, generally confirm the relative chronology of the sequence from tubular rim to rounded rim within this period.

The problem is one of explaining the compression of this development in relation to the broader span of time interpreted from Scandinavian depositions. Two probable causes of this disparity can be identified; firstly that the Hamwic material is not precisely comparable on typological grounds with the Scandinavian material, or secondly, that the depositional chronology of one of the groups has been influenced by unidentified factors. The first of these alternatives can be countered by the fact that the general forms are similar, despite minor decorative and contour attributes, and by the presence of other similar forms in continental contexts. An overview shows the palm cup/funnel beaker vessel series to have been commonplace throughout north-west Europe, and thus the second cause is a more realistic alternative. Problems are exacerbated by the difficulty of dating the palm cup/funnel beaker contexts outside Hamwic: the Helgö pieces were recovered from layers spanning several centuries; the Birka types were dated according to the typological/art historical criteria of associated artefacts; and those at Dorestad appear to have been located within a timescale formulated by a similar derived chronology. Only at Hamwic for the reasons outlined above may the contexts be used as a reliable yardstick. In the absence of detailed dating evidence from other sites it would appear that the full sequence of types had been achieved by the earlier 9th century. Given the apparent common distribution of types elsewhere, this dating range is of some significance. Although, for example, this compression of the seriation can be absorbed within the broad framework of the Helgö stratigraphy, it poses certain problems regarding the presence of glass in the Birka cemetery; there the palm cup/funnel beaker forms in the later part of the seriation might be seen as being old at the time of deposition. Work has already shown that many glasses in Scandinavian burials might be interpreted as having an intrinsic 'heirloom' or 'special' significance (Hunter 1975) on the basis of their physical position within the funerary context. This could certainly apply to many of the Birka vessels whose grave positions are distinctive. In turn this suggests a rarity value and infers a certain Scandinavian remoteness from the manufacturer or manufacturers supplying Hamwic – a possibility already suggested above from compositional analysis.

The implications of this are more far-reaching for Scandinavian archaeology than for British archaeology, but the issue serves to emphasise the importance of the contextual integrity of the Hamwic material and its resultant significance in early glass studies. As far as this specific vessel group is concerned, a number of features might now be noted as being characteristic of this early 9th century period; these include the presence of both marvered opaque yellow and opaque white trails, the tendency for yellow marvering to occur in combination with the application of reticella rods, and the reticella rods themselves which appear to represent a popular and conventional decorative technique. Whether or not these features are characteristic of Hamwic alone (or its source), or to north-west Europe as a whole will be demonstrated only by excavation of other contemporary sites.

Other vessel forms were in a considerable minority and this tends to suggest, assuming the material to be representative, that the number of forms being produced in the Middle Saxon period was somewhat less than in pagan times. The major identifiable groups consist of small flasks or jars, bowls and tall beakers, together comprising less than 10% of the total corpus by either count or weight. Of these the flask/jar forms were most easily identifiable from pushed base fragments (the most durable part of the vessel) and can be compared with complete forms from a number of 7th and 8th century contexts (such as Gotland (Nerman 1969, pl 85 no 740), Kent (Harden 1956, pl XVIII k) and with fragmentary remains from Helgö (Holmqvist and Arrhenius 1964, 253 pl 113). The distribution of this type has recently been discussed by Näsman (1986, 70–3). The dated examples from burial contexts are acceptable within the Hamwic chronology but are better suited to the earlier rather than the later part of the chronological range. They occur in Hamwic pit contexts in association with the full spectrum of palm cup/funnel beaker forms but this can be reconciled to some extent with the clearance nature of many of the deposits. A particular characteristic of these types, already evident from Scandinavian examples and emphasised further here, is their bright or varied colouring. This might now be extended to include the application of self-coloured reticella rods.

Tall beakers could only be identified from rim fragments in those instances where the contour of the surviving body portion suggested an overall conical form. In most cases the vessels are of a deep colour (blue, red or green) with one example showing marvered trailing and several exhibiting the zones of applied self-colouring trails (for example 177 498, see Plate 4 and Fig 9) more typical of the claw beaker forms. Similarly coloured and decorated fragments from Eketorp, Öland, have also been interpreted as belonging to claw beakers (Näsman 1986, 62–3). Other than one possible 'claw' (24 570) no lower body fragments were identified but the presence of claw beakers cannot totally be discounted despite this relatively late date of occurrence. Tall beakers tend not to appear beyond late 7th century contexts, but this in itself is no reason to preclude their existence either in survival form or as cullet within the earlier part of the period considered here. Indeed a small group of fragments exhibiting a pronounced carination in the body may even belong to bell beaker forms; they pose a similar chronological problem (see also Näsman 1986, 74). Like the claw beaker, this type is normally to be found in contexts no later than the 7th century, but has since been discovered in deposits contemporary with palm cup/funnel beaker forms at Dorestad where an 8th century date has been postulated and where the persistence of the bell beaker form has been queried (Isings 1980, 226). The cullet argument might apply equally, but there is, nonetheless, a growing inference that a number of vessel forms persisted in use, if not in manufacture, into the 8th century. Another possibility for these fragments lies in a type identified by Holmqvist (1964, 257) from Helgö, probably of bottle form, but without close dating.

An earlier rather than later date seems likely for these non-palm cup/funnel beaker forms, suggesting a number of possibilities which include loss of contact with a particular production centre, or, more plausibly from the evidence noted above, a further decrease in forms available by the 9th century. The only vessel type possibly exceptional to this is the bowl form, the chronology and distribution of which is now becoming more understood as new finds are discovered. Examples of the Valsgärde-type bowl were identified from Hamwic from characteristic rim pieces and suitably contoured body fragments showing bands of applied reticella rods. Similar forms are recorded from Helgö (Holmqvist 1964, 253), Fishergate in York (Hunter and Jackson 1993) and from both Dorestad (Isings 1980, fig 154) and Esslingen (Haevernick 1979, 168); the type has been reviewed in some detail by Evison (1988a, 241). These are acceptable in 8th century contexts, or even before (Näsman 1980, 80), thus emphasising an earlier rather than later variety of available forms. More difficult to interpret, however, is a group of fragments from Hamwic, undoubtably of bowl profile, for which there are few obvious parallels. These fragments are of either blue or lightly tinted glass with two of the examples exhibiting combed marvered decoration. A similar piece was discovered at Melbourne Street (Hunter 1980, 70, fragment 4 31) and was attributed to probable eastern manufacture with the less likely possibility of a north Italian provenance. Since then additional pieces showing similar combing have been recovered at Dorestad (Isings 1980, fig 155), at Whithorn (Hold 1990) and at Maastricht (van Lith 1988, for example fig 41); at the last of these the fragment is argued to belong to a small bowl of Belgian type with a context post-dating the 6th century (ibid, 72). Problems in identifying the nature and origins of these vessels will undoubtedly lessen as more examples are recovered; current evidence suggests that they are more likely to appear in 5th and 6th century contexts than those of the 7th or 8th century. Holmqvist (1964, 253) was able to reconstruct a small number of bowl forms from the Helgö material and these might be used as a basis for contemporary types and developments.

The decrease in the range of vessel types by the 8th and 9th centuries seems well enough established from current excavated data, yet those types which appear to have diminished in variety are those which ostensibly pertain to one specific function, namely that of drinking. If a smaller range of items was produced one might justifiably expect that the resulting vessels would still perform the minimum number of vessel functions necessary. It might be anticipated that while a single drinking form persisted (the palm cup/funnel beaker vessel series), a bowl form, satisfying a completely different function, might also have continued well into the 9th century. If it did not, the point is of interest in assessing the role played by glass, its status, its availability and the likely presence of contemporary vessels produced from competing materials. From the evidence here, however, it would seem that the few bowl fragments recovered could not be used to indicate the retention of that specific function. Accordingly, there seems to be a decrease in typological variety by the 9th century. The only exception, represented by two items hesitantly interpreted as lamps, is virtually unparalleled and thus undatable beyond the broad chronology of the Hamwic contexts. Both fragments exhibit perforations at the base in combination with internal decoration. They represent the only evidence for innovation in an otherwise decreasing range of products.

6.1 Contextual significance

These issues of form and chronology are, however, not confined solely to aspects of visual typology; a number of other factors require amplification, the most pressing being that of the contextual significance of the assemblage as a whole. The decorative quality seen from many of the pieces, both of coloured glass and of ornamented lightly tinted glass, shows many similarities to other contemporary glass assemblages (such as at Ribe and Helgö) where beadmaking or other secondary activities have been mooted. This issue of function, determined by whether the glasses were complete or fragmentary in their original role on the site of recovery, has considerable bearing on both the status of glass within the town and on the nature of the population that used it.

There are a number of distributional factors which are of some value in this respect. It seems reasonably certain, for example, that the palm cup/funnel beaker vessel series was a popular form throughout north-west Europe, and equally that other vessel forms (by comparison highly coloured) were rarer within the same contemporary distribution areas. By the 9th century the palm cup/funnel beaker alone continued to be manufactured, and thus any individual assemblages of cullet containing developed funnel fragments are unlikely to have been collected earlier than that time. The site contexts, however, demonstrate a chronological distribution of fragments which broadly conforms (with some overlap) to the evolution of the palm cup/funnel beaker vessel series; hence the deposition of fragments might be interpreted as having been individual and continuous, rather than collective and sporadic. In turn this suggests unbroken contact with suppliers until the earlier or middle part of the 9th century after which time glass was either not produced, or, was not supplied, or perhaps was not even required. The general absence of nondurable glass which is first recorded at nearby Winchester from the late 9th or early 10th century (Biddle and Hunter 1990, 362) might also be used to suggest that such contacts were broken by this time, possibly indicating that the main period of occupation at Hamwic had already been passed. There appears to be a general scatter of glass across the sites excavated, particularly at *Six Dials*, and apart from a few specific concentrations of remains (notably at SOUs 24, 31 and 169 – all within *Six Dials*), the greater part of the assemblage derives from pit deposits and presumably represents clearance debris.

The disposal of glass fragments in debris contexts itself suggests that the items were of little value, or alternatively that the disposal process was carried out without the fragments being observed – an unlikely factor considering the bright colouring of many of the pieces. Indeed, one of the main arguments against an original cullet function is the ubiquity of this fragmentary waste material which seems incongruous with that of a tradable commodity.

Another factor which tends to argue against a cullet function is the virtual absence of non-vessel glass items which tend to characterise those assemblages where secondary activity has been identified. Pieces of coloured tesserae which could be used as a basic material for beadmaking, such as have been found at for example Paviken, Gotland (Lundström 1974), at Ribe (Näsman 1979, 127–8), in smaller quantities at Helgö (Lundström 1981, 17), Kaupang (Hougen 1969) and at Whithorn (Hold 1991) were not recorded at Hamwic. The colouring merits of tesserae were noted by Theophilus (II XII) and the colours of the Paviken pieces could be closely correlated with the beads produced. At Åhus, Sweden, tesserae were supplemented by flakes of coloured glass struck from blocks or cakes, and the significance of these has been discussed in some detail (see Callmer 1982, 149). It is interesting to note that at Åhus the vessel fragments constituted only a minor part of the excavated assemblage and thus contrast starkly with the Hamwic material. The inhabitants of Åhus were also proficient in the production of reticella rods, and the site might be viewed as a sophisticated reworking centre with which, on the basis of excavated evidence, Hamwic cannot compare. Ribe has produced a slightly different assemblage (Näsman 1979) in which both vessel fragments and finished products (for example beads) were common, but the nature of the material is nevertheless different from that of Hamwic.

It is difficult to determine the type of yield that a 'typical' reprocessing or semi-manufacturing site might offer, and previous discussions have viewed the problem in terms of trade backgrounds, available skills and recovered materials (for example Hougen 1969, 128; Lundström 1981, 17). Approaches of that type best serve to interpret sites such as that at Staraja Ladoga, in the USSR, where tesserae were absent but where beadmaking was identified from a primary glass-manufacturing process (L'Vova 1970), no doubt intended for vessels, but extended to include other glass items. Other common remains in the form of wasters and rods are also mostly absent at Hamwic, but notable exceptions include a single twisted rod from Melbourne Street (Hunter 1980, fig 11, 2 no 6) and a substantial waster here (31 1013). Both items are normally diagnostic of secondary activity, the rods often exhibiting tong marks such as at Helgö, Paviken, Hedeby, Ribe and Kaupang (Lundström 1976, 8). The evidence of glass reuse on any scale is thus difficult to identify at Hamwic and is further emphasised by a general dearth of likely secondary products, especially beads. Although the small number of beads recovered showed a range of opaque colours and decorative effects that might have resulted from fragments typical of the assemblage, there were no rejects or unfinished pieces which might point towards a localised beadmaking activity.

The predominance of vessel fragments among the Hamwic glass material is not evidenced elsewhere to the same extent; the closest parallel lies at Helgö where vessel fragments constituted the greater part of the glass assemblage throughout the sequence of occupation, but where other items were specifically indicative of beadmaking. The resulting interpretation (Lundström 1981, 21) was one which took into account the trading and commercial importance of the settlement, suggesting that glass was imported in complete form with the intention of resale, but that small-scale beadmaking also took place, probably utilising items which were broken in the trade process. This 'warehouse' theory is an acceptable compromise solution for that site and might offer some direction to the problem here. If applied, it would effectively reduce the standing of Middle Saxon Hamwic to little more than a repository for glass vessels, but at the same time might go some way to explain why glass was so ubiquitous on the sites excavated. In any event, given the trading and manufacturing prowess of the Hamwic community as indicated by other artefacts, and in the absence of any overt evidence of glassworking activity, the presence of complete vessels in the first instance might reasonably be assumed.

There are, however, problems in such an assumption. These include the low minimum number of palm cup/funnel beaker vessels calculated from base fragments; the presence of window fragments within the corpus; and the occurrence of small glass items, notably reticella rods, which appear to have been deliberately separated from adhering body fragments. For the first of these, the relative absence of palm cup/funnel beaker bases is difficult to explain; in theory their durability and toughness should have guaranteed a greater probability of archaeological survival as appears to have been the case in the Birka 'Schwartz Erde' (Arbman 1937, 52). If the material originated as cullet their relative absence is explicable, but if considered as original complete vessels on or near the location of discovery, and assuming the assemblages to be representative, it might be concluded that broken bases were deliberately removed. This removal may have been undertaken at a simple level, for example in the separate disposal of large and obvious items, but conversely the bases may have been useful for some other purpose. It might tentatively be concluded that the palm cup/funnel beaker bases were somehow significant, either by virtue of their bulk or their lightly tinted colour, or by a combination of both.

The presence of a small quantity of window glass is equally difficult to reconcile with a non-cullet group. Glazing, even in the 8th and 9th centuries, was still rare in Anglo-Saxon England (Hunter

Table 15   Mean sherd weights from two Hamwic sites excavated under different conditions

Site	Number of fragments	Mean Weight (g)
SOU 36	73	1.112
SOU 169 (without sieved portion)	246	0.820
SOU 169 (total recovery)	567	0.462

1981, 143–4) and seems to have been wholly restricted to ecclesiastical buildings, or more specifically, to those constructed of stone. Window glass is evidenced from Winchester at this time, from locations appropriate to an ecclesiastical context, but its use seems unlikely at Hamwic where the structures appear to have been timber-supported (Brisbane 1988). Several of the fragments occurred in pit contexts together with vessel glass and, although there was an 8th or 9th century church at SOU 13 (Morton 1992, 123), there is no firm evidence to support the notion of an original glazing function for the fragments recovered.

Different problems are presented by several of the small, highly ornamented pieces, notably fragments of reticella rods or applied arcaded trails. Several of these show evidence of having been deliberately trimmed by breakage in order to leave as little of the vessel body as possible adhering to the ornament. Although these pieces are naturally more durable than the body portions by virtue of their thickness, the manner of the breakage, which in many instances leaves only that part of the vessel wall which physically touches the ornament, is uncharacteristic of a natural fracture. The implications are that this process was undertaken either to retain the ornamented part or, conversely, to retain undecorated parts of the vessel and reject the ornamentation. If the retention of the ornamentation was intended, perhaps for colouring purposes or for decoration in a re-working process, the items fall into the category of cullet and are not easily explained in the context of disposal. If, on the other hand, the ornamented parts were deliberately discarded, the depositional contexts are wholly in keeping with this interpretation. Harder to explain are the reasons why this might have been carried out.

If the interpretation is extended to cover all the material, it could be argued that many of the items recovered might also have been de-selected in a similar manner, that is to say, they represent the residue from a specific selection process. These would include both trailed and coloured areas, clouded or streaked portions of the body and zones of decoration immediately below the rim. These decorative and colouring aspects may, for example, have offered specific problems in any subsequent glass-based process. It might therefore be useful to consider what is not present in the material, assum-

ing many of the items to represent 'waste'. One possibility is that the lightly tinted fragments were removed for assisting in a primary glassmaking process where they were of traditional value in forming the batch without significantly affecting the colour. The most suitable cullet for rapid melting would have been thin-walled fragments and the selection would have entailed the rejection of thicker items (rims and bases) together with coloured pieces which might have darkened an intended clear product. Research into this possibility would entail examination of the size and weight of individual items in an attempt to identify fragment types missing from the assemblage.

Such an exercise is inevitably limited, not only by breakage factors but also by the difficulties in determining the degree to which a particular site assemblage can be considered representative in terms of the recovery system used. Material from the sites excavated in the 1940s, eg SOUs 36, 38 and 39, is, for example, markedly distinct from material recorded from later investigations in that the items are invariably larger and the corpus smaller. This is likely to have been due to the recovery system at the time. The point is exemplified by reference to Table 15 which considers the mean weights of fragments from two separate excavated areas, one examined in 1946–50 (SOU 36) and the other in 1983 (SOU 169). For the latter site the fragments derived from sieving have been measured separately.

Not unnaturally the results indicate the lowering of the mean fragment weight according to the sophistication of recovery and thus emphasise the difficulty of interpreting any overall de-selection process for which size/thickness may have been a criterion. It does, nevertheless, indicate a possible future approach to assemblages of this type where function is largely open to question.

6.2 Conclusions

The conclusions regarding the original function of the Hamwic glass are necessarily confused, the most fitting interpretation probably lying in a combination of factors. Any evidence for secondary working in the form of beadmaking is small, and, while this localised activity may have occurred in the vicinity, it cannot be seen as the major purpose behind the presence of the glass. The greater proportion of the fragments must be assumed to represent complete vessels within the town, either in use as domestic items or as broken stock according to the 'warehouse' interpretation. Given the ubiquity of the pieces throughout every site excavated the latter possibility seems unlikely for all but a part of the assemblage; the presence of domestic items in the first instance is a more satisfactory interpretation for the bulk of the material. This, however, carries with it a possible inconsistency on the grounds that the items are from vessels of considerable quality and presumably of equally high value. Their presence might be seen, perhaps inaccurately, as testimony of wealth in a merchant context. No other Middle Saxon town has been investigated on the same scale as Hamwic, and whether the nature of this assemblage conforms to, or departs from, a contemporary norm remains unknown.

On the other hand the concept of de-selection which might be inferred from the fragments gives rise to the possibility of localised glass production in or near the town itself. At this stage the point can be neither proved nor disproved, but it may be noted that few of the criteria outlined by Lundström (1981, 22) as being essential for production can be met from the Hamwic remains. Some support for this, however, exists in the presence of a small number of ceramic sherds and stones exhibiting glass droplets, residues or 'industrial' concretions; these were mostly scattered, although a concentration of items was noted within SOU 169. The same site revealed two hearth or furnace features but neither was of a type considered appropriate to glassmaking or working and working debris was not identified. The items recovered seem unlikely to have travelled far from the location of use and would suggest the presence of 'industrial' activity nearby. Unfortunately, the nature of this activity is unclear; glass was certainly melted but the concretions on a few of the items could also be argued to have originated from a fritting process which would indicate primary glassmaking. Siliceous deposits, however, are also produced by other industrial processes and the argument might be tempered accordingly.

Indirect support for the argument can be derived from the overview of analytical data which suggests a compositional distinctiveness for the Hamwic group in relation to Scandinavian material analysed. The results of both major/minor and trace element analysis could be used to suggest that the Hamwic palm cup/funnel beakers were derived from a different source from those vessels recovered from Dorestad, and probably also from Helgö. The fact that the overall compositional data from Hamwic using ICPS, based on a suite of 28 elements, was comparable with that of a Winchester window group of roughly the same date might also point towards a common production origin. Any localised industry, even based within the region itself, would additionally serve to explain not only why glass was so common in the town, but also why any de-selection process might have taken place. It is otherwise difficult to explain why so few of the fragments recovered can be reconstructed into complete forms. Conversely, however, if palm cup/funnel beaker vessel types were produced locally it becomes difficult to establish exactly where distribution was intended. According to the excavated evidence, Hamwic itself received the glass, but it seems unreasonable to suppose that production was intended for that town alone. However, according to the analytical data, Helgö and Dorestad, both recently argued to have been supplied from British sources (Näsman 1986, 88–9), received their glass from elsewhere than Hamwic; and no proof has yet been found that the glass was exported to, for instance, France and the south-western areas of the Continent. A group of Winchester window glass may have been made by the same workshops as Hamwic's but on present evidence not one palm cup/funnel beaker type found its way to Winchester, although at least part of the reason may lie in an excavation bias in the later part of the Anglo-Saxon town. The picture is far from simple and does not necessarily explain the presence of non-palm cup/funnel beaker forms within Hamwic, or even suggest their point of origin. The solution, if there is one, probably lies in an understanding of sub-divisions of groups, both typologically and chronologically, currently undefinable but perhaps hinted at by the compositional distinction between the light green and the light blue fragments.

For the present, the Hamwic material stands as the single most important assemblage of European glass of the 7th to 9th centuries. Irrespective of the conflicting interpretations regarding function, the sophistication and quality of many of the pieces is undeniable; they represent a high point in post-Roman glass and reflect levels of craftsmanship and technology unequalled until the Middle Ages. In some respects this corpus marks the last flowering of durable glass in the first millennium: no other forms are seen here or elsewhere, and the tradition, although continuing in some of the later Winchester window glass, appears to have given way to vessels made from more readily available materials. The recovery of this glass is of considerable importance for the overall understanding of Middle Saxon Hamwic and may have far-reaching implications, not only for the direction and nature of the town's trade, but also for other contemporary towns and the trading networks on which they depended.

Bibliography

Alcock, L, 1963, *Dinas Powys, an Iron Age, Dark Age, and early medieval settlement in Glamorgan*, Cardiff.

Andrews, P (ed), 1997, *Excavations at Hamwic: volume 2*, CBA Res Rep **109**

Arbman, H, 1937, *Schweden und das karolingische Reich*, Stockholm.

Arbman, H, 1943, *Birka*, **1**, Stockholm.

Arwidsson, G, 1932, Some glass vessel from the boat grave cemetery at Valsgärde, *Acta Archaeologia*, **3**, 251–66.

Arwidsson, G, 1942, *Vendelstile, email und glas*, Stockholm.

Aspinall, A, Feather, S W and Renfrew, C, 1972, Neutron activation analysis of Aegean obsidians, *Nature*, **337**, 333.

Bayley, J, 1995, *Notes on the composition of coloured glasses*, in K Blockley *et al*, *Excavations in the Marlowe Car Park and surrounding areas. The archaeology of Canterbury*, **5**, 1194–9.

Bayley, J, 1987, Viking glassworking: the evidence from York, in *Annales du 10ᵉ congrès de l'Association Internationale pour l'Histoire du Verre, Madrid 1985*, Amsterdam, 245–54.

Bayley, J, 1991, La verrerie en Angleterre pendant l'époque Anglo-Saxonne, in D Foy and G Sennequier (eds), *Ateliers de verriers de l'antiquité à la période pré-industrielle*, Rouen, 31–4.

Bede, *Historia abbatum*, C Plummer (ed), 1896.

Biddle, M and Hunter, J R, 1990, Window glass, in M Biddle (ed), *Object and economy in medieval Winchester*, Winchester Studies, **7**(ii), Oxford, 350–86.

Biek, L, 1983, The ethnic factor in archaeotechnology, in A Aspinall and S E Warren (eds), *Proc 22nd international symposium on archaeometry*, Bradford, 303–15.

Biek, L and Bayley, J, 1979, Glass and other vitreous materials, *World Archaeol*, **11**(1), 1–25.

Biek, L, Bayley, J and Gilmore, G, 1986, Scientific examination of the glass beads, in S M Hirst (ed), *An Anglo-Saxon inhumation cemetery at Sewerby, E Yorkshire*, York University Publications, **4**, 77–85.

Bimson, M, 1978, Coloured glass and millefiori in the Sutton Hoo ship burial, *Annales du 7e congrès international d'étude historique du verre, Berlin-Leipzig 1977*, Liège, 427–33.

Brighton, T and Newton, R, 1986, William Peckitt's red glasses, *Stained Glass Quarterly*, **81**, 213–20.

Brisbane, M, 1988, Hamwic (Saxon Southampton): an 8th century port and production centre, in R Hodges and B Hobley (eds), *The rebirth of towns in the West AD 700 – 1050*, CBA Res Rep, **68**, 101–8.

Callmer, J, 1977, *Trade beads and bead trade in Scandinavia ca 800–1000 AD*, Acta Archaeologica Lundensia, Lund.

Callmer, J, 1982, Production site and market area, *Meddelanden från Lunds Universitets Historika Museums* (1981–2), 135–65.

Chase, P G, 1985, Whole vessels and sherds: an experimental investigation of their quantitative relationships, *J Field Archaeol*, **12**, 213–18.

CIE, 1970, *Principles of light measurement*, Paris.

Cramp, R, 1970, Decorated window glass and millefiori from Monkwearmouth, *Antiq J*, **50**, 327–35.

Cramp, R, 1975, Window glass from the monastic site of Jarrow: problems of interpretation, *J Glass Stud*, **17**, 88–96.

Evison, V I, 1982, Anglo Saxon glass claw beakers, *Archaeologia*, **107**, 43–76.

Evison, V I, 1983, Bichrome glass vessels of the seventh and eighth centuries, *Studien zur Sachsenforschung*, **3**, 7–21.

Evison, V I, 1988a, Some Vendel, Viking and Saxon glass, in B Hårdh, L Larsson, D Olausson, and R Petré (eds), *Trade and exchange in prehistory*, Acta Archaeologia Lundensia, **16**, 237–245.

Evison, V I, 1988b, Vieux-Marche, Place Saint-Lambert, Liège – The glass, in M Otte (ed), *Les fouilles de la Place Sainte-Lambert à Liège 2, Le vieux marche*, Etudes et Recherches Archeologiques de l'Université de Liège **13**, 215–9.

Evison, V I, 1990, Red marbled glass, Roman to Carolingian, *Annales du 11ᵉ congrès de l'Association Internationale pour l'Histoire du Verre, Basel 1988*, Amsterdam, 217–28.

Evison, V I, forthcoming, The glass from Ipswich.

Fletcher, W and Heyworth, M P, 1987, The quantification of ceramic types, in C F Gaffney and V L Gaffney (eds), *Pragmatic archaeology: theory in crisis?*, BAR British Ser, **167**, 35–46.

Fulford, M, 1973, Excavation of three Romano-British pottery kilns in Amberwood enclosure, near Fortham, New Forest, *Proc Hampshire Fld Club Archaeol Soc*, **28**, 5–28.

Geilmann, W and Bruckbauer, T, 1954, Der mangangehalt alter gläser, *Glastechnische Berichte*, **27**, 456–9.

Guido, M, Henderson, J, Cable, M, Bayley, J and Biek, L, 1984, A Bronze Age glass bead from Wilsford, Wiltshire: barrow G42 in the Lake Group, *Proc Pre Soc*, **50**, 245–54.

Haevernick, T E, 1979, Karolingisches glas aus St Dionysius in Esslingen, *Forschungen und Berichte der Archaeologie des Mittelalters in Baden-Wurttemburg*, **6**, 157–71.

Harden, D B, 1956, Glass vessels in Britain and Ireland AD 400–1000, in D B Harden (ed), *Dark Age Britain: studies presented to E T Leeds*, London, 132–67.

Harden, D B, 1978, Anglo-Saxon and later medieval glass in Britain: some recent developments, *Medieval Archaeol*, **22**, 1–24.

Henderson, J, 1988, The nature of the Early Christian glass industry in Ireland: some evidence from Dunmisk fort, Co Tyrone, *Ulster J Archaeol*, **51**, 115–26.

Henderson, J and Holand, I, 1992, The glass from Borg, an early medieval chieftain's farm in northern Norway, *Medieval Archaeol*, **36**, 29–58.

Henderson, J and Warren, S E, 1983, Analysis of prehistoric lead glass, in A Aspinall and S E Warren (eds), *Proc 22nd international symposium on archaeometry*, Bradford, 168–80.

Henderson, J and Warren, S E, 1986, Analysis of the glass and glassy waste, in D Tweddle (ed), *Finds from Parliament Street and other sites in the city centre, The Archaeology of York: the small finds*, **17**(4), London, 224–5.

Heyworth, M P, 1988, Glass from *Quentovic*, *Stained Glass*, Spring 1988, 16.

Heyworth, M P, 1991, *An archaeological and compositional study of early medieval glass from north-west Europe*, unpublished PhD thesis, University of Bradford.

Heyworth, M P, 1992, *Evidence for early medieval glass production in north-west Europe*, in *Medieval Europe 1992: technology and innovation*, pre-printed conference papers, **3**, 169–74.

Heyworth, M P, Hunter, J R and Warren, S E, 1984a, *ICPS as an analytical tool in archaeometry*, contribution prepared for meeting on the Chemical Analysis of Roman Pottery held at King's College, London.

Heyworth, M P, Hunter, J R and Warren, S E, 1984b, *Calibration of the IC plasma spectrometer for the analysis of high soda content glasses*, unpublished laboratory report, University of Bradford.

Heyworth, M P, Hunter, J R and Warren, S E, 1986, *Inductively coupled plasma spectrometry of archaeological materials*, final grant report to SERC, University of Bradford.

Heyworth, M P, Hunter, J R, Warren, S E and Walsh, J N, 1989, The role of inductively coupled plasma spectrometry in glass provenance studies, in Y Maniatis (ed), *Archaeometry: proceedings of the 25th International Symposium*, Amsterdam, 661–70.

Heyworth, M P, Hunter, J R, Warren, S E and Walsh, J N, 1991, ICPS and glass: the multi-element approach, in M J Hughes, M R Cowell and D R Hook (eds), *Neutron activation and plasma emission spectrometric analysis in archaeology: techniques and applications*, Brit Mus Occas Pap, **82**, London, 143–54.

Heyworth, M P and Warren, S E, 1990, Scientific analysis of the window glass using inductively coupled plasma spectrometry, in M Biddle (ed), *Object and economy in medieval Winchester*, Winchester Stud, **7**(ii), Oxford.

Heyworth, M P and Warren, S E, forthcoming, Scientific analysis of the window glass, in M Biddle and N Wickenden (eds), *Investigations at Repton volume 3: the material cultures of Repton*.

Hill, D, Barrett, D, Maude, K, Warburton, J and Worthington, M, 1990, Quentovic defined, *Antiquity*, **64**, 51–8.

Hinton, D, 1983, *25 years of medieval archaeology*, Sheffield University.

Hodges, R, 1982, *Dark Age economics*, London.

Hold, A G, 1991, *The study of the Anglian vessel and window glass from Whithorn using ICPS analysis*, unpublished undergraduate dissertation, Department of Archaeological Sciences, University of Bradford.

Holmqvist, W, 1964, Glass, in W Holmqvist and B Arrhenius (eds), *Excavations at Helgö II*, Stockholm, 242–59.

Holmqvist, W and Arrhenius, B, 1964, *Excavations at Helgö II*, Stockholm.

Hougen, E, 1968, Glassbegre i Norge fra Sjetta til Tiende Århundre, *Viking*, **32**, 85–110.

Hougen, E, 1969, Glassmaterialet fra Kaupang, *Viking*, **33**, 119–37.

Hulthen, B, 1974, On choice of element for determination of quantity of pottery, *Norwegian Archaeol Rev*, **7**, 1–5.

Hunter, J R, 1975, Glass from Scandinavian burials in the first millennium AD, *World Archaeol*, **7**(1), 79–86.

Hunter, J R, 1979, The glass, in J Williams (ed), *St Peter's Street, Northampton, Excavations 1973–76*, 297.

Hunter, J R, 1980, The glass, in P Holdsworth (ed), *Excavations at Melbourne Street, Southampton, 1971–76*, CBA Res Rep, **33**, London, 59–72.

Hunter, J R, 1981, The medieval glass industry, in D Crossley (ed), *Medieval industry*, CBA Res Rep, **40**, London, 143–50.

Hunter, J R, 1982, The glass, in C L Curle, *Pictish and Norse Finds from the Brough of Birsay 1934–1974*, Soc Antiq Scot Monogr Ser, **1**, 46–7.

Hunter, J R, 1985, Glass and glassmaking, in P Phillips (ed), *The Archaeologist and the Laboratory*, CBA Res Rep, **58**, London, 63–6.

Hunter, J R and Jackson, C M, 1993, Glass, in N S H Rogers (ed), *Anglian and other finds from Fishergate, The Archaeology of York*, **17**(9), York Archaeological Trust, York, 1331–1344.

Hunter, J R and Sanderson, D C W, 1982, The Snartemo/Kempston problem, *Fornvännen*, **77**, 22–9.

Hunter, J R and Sanderson, D C W, 1983, The investigation of early glass, in A Aspinall and S E Warren (eds), *Proc 22nd international symposium on archaeometry*, Bradford, 158–67.

Isings, C, 1980, Glass finds from Dorestadt, Hoogstraat I, in A Van Es and W J H Verwers (eds), *Excavations at Dorestadt I. The Harbour:*

Hoogstraat I, Nederlandse Oudheden, **9**, Amersfoort, 225–37.

Jackson, C M, Hunter, J R, Warren, S E and Cool, H E M, 1990, The analysis of blue-green glass and glassy waste from two Romano-British glass working sites, in E Pernicka and E A Wagner (eds) *Archaeometry '90 – International Symposium of Archaeometry*, Basle, 295–305.

Jackson, C M, Hunter, J R and Warren, S E, 1991, The analysis of glass from Coppergate, York by inductively coupled plasma spectrometry, in P Budd, B Chapman, C M Jackson, R C Janaway and B S Ottaway (eds) *Archaeological Sciences 1989*, Oxford, 76–82.

Jensen, S, 1991, *The Vikings of Ribe*, Antikvariske Samling, Ribe.

L'Vova, Z A, 1970, Stekhjanne busy Staroj Ladogi. Cast II. Proischozdenie busoga. *Archeologceskij Sbornik*, **12**, Leningrad.

van Lith, S M E, 1988, Late Roman and Early Merovingian glass from a settlement site at Maastricht (Dutch South Limberg) – Part 2, *J Glass Stud*, **30**, 62–76.

Lundström, A, 1976, Bead-making in Scandinavia in the Early Middle Ages, *Early Medieval Studies*, **9**, Stockholm.

Lundström, A, 1981, Survey of the glass from Helgö, in A Lundström, G Werner, A Knape, H B Madsen and S Reisbord (eds), *Excavations at Helgö VII: glass–iron–clay*, Stockholm, 1–38.

Lundström, P, 1974, Paviken I bei Vastergarn. Hafen, Handelsplate under Werft, *Vor- und Fruhformen der Europaischen Stadt im Mittelalte*r, Gottingen.

Metcalf, M, 1988, The coins, in P Andrews (ed), *Southampton Finds, Vol 1: The coins and pottery from Hamwic, Southampton Archaeol Monogr Ser*, **4**, Southampton, 17–59.

Millet, M, 1979, How much pottery?, in M Millet (ed) *Pottery and the Archaeologist, Institute of Archaeology, University of London, Occasional Paper*, **4**, 30–5.

Moreland, J, 1985, A monastic workshop and glass production at San Vincenzo al Volturno, Molise, Italy, in R Hodges and J Mitchell (eds), *San Vincenzo al Volturno. The Archaeology, Art and Territory of an Early Medieval Monastery, BAR Int Ser*, **252**, 37–60.

Morton, A D (ed), 1992, *Excavations at Hamwic volume 1: excavations 1946–83 excluding Six Dials and Melbourne Street, CBA Res Rep* **84**, London.

Näsman, U, 1979, Die Herstellung von Glasperlen, in M Bencard, K Ambrosiani, L B Jorgensen, M B Madsen, I Nielsen and U Näsman, Wikingerzeitliches Handwerk in Ribe: eine ubersicht, *Acta Archaeologia*, **49**, 113–38.

Näsman, U, 1986, Vendel period Glass from Eketorp-II, Oland, Sweden, *Acta Archaeologica*, **55, 55–116**.

Näsman, U, 1990, Om fjärrhandel i Sydskandinaviens yngre järnålder. Handel med glas under germansk jarnalder och vikingetid, *Hikuin*, **16**, 89–118.

Nerman, B, 1969, *Die Vendelzeit Gotlands*, Stockholm.

Newton, R G, 1978, Colouring agents used by medieval glassmakers, *Glass Technol*, **19**(3), 59–60.

Olczak, J, 1971, *Bemerkungen zur technologie der glasproduktion in Polen im fruhen mittelalter*, Veroffentlichungen des Museums fur Ur– und Fruhgeschichte, Potsdam.

Orton, C, 1975, Quantitative pottery studies: some progress, problems and prospects, *Sci & Archaeol*, **16**, 30–5.

Orton, C, 1980, *Mathematics in archaeology*, London.

Orton, C and Tyers, P, 1991, A technique for reducing the size of sparse contingency tables, in K Lockyear and S P Q Rahtz (eds), *Computer Applications and Quantitative Methods in Archaeology 1990, BAR Int Ser*, **565**, Oxford, 121–6.

Paul, A, 1982, *Chemistry of Glasses*, London.

Price, J, forthcoming, Late Roman vessel glass, in M Biddle (ed), *Roman Winchester*, Winchester Studies series

Rademacher, F, 1942, Frankische glaser aus dem Rheinland, *Bonner Jahrbucher*, **147**, 285–344.

Radford, C A R, 1958, The excavations at Glastonbury Abbey 1956–7, *Somerset Dorset Notes Queries*, **27**, 165–9.

Rooksby, H P, 1964, A yellow cubic lead tin oxide opacifier in ancient glasses, *J Sci & Technol*, **29**, 20–6.

Sanderson, D C W and Hunter, J R, 1980, Major element glass type specification for Roman, post-Roman and medieval glasses, *Revue d'Archaeometrie*, **3**, 255–64.

Sanderson, D C W and Hunter, J R, 1982, Neutron activation analysis of glass from Britain and Scandinavia, *PACT*, **7**, 401–11.

Sanderson, D C W, Hunter, J R and Warren, S E, 1984, Energy dispersive X-ray fluorescence analysis of 1st millenium AD glass from Britain, *J Archaeol Sci*, **11**, 53–69.

Sanderson, D C W and Hutchings, J B, 1987, The origins and measurement of colour in archaeological glasses, *Glass Technol*, **28**(2), 99–105.

Sayre, E V, 1963, The intentional use of antimony and manganese in ancient glasses, in F Matson and G E Rindone (eds), *Advances in Glass Technol*, **2**, 263–82.

Sayre, E V and Smith, R W, 1961, Compositional categories of ancient glass, *Science*, **123**, 1824–6.

Stolpe, H, and Arne, T J, 1927, *La Necropole de Vendel*, Stockholm.

Tabacynska, E, 1965, Glasshutte aus dem VII-VIII Jhrt auf Torcello, Communication faite au VIIe congrès de l'International Commission au Glass, Brussels.

Theophilus, *De Diversis Artibus*, C R Dodwell

(trans), 1961.

Turner, W E S, 1956, Studies in ancient glasses and glassmaking processes part IV, *J Soc Glass Technol*, **40**, 162–86.

Turner, W E S and Rooksby, H P, 1961, Further historical studies based on X-ray diffraction methods of the reagents employed in making opal and opaque glasses, *Jahrbuch des Romisch-Germanisches Zentralmuseums*, **8**, 1–6.

Tyers, P and Orton, C, 1991, Statistical analysis of ceramic assemblages, in K Lockyear and S.P.Q.Rahtz (eds), *Computer Applications and Quantitative Methods in Archaeology 1990*, *BAR Int Ser*, **565**, Oxford, 117–20.

Wade, Keith, 1988, Ipswich, in R Hodges and B Hobley (eds), *The rebirth of towns in the west AD 700–1050*, *CBA Res Rep*, **68**, 93–100.

Ypey, Y, 1963, Die funde aus dem frumittelalterlichen graberfeld Huinerveld bei Putten im Museum Nairac zu Barnveld, *Berichten R O B*, **12/13**, 99–152.

Appendix One. Colour measurement of the Hamwic glass

In all, 195 sherds of lightly tinted glass were analysed for colour and composition. The samples were selected from many different sites within Hamwic using the following criteria:

i) Size and shape. Minimum size was 6mm diameter, and, as the pieces were all vessel fragments, flatter pieces were chosen.
ii) Surface and homogeneity. Badly scratched and highly seeded ('bubbled') pieces were avoided.
iii) Colour. Only lightly tinted blue/green pieces were selected. Non-uniformly coloured pieces (those with streaked decoration) were excluded.

There is no universally accepted method of colour determination for actual measurement, units of colour or standards. However there are preferred methods, units and standards. In this analysis the following were used:

Instrument

Pretema FS-3A spectrophotometer, interfaced to a Hewlett-Packard HP85 micro-computer using dedicated software.

Method

Diffuse illumination using a Xenon light source onto the sample embedded in a tray of pure $BaSO_4$ (a 100% diffuse 'white' reflector). The resulting reflected beam was passed through a series of 33 interference filters (range 390nm–710nm in 10nm steps) to be eventually detected by a photo-multiplier. The micro-computer handles all calibration and running conditions and outputs both colour units and graphics (reflectance/absorbance spectrum for visible light per sample).

Units

There are very many units of colour. For the majority of them however, the samples measured need to be perfect (no bubbles) and have optically parallel sides. This does not apply to the Hamwic glass, and hence units were chosen accordingly. The parameters used were CIE (Communitée International d'Éclairage) 1931 units x, y and λd. The unit λd (dominant wavelength measured in nm) lies in the range 380–780nm and represents the 'colour' of the sample. It is calculated from colour units x, y.

Standards

The samples were referenced to CIE Illuminant C (North Sky-light) and to a $BaSO_4$ 'white' standard. The XRF analysis was carried out on a Philips PV9500 energy dispersive (EDAX) analysis system. Samples were buffed and polished before analysis in order to remove any surface effects that may affect the analysis. Suitable standards were used to provide a calibration for the following elements: sodium, magnesium, aluminium, silica, phosphorus, potassium, calcium, titanium, manganese, iron, copper, zinc, arsenic, lead, strontium, zirconium, tin, and antimony (as oxides).

Preliminary results indicate a continuum of colour in the blue/green range. However there seem to be two large groups with colour means of 496nm (light blue) and 561nm (light green) in the proportion of sherds of 3:1, light blue:light green (Fig 19). Due to the skewed nature of the colour units, similar groups can be achieved using a random scatter of points, but tests of statistical significance show the two Hamwic colour groups to be significant.

The XRF analysis showed that the Fe:Mn ratio (the major colouring agents) for the two groups is noticeably different for the two colour groups, that is 2.1:1 Fe:Mn for light blue glass and 1.1:1 Fe:Mn for light green glass. The absolute quantities show this well (see also Fig 20):

Light Blue : Fe_2O_3 1.39%   MnO   0.65%
Light Green: Fe_2O_3 1.16%   MnO   0.97%

The differences are very small and it is difficult to believe in a deliberate addition of 0.32% MnO. It is far easier to accept that another sand source was used to make light green glass which had a different Fe:Mn composition (whether this was done deliberately is another question). Other elements show slight variations, noticeably K, Ca, Cu, Pb, Sn, and Sb. Of these Cu and Sb show most promise in explaining colour change, although at a level of approximately 0.2% (average) it is difficult to say that these are deliberate additions (there are some sherds where this level is higher, for example 0.5% Sb_2O_3 and 1.0% CuO). Even though the absolute levels may be small, their contribution to the final colour of the glass is significant.

Interestingly, there are some light green sherds which have typical 'light blue' composition and vice versa. These colours cannot be explained by compositional differences. However, such differences could be explained by a particular batch being melted differently in the furnace. For instance a light blue batch may be turned light green in a rather less reducing atmosphere furnace and vice versa. Again it is difficult to know whether to interpret this as due to deliberate control.

In conclusion there do seem to be two types of lightly tinted 'clear' glass differentiated by colour measurement and in most cases by compositional analysis. As yet it is difficult to ascertain whether any of the above compositional/furnace differences were deliberate attempts to 'decolour' iron-tinted glass. The evidence so far seems to imply the glass-makers were constrained by their raw materials and the efficiency of an individual furnace on the day of firing.

The information listed here is the dominant wavelength for each fragment, obtained by colour measurement, measured in λd; the MnO and Fe_2O_3 contents for each fragment, obtained by surface EDXRF analysis; and the iron/manganese ratio figure calculated from the EDXRF data.

The fragments are divided into two groups with the light blue fragments listed first, followed by the light green fragments.

Light blue glass

Fragment No			λd	Fe/Mn	MnO%	Fe_2O_3%
SOU	7	No 31	500.7	1.762	.63	1.11
SOU	11	No 157	493.9	1.970	.67	1.32
SOU	11	No 162	495.8	2.098	.61	1.28
SOU	11	No 164	496.3	1.524	.84	1.28
SOU	11	No 180	503.9	2.885	.52	1.50
SOU	11	No 182	492.0	1.889	.63	1.19
SOU	13	No 64	494.5	1.797	.69	1.24
SOU	14	No 211	494.2	1.955	.67	1.31
SOU	14	No 218	495.9	2.407	.54	1.30
SOU	14	No 237	494.5	1.877	.65	1.22
SOU	14	No 240	496.0	2.894	.66	1.91
SOU	14	No 253	495.4	2.000	.62	1.24
SOU	14	No 258	494.0	2.047	.64	1.31
SOU	14	No 260	493.2	1.893	.56	1.06
SOU	14	No 272	494.9	1.762	.63	1.11
SOU	14	No 273	494.5	3.231	.26	.84
SOU	14	No 281	505.7	2.414	.58	1.40
SOU	14	No 284	496.4	1.645	.76	1.25
SOU	14	No 287	496.5	1.956	.68	1.33
SOU	14	No 289	493.8	1.877	.57	1.07
SOU	14	No 292	499.3	2.397	.58	1.39
SOU	15	No 393	492.8	1.894	.66	1.25
SOU	15	No 400	494.1	2.044	.68	1.39
SOU	15	No 420	498.2	1.757	.74	1.30
SOU	23	No 11	494.5	1.955	.67	1.31
SOU	23	No 13	494.4	1.734	.64	1.11
SOU	23	No 20	495.0	1.897	.68	1.29
SOU	23	No 22	494.1	1.860	.50	.93
SOU	23	No 25	496.2	1.814	.70	1.27
SOU	23	No 26	500.8	2.016	.63	1.27
SOU	23	No 33	494.3	1.923	.65	1.25
SOU	23	No 35	494.6	3.167	.36	1.14
SOU	23	No 36	495.0	3.742	.31	1.16
SOU	23	No 37	497.5	1.853	.68	1.26
SOU	24	No 159	493.9	1.868	.68	1.27
SOU	24	No 429	494.3	2.690	.42	1.13
SOU	24	No 431	493.8	2.605	.43	1.12
SOU	24	No 432	494.6	1.600	.70	1.12
SOU	24	No 448	497.5	2.529	.51	1.29
SOU	24	No 454	496.3	1.588	.80	1.27
SOU	24	No 459	494.2	1.958	.71	1.39
SOU	24	No 464	495.5	2.016	.62	1.25
SOU	24	No 470	493.5	1.790	.62	1.11
SOU	24	No 473	499.0	2.500	.46	1.15
SOU	24	No 474	494.6	1.661	.56	.93
SOU	24	No 477	494.9	2.032	.63	1.28
SOU	24	No 480	492.7	1.691	.68	1.15
SOU	24	No 489	494.4	1.972	.71	1.40
SOU	24	No 499	494.7	1.683	.63	1.06
SOU	24	No 505	495.8	2.000	.73	1.46

Fragment No			λd	Fe/Mn	MnO%	Fe₂0₃%
SOU	24	No 511	493.7	1.959	.73	1.43
SOU	24	No 523	494.4	1.808	.73	1.32
SOU	24	No 536	494.7	1.423	.71	1.01
SOU	24	No 538	494.7	1.870	.69	1.29
SOU	24	No 539	496.1	2.188	.64	1.40
SOU	24	No 545	494.1	1.903	.72	1.37
SOU	24	No 547	493.4	1.625	.72	1.17
SOU	24	No 557	498.6	1.955	.66	1.29
SOU	24	No 571	496.0	2.119	.67	1.42
SOU	24	No 575	497.5	2.203	.64	1.41
SOU	24	No 583	491.8	1.576	.66	1.04
SOU	24	No 586	495.3	2.239	.67	1.50
SOU	24	No 596	494.1	1.828	.64	1.17
SOU	24	No 604	497.5	2.000	.66	1.32
SOU	24	No 612	495.0	2.045	.67	1.37
SOU	24	No 623	494.3	1.800	.65	1.17
SOU	24	No 627	494.9	2.404	.57	1.37
SOU	24	No 630	495.9	2.094	.64	1.34
SOU	26	No 100	493.6	1.922	.64	1.23
SOU	26	No 156	494.7	1.956	.68	1.33
SOU	26	No 562	494.6	1.952	.63	1.23
SOU	26	No 615	494.0	1.825	.63	1.15
SOU	26	No 623	492.3	2.296	.54	1.24
SOU	26	No 657	495.9	2.397	.63	1.51
SOU	26	No 693	496.2	2.000	.56	1.12
SOU	26	No 753	493.4	2.153	.59	1.27
SOU	26	No 761	494.8	2.000	.61	1.22
SOU	26	No 776	494.3	2.046	.65	1.33
SOU	30	No 45	494.9	1.905	.63	1.20
SOU	30	No 115	493.8	2.020	.49	.99
SOU	30	No 291	501.3	1.712	.73	1.25
SOU	30	No 330	505.1	1.704	.71	1.21
SOU	30	No 432	496.2	1.867	.60	1.12
SOU	30	No 538	494.7	1.955	.44	.86
SOU	31	No 17	493.8	1.736	.72	1.25
SOU	31	No 30	516.0	1.411	.95	1.34
SOU	31	No 110	494.0	1.733	.60	1.04
SOU	31	No 256	497.6	1.912	.57	1.09
SOU	31	No 282	494.0	1.613	.75	1.21
SOU	31	No 534	495.0	2.030	.66	1.34
SOU	31	No 540	495.5	1.953	.64	1.25
SOU	31	No 555	495.5	1.862	.65	1.21
SOU	31	No 578	509.6	1.495	.93	1.39
SOU	31	No 585	495.0	2.086	.58	1.21
SOU	31	No 748	495.2	2.051	.59	1.21
SOU	31	No 749	494.8	2.082	.61	1.27
SOU	31	No 1131	498.4	2.420	.50	1.21
SOU	31	No 1253	498.3	2.673	.49	1.31
SOU	31	No 1462	493.9	1.713	.80	1.37
SOU	31	No 1509	495.4	1.786	.70	1.25
SOU	31	No 1604	502.6	3.551	.49	1.74
SOU	31	No 2590	519.5	2.230	.61	1.36
SOU	99	No 21	493.9	2.095	.63	1.32
SOU	99	No 32	494.3	1.815	.65	1.18
SOU	99	No 116	492.5	1.955	.66	1.29
SOU	99	No 127	500.2	2.016	.64	1.29
SOU	169	No 5	493.7	2.015	.68	1.37
SOU	169	No 29	495.7	1.730	.74	1.28
SOU	169	No 186	495.6	1.682	.85	1.43
SOU	169	No 229	496.3	1.789	.76	1.36
SOU	169	No 231	494.4	1.836	.67	1.23
SOU	169	No 440	492.3	1.761	.67	1.18
SOU	169	No 676	494.9	1.938	.64	1.24
SOU	169	No 875	493.9	1.742	.66	1.15
SOU	169	No 951	499.0	1.864	.66	1.23
SOU	169	No 1009	510.0	2.092	.65	1.36
SOU	169	No 1152	494.0	1.953	.64	1.25
SOU	169	No 1413	496.3	2.780	.41	1.14
SOU	169	No 1622	494.3	1.697	.66	1.12

Fragment No			λd	Fe/Mn	MnO%	Fe₂0₃%
SOU	169	No 1956	495.2	1.894	.66	1.25
SOU	169	No 1982	492.8	1.883	.77	1.45
SOU	169	No 2097	496.3	1.506	.77	1.16
SOU	169	No 2253	496.1	1.754	.69	1.21
SOU	169	No 2272	493.6	1.851	.74	1.37
SOU	169	No 3040	494.6	1.701	.67	1.14
SOU	169	No 3208	517.9	2.075	.67	1.39
SOU	169	No 3073	494.8	1.750	.72	1.26
SOU	177	No 311	496.2	1.893	.75	1.42
SOU	177	No 408	494.1	1.946	.74	1.44
SOU	177	No 409	494.2	2.000	.78	1.56
SOU	177	No 419	495.6	1.920	.75	1.44
SOU	177	No 561	495.0	2.221	.77	1.71
SOU	177	No 649	506.5	2.353	.51	1.20
SOU	184	No 65	496.2	1.250	.84	1.05

Light green glass

Fragment No			λd	Fe/Mn	MnO%	Fe₂0₃%
SOU	11	No 154	548.3	1.455	1.10	1.60
SOU	11	No 168	565.2	1.165	.85	.99
SOU	11	No 175	566.9	.992	1.31	1.30
SOU	11	No 177	568.8	1.018	1.11	1.13
SOU	13	No 70	548.9	1.103	1.07	1.18
SOU	14	No 201	569.5	.847	1.63	1.38
SOU	14	No 204	543.0	1.161	.87	1.01
SOU	14	No 204	543.0	1.161	.87	1.01
SOU	14	No 215	544.5	1.135	.96	1.09
SOU	14	No 238	568.7	1.098	.92	1.01
SOU	14	No 239	557.5	2.339	.56	1.31
SOU	14	No 256	568.9	1.009	1.06	1.07
SOU	14	No 268	562.5	1.235	.85	1.05
SOU	14	No 283	569.4	2.293	.58	1.33
SOU	15	No 390	570.0	.880	1.17	1.03
SOU	24	No 475	565.3	1.125	.96	1.08
SOU	24	No 520	555.2	1.115	1.13	1.26
SOU	24	No 528	534.8	1.193	.57	.68
SOU	24	No 600	565.0	2.415	.65	1.57
SOU	24	No 603	556.2	1.096	1.04	1.14
SOU	26	No 552	573.0	2.647	.51	1.35
SOU	26	No 582	548.9	1.123	1.06	1.19
SOU	26	No 622	565.0	1.233	.86	1.06
SOU	26	No 649	567.8	1.000	1.46	1.46
SOU	26	No 773	545.4	1.123	1.14	1.28
SOU	30	No 17	568.3	.849	1.65	1.40
SOU	30	No 44	561.7	1.115	1.13	1.26
SOU	30	No 52	569.3	1.272	.81	1.03
SOU	30	No 92	570.3	1.065	.77	.82
SOU	30	No 120	550.9	1.182	.88	1.04
SOU	30	No 262	569.6	1.148	.88	1.01
SOU	31	No 7	561.3	2.114	.70	1.48
SOU	31	No 366	569.1	1.247	.85	1.06
SOU	31	No 368	572.5	1.025	.79	.81
SOU	31	No 543	570.8	1.206	1.02	1.23
SOU	31	No 645	568.0	1.118	1.36	1.52
SOU	31	No 665	567.0	1.350	1.00	1.35
SOU	31	No 966	559.8	1.153	.72	.83
SOU	31	No 1173	570.2	1.015	1.33	1.35
SOU	31	No 1484	571.4	1.054	.93	.98
SOU	31	No 1878	568.0	1.076	.92	.99
SOU	31	No 2587	568.5	1.130	1.08	1.22
SOU	31	No 2589	570.5	1.128	.94	1.06
SOU	31	No 2592	566.9	1.151	1.06	1.22
SOU	31	No 2593	570.1	1.089	1.01	1.10
SOU	31	No 2594	570.1	.937	.95	.89
SOU	169	No 133	548.0	1.232	99	1.22
SOU	169	No 230	554.3	.973	1.11	1.08
SOU	169	No 314	562.8	1.823	.79	1.44
SOU	169	No 335	563.3	1.018	1.09	1.11

Fragment No			λd	Fe/Mn	MnO%	Fe₂0₃%
SOU	169	No 467	569.3	1.468	.62	.91
SOU	169	No 551	524.2	.626	1.63	1.02
SOU	169	No 683	556.8	1.295	1.05	1.36
SOU	169	No 826	560.2	.882	1.35	1.19
SOU	169	No 1483	562.8	1.088	1.14	1.24
SOU	169	No 1592	567.2	1.030	1.33	1.37
SOU	169	No 2066	568.5	1.096	1.36	1.49
SOU	169	No 3347	561.6	1.621	.95	1.54
SOU	177	No 436	546.1	1.917	.72	1.38
SOU	177	No 514	559.2	1.086	1.16	1.26
SOU	177	No 782	526.6	1.960	.75	1.47
SOU	177	No 839	565.2	1.419	.62	.88
SOU	169	No 2066	568.5	1.096	1.36	1.49
SOU	169	No 3347	561.6	1.621	.95	1.54
SOU	177	No 436	546.1	1.917	.72	1.38
SOU	177	No 514	559.2	1.086	1.16	1.26
SOU	177	No 782	526.6	1.960	.75	1.47
SOU	177	No 839	565.2	1.419	.62	.88

Fragment No			λd	Fe/Mn	MnO%	Fe₂0₃%

Appendix Two. Scientific analysis of the Hamwic glass

X-Ray Fluorescence Analysis
(from Sanderson *et al* 1984)

The previous analyses by X-ray fluorescence (XRF) were performed at the University of Bradford using an Edax II energy dispersive system with a transmission Rhodium tube run at 25kV and 500mA and a Si:Li detector with a resolution of 170eV at Mn Kα protected by a 0.00033" Be window. The angles of incidence and take-off were equal at 22.5° from Normal and the beam was collimated to form a 3mm x 4mm ellipse at the sample. Spectra were recorded with the sample chamber evacuated to 0.1 Torr. The spectra were accumulated in an Edax 711 analyser and transferred to a Data General Nova 2 computer for background subtraction and peak stripping. In a single 800 sec counting period, signals could be obtained from sodium, magnesium, aluminium, silicon, phosphorus, sulphur, potassium, calcium, titanium, manganese, iron, cobalt, nickel, copper, zinc, arsenic, lead and strontium.

Sample preparation was achieved by grinding the surface of the samples with a carborundum disc typically to a depth of about 300 microns followed by

Sherd No	Na_2O	MgO	Al_2O_3	SiO_2	K_2O	CaO	TiO_2	MnO	Fe_2O_3
1	12.4	0.97	4.8	74.0	0.46	6.86	0.06	0.01	0.38
2	13.7	1.16	4.6	69.0	1.18	7.30	0.14	0.45	1.18
3	12.2	0.70	4.9	70.8	1.16	7.30	0.15	0.58	1.15
4	12.8	0.86	4.8	70.8	1.18	7.38	0.15	0.43	1.04
5	13.8	0.98	4.7	69.7	1.19	6.99	0.13	0.44	1.12
6	8.9	0.48	4.7	73.8	1.28	8.08	0.16	0.60	1.22
7	8.8	1.00	5.7	71.3	3.01	6.91	0.29	0.42	2.36
8	12.7	0.99	4.7	70.8	1.14	7.07	0.13	0.55	1.16
9	13.0	0.78	4.7	70.5	1.02	6.82	0.14	0.61	1.16
10	15.4	0.96	4.4	69.6	0.95	6.41	0.13	0.65	0.94
11	12.9	0.96	4.6	71.9	1.06	6.43	0.12	0.38	0.97
12	13.7	0.47	4.5	71.3	0.92	6.19	0.11	0.41	1.00
13	10.6	0.44	3.9	71.3	1.10	9.56	0.15	0.60	1.38
14	14.1	0.22	3.7	69.4	1.07	8.76	0.15	0.57	1.17
15	15.7	0.50	3.7	67.9	0.82	8.31	0.14	0.60	1.09
16	16.1	0.62	3.4	68.6	0.90	8.21	0.14	0.62	0.89
17	12.6	0.39	3.9	68.9	1.63	9.60	0.17	0.46	1.28
18	16.9	0.35	3.4	68.3	0.67	8.04	0.14	0.67	0.83
19	13.9	0.65	3.9	67.5	1.25	9.70	0.18	0.63	1.28
20	13.7	0.51	2.5	69.8	0.65	8.93	0.18	0.99	1.15
21	15.7	0.67	3.9	66.6	0.88	8.80	0.10	0.54	1.18
22	14.7	0.61	4.1	69.0	1.11	8.50	0.16	0.38	0.98
23	12.8	0.97	4.7	71.4	0.50	9.05	0.08	0.01	0.56
24	11.7	0.42	3.9	73.3	0.65	7.62	0.11	0.54	1.29
25	10.3	0.63	4.3	73.6	0.50	8.81	0.08	0.21	0.94
Mean	13.2	0.7	4.25	70.4	1.05	7.91	0.14	0.49	1.11
S D	2.1	0.3	0.66	2.0	0.50	1.07	0.04	0.20	0.34

polishing with a fine buffing pad or a diamond lap. Standards were treated in the same way, being repolished periodically and stored in a dessicator. Specimens were rinsed in acetone before measurement. The sample chamber could accommodate samples up to 10cm in diameter although those examined were substantially smaller than this. Possible errors caused by curvature of samples were minimised by selection of flatter areas for analysis, by analysis of a small 3mm x 4mm elliptical area, and by polishing.

The errors in the XRF compositions calculated from simplified fundamental parameters procedure arise from three sources. There is a random error arising from the comparison of sample and standard intensities; a cross term combining random and systematic errors through the mass absorption coefficient estimates; and finally, the systematic errors due to errors in the composition of the standards. The random errors can be predicted by applying Poisson statistics to the spectral data, or determined empirically by repeated measurements. However, it is difficult to separate the other two sources from each other, although their combined effect can be estimated from cross-analyses using a set of standards. At typical compositions the average predicted precision for the ten elements was 4.5%, whilst the observed precision was 8.4%. As far as accuracy is concerned cross-analysis with other glass standards shows that the fundamental parameters procedure used here is accurate to 5%–10% for most elements subject to the results being tied to the published composition for the ESF/Pilkington's standard 151.

The XRF data for the 25 glass fragments analysed from Southampton are listed on the previous page (from Sanderson *et al*, 1984). The item number of each fragment analysed is not known.

Neutron activation analysis
(from Sanderson and Hunter 1982)

The neutron activation analysis (NAA) was carried out at the University of Bradford, using irradiation facilities at AERE Aldermaston. Irradiations were carried out in a mixed neutron flux with a thermal component of 2×10^{12} ns^{-1} cm^{-2} for a period of 48 hours. After irradiation, samples were held for a few days and returned to Bradford, usually arriving about a week after irradiation. Gamma-ray spectra were recorded in two counting periods, one immediately on arrival and one after a cooling period of about a month, using an automated high-resolution gamma spectrometer developed in the School of Physics at Bradford. The apparatus consisted of a shielded Ge:Li detector and associated electronics, a multichannel analyser with a digital cassette output and a remote mechanical sample changer controlled by a microprocessor. Spectra were collected in 1024 channels spanning the energy range 50keV to 1800keV and were recorded on cassettes for later processing. The spectra were processed on an HP 1000 computer.

Samples were prepared by taking a small piece from the glass fragments with a diamond saw after abrasion with a carborundum drill to remove surface layers. Sample mass ranged between 20mg–150mg. They were then rinsed in acetone, weighed to a precision of 10μg, wrapped in aluminium foil together with flux monitors, and numbered. Batches of about twenty samples were packed in polythene tubs with standards and sent to the reactor.

The standard used was a secondary pottery standard (UB NPS1) calibrated to primary USGS standards and specpure materials in previous work. The second pottery standard in each batch of samples was used as an internal check on the quality of the analyses, and a sample of modern window glass which was included in each batch of samples was used to check batch-to-batch reproducibility. Flux monitors consisted of a small chip of specpure zinc (c 5mg) placed in direct contact with each sample to measure any variation in local flux density within the irradiation tub. Flux variations within one batch averaged out at between 5% and 10% over nine irradiations, although occasionally corrections up to 20% were necessary.

The number of elements quantified by the computer varied considerably from sample to sample, giving a data block with many gaps. Occasionally the computer failed to identify peaks and these peaks were calculated by hand. When this was not possible, a minimum detectable level was calculated as the concentration equivalent to three times the square root of the background. Minimum detectable levels varied considerably through the sample batches owing to differences in mass and composition. In the analyses the main element for compositional dependence of minimum detectable level was antimony which varied by nearly three orders of magnitude over the samples and which had a marked effect on the background rates for other peaks in both short and long lived spectra.

The NAA data for the six glass fragments analysed from Southampton is listed in Table 7.

Inductively coupled plasma spectrometry
(from Heyworth *et al* 1986)

The ICPS analyses were carried out at King's College, London, with the cooperation of Dr Walsh of the Department of Geochemistry. The ICP system used was a Philips PV8210 air path spectrometer, with a 1.5m diffraction grating, and 49 spectral lines analysed simultaneously. Each complete analysis required only 1–2 minutes (excluding sample preparation time), and the results were output on a computer as concentrations, using calibration data stored in the computer.

Small samples were cut from the glass fragments using a diamond saw and crushed in a ball mill. The samples were prepared for analysis using methods and equipment set up at the University of Bradford, modelled on the King's College system. For the normal analytical programme a powdered sample of 100mg is evaporated to dryness with 1ml perchloric acid and 2ml hydrofluoric acid, and the residue dissolved in 1ml hydrochlowater before diluting to 10ml. Silicon is removed in the evaporation, but all the other major/minor elements, except oxygen, and many trace elements, can be determined in this solution.

ICPS offers the prospect of good accuracy and high precision for major and minor elements in silicates and good precision for many trace elements down to the 1ppm level. The method is also relatively free from all inter-element interferences. Calibrations are linear over several orders of magnitude for most elements, though a separate calibration was necessary for the analysis of the high soda glasses (Heyworth *et al* 1984b). Once the calibration was established, a rapid throughput of samples was possible, averaging 50 samples an hour through the spectrometer. The apparatus was prone to short-term instabilities and to longer-term drift. In practice recalibration for longer-term larger drift and frequent normalisation to a multi-element standard for smaller-term drift gave reasonable precisions and accuracies. The average precision for the elements routinely analysed was 8.1%, and the average accuracy of analysis for major and minor elements was 4.4%, and for trace elements was 9.4%.

As some fragments were analysed by more than one analytical technique it is possible to compare the compositional data obtained in each study. Between the XRF analyses listed above and the ICPS data there is good agreement for the majority of oxides, though the ICPS figures for soda are rather higher than those obtained by XRF, and the alumina figures are correspondingly lower. Sodium and aluminium are two of the lightest elements analysed in the glass and are most likely to have leached from the surface of the glass during burial. It is possible that this explains the lower soda figures obtained by XRF, which is a surface analysis technique. However, this would not explain the higher alumina figure obtained by XRF, which may be related to the calculations by which the concentration is derived from the intensity of the aluminium signal in XRF analysis.

The ICPS data for the 273 glass fragments analysed from Southampton is listed here, together with some basic information concerning the context from which the glass came, the colour and type of fragment which was analysed and any decoration which it showed. The following codes are used:

Colour

LB	-	Light Blue
LG	-	Light Green
B	–	Blue
G	–	Green
R	–	Red
G/Y	–	Green/Yellow
B/Y	–	Brown/Yellow
P	–	Polychrome
DO	–	Dark Opaque
C	–	Colourless

Fragment type code

11	–	Palm cup/Funnel beaker vessel series: Tubular rim with cavity
12	–	Palm cup/Funnel beaker vessel series: Tubular rim without cavity
13	–	Palm cup/Funnel beaker vessel series: Rounded rim
14	–	Palm cup/Funnel beaker vessel series: Base
15	–	Other vessel type
16	–	Decorated, non-diagnostic vessel body fragment
17	–	Non-diagnostic vessel body fragment
20	–	Flat (window) fragment

Decoration code

4	–	Streaking in metal
5	–	Fluted/Ribbed
6	–	Twisted
7	–	Clouded
8	–	Cut edge/grozed
9	–	Carination in vessel body
10	–	Reticella rod(s) and applied trail(s)
11	–	Opaque yellow reticella rod(s)
12	–	Opaque white reticella rod(s)
13	–	Opaque yellow and white reticella rod(s)
20	–	Applied trail(s)
24	–	Applied trail(s) and streaking in metal
30	–	Marvered trail(s)
34	–	Marvered trail(s) and streaking in metal
39	–	Marvered trail(s) and carination in vessel body

Sherd No		11/177	14/311	169/230	31/759	99/52	177/393	31/759	169/1390	24/456	14/280	7/33	169/1982
Al_2O_3	(%)	2.34	2.82	2.25	3.04	3.30	2.99	2.38	3.11	2.91	3.29	3.14	2.86
Fe_2O_3	(%)	0.86	1.11	0.87	1.41	1.63	1.25	1.19	1.20	1.14	1.36	0.58	1.24
MgO	(%)	0.74	0.81	0.68	0.89	0.92	0.82	0.69	0.82	0.85	1.01	0.60	0.83
CaO	(%)	6.36	7.38	6.63	7.05	6.25	7.37	6.60	6.31	7.29	7.47	7.47	7.54
Na_2O	(%)	16.94	15.34	16.55	14.00	14.89	15.08	15.74	17.05	15.89	14.38	13.85	14.24
K_2O	(%)	0.76	1.28	0.74	1.48	1.28	1.44	0.70	0.76	1.40	2.06	0.59	1.40
TiO_2	(%)	0.12	0.13	0.14	0.16	0.20	0.14	0.11	0.17	0.14	0.15	0.08	0.14
P_2O_5	(%)	0.31	0.46	0.10	0.59	1.79	0.63	1.84	0.82	0.44	0.47	0.02	0.45
MnO	(%)	0.63	0.48	0.64	0.35	0.38	0.46	0.45	0.60	0.46	0.38	0.02	0.46
Pb	(%)	0.53	0.49	0.13	1.03	4.86	0.66	1.03	1.09	0.56	0.23	0.10	0.72
Sb	(%)	0.28	0.16	0.18	0.75	0.24	0.14	0.75	0.41	0.16	0.11	0.02	0.15
Ba	(ppm)	285	294	303	299	263	311	240	286	333	416	235	314
Ce	(ppm)	14	17	16	22	18	20	18	18	17	20	16	20
Co	(ppm)	12	20	11	14	37	16	226	18	20	12	7	20
Cr	(ppm)	43	47	53	53	51	49	46	56	50	56	42	54
Cu	(ppm)	1000	1158	230	1452	5539	1775	5510	2821	1104	834	55	1014
La	(ppm)	6	6	5	7	7	6	6	8	6	8	4	7
Li	(ppm)	7	15	9	21	15	20	7	8	17	21	8	17
Nb	(ppm)	0	0	0	0	0	0	0	0	0	0	0	0
Ni	(ppm)	30	31	26	31	36	32	64	32	31	30	21	33
Sc	(ppm)	2	2	2	2	3	2	2	2	2	2	1	2
Sr	(ppm)	446	436	424	389	396	422	399	432	438	462	401	418
V	(ppm)	19	19	20	21	25	20	17	23	20	21	9	21
Y	(ppm)	8	10	8	11	11	11	8	11	11	11	8	11
Zn	(ppm)	54	71	42	88	404	80	133	150	77	80	11	75
Zr	(ppm)	63	71	69	69	85	58	57	76	69	75	43	65
SiO_2	(%)	69.93	69.32	70.97	69.00	63.57	68.74	67.85	67.27	68.54	68.89	73.44	69.76
Colour		LG	LB	LG	B	R	LB	B	LB	LB	LB	B/Y	LB
Type		13	14	13	15	16	13	15	16	11	17	15	13
Decoration		-	-	-	-	4	4	-	4	-	-	-	12

Sherd No		169/ 3069	31/ 282	169/ 314a	177/ 203	169/ 133	24/ 540	24/ 527	177/ 561	99/ 21	184/ 129	15/ 389	24/ 449
Al₂O₃	(%)	3.30	2.77	2.87	2.83	2.50	2.88	2.44	3.01	2.94	3.06	3-39	2.58
Fe₂O₃	(%)	1.77	1.29	1.29	1.09	1.01	1.18	0.57	1.43	1.33	1.50	1.65	0.96
MgO	(%)	1.05	0.80	0.94	0.83	0.76	0.82	0.52	0.91	0.83	0.95	1.27	0.69
CaO	(%)	8.33	7.22	7.62	6.84	7.06	7.26	6.70	8.06	7.26	8.08	9.06	6.98
Na₂O	(%)	12.68	14.51	14.01	17.17	16.07	15.40	15.86	13.96	15.01	13.91	11.67	15.06
K₂O	(%)	2.14	1.28	1.69	1.24	0.89	1.34	0.68	1.56	1.38	1.77	2.87	1.04
TiO₂	(%)	0.15	0.13	0.15	0.13	0.12	0.14	0.08	0.16	0.15	0.17	0.22	0.12
P₂O₅	(%)	0.60	0.43	0.50	0.53	0.39	0.42	0.13	0.59	0.60	0.62	0.56	0.29
MnO	(%)	0.48	0.46	0.54	0.50	0.63	0.43	0.45	0.49	0.45	0.50	0.57	0.40
Pb	(%)	0.96	0.89	0.69	0.78	0.64	0.62	0.08	0.80	0.76	0.78	0.34	0.41
Sb	(%)	0.08	0.13	0.12	0.21	0.17	0.16	0.09	0.16	0.19	0.14	0.09	0.37
Ba	(ppm)	369	286	392	336	317	324	240	353	327	559	949	418
Ce	(ppm)	25	19	21	16	18	19	17	24	23	24	30	21
Co	(ppm)	18	18	18	21	16	16	14	17	18	17	17	12
Cr	(ppm)	57	49	49	48	47	47	48	52	53	55	59	52
Cu	(ppm)	1048	1081	1112	1530	1074	943	179	1015	1449	1115	563	553
La	(ppm)	8	6	7	7	6	7	5	7	7	7	8	6
Li	(ppm)	24	17	24	19	12	16	5	22	19	21	29	13
Nb	(ppm)	0	0	0	0	0	0	0	1	1	1	3	0
Ni	(ppm)	35	33	33	35	30	30	25	36	34	34	39	28
Sc	(ppm)	2	2	2	2	2	2	1	2	2	2	3	2
Sr	(ppm)	396	404	421	456	438	420	383	411	413	414	427	394
V	(ppm)	24	20	22	19	21	20	14	22	21	23	27	18
Y	(ppm)	13	10	10	10	10	11	8	11	11	12	13	10
Zn	(ppm)	102	80	83	82	94	75	24	83	95	85	75	55
Zr	(ppm)	51	46	58	59	59	71	38	90	70	73	99	56
SiO₂	(%)	68.24	69.88	69.35	67.59	69.55	69.15	72.30	68.66	68.85	68.28	68.08	70.94
Colour		G	LB	LB	LB	LG	LB	LB	LB	LB	LB	LB	LB
Type		15	11	13	11	17	16	15	17	14	11	17	15
Decoration		30	-	-	-	-	20	-	-	-	-	-	9

Sherd No		169/ 554	31/ 1032	177/ 611	184/ 65	31/ 1392	11/ 172	7/ 28	14/ 273	177/ 436	177/ 311	14/ 302	177/ 782
Al_2O_3	(%)	2.62	2.35	2.26	2.50	2.78	2.55	2.66	3.19	2.96	2.94	2.77	3.42
Fe_2O_3	(%)	1.08	0.92	0.80	0.80	1.12	1.03	0.97	0.76	1.27	1.24	1.11	1.50
MgO	(%)	0.75	0.78	0.65	0.60	0.85	0.77	0.77	0.60	0.85	0.84	0.74	0.95
CaO	(%)	7.13	6.50	6.43	7.04	7.65	7.07	6.92	7.12	7.61	7.42	6.55	7.98
Na_2O	(%)	13.81	16.08	17.00	15.45	14.55	14.86	15.33	15.24	15.69	15.21	15.36	17.35
K_2O	(%)	1.17	0.82	0.74	0.83	1.38	1.09	1.06	0.96	1.47	1.46	1.03	1.56
TiO_2	(%)	0.13	0.12	0.13	0.11	0.14	0.13	0.13	0.12	0.15	0.16	0.14	0.18
P_2O_5	(%)	0.38	0.67	0.17	0.08	0.46	0.50	0.54	0.13	0.55	0.50	0.37	0.67
MnO	(%)	0.42	0.51	0.52	0.45	0.45	0.52	0.41	0.13	0.47	0.47	0.36	0.42
Pb	(%)	0.49	0.78	0.15	0.08	0.47	0.72	0.70	0.10	0.47	0.72	0.54	0.86
Sb	(%)	0.18	0.41	0.23	0.21	0.15	0.23	0.25	0.05	0.16	0.16	0.14	0.11
Ba	(ppm)	407	396	423	381	479	454	285	285	338	334	281	342
Ce	(ppm)	23	19	18	20	22	21	19	19	23	21	19	23
Co	(ppm)	15	18	10	10	17	22	14	9	17	16	13	18
Cr	(ppm)	55	52	50	50	56	55	51	53	55	52	53	68
Cu	(ppm)	720	1893	427	88	891	1262	1452	270	1126	1024	846	1561
La	(ppm)	6	6	6	6	7	6	6	6	7	7	7	14
Li	(ppm)	14	13	9	14	17	16	15	11	20	18	13	17
Nb	(ppm)	1	0	0	0	1	1	0	0	1	1	0	0
Ni	(ppm)	32	33	31	28	33	33	30	23	34	32	30	41
Sc	(ppm)	2	2	2	2	2	2	2	2	2	2	2	2
Sr	(ppm)	382	413	414	402	405	411	417	413	432	432	384	448
V	(ppm)	19	18	18	17	20	20	19	13	22	21	18	23
Y	(ppm)	10	8	8	10	10	10	10	10	11	11	10	11
Zn	(ppm)	66	100	43	35	77	89	76	27	83	82	76	114
Zr	(ppm)	70	46	64	51	63	68	62	55	72	79	64	68
SiO_2	(%)	71.66	69.76	70.77	71.74	69.79	70.28	70.01	71.48	68.13	68.67	70.71	64.73
Colour		LB	LG	LG	LB	LB	LB	LG	LB	LB	LB	B/Y	LB
Type		16	11	11	20	17	11	16	17	16	13	15	16
Decoration		20	-	-	8	-	-	13	-	4	12	11	10

Sherd No		24/457	99/96	99/116	169/1906	177/409	11/189	169/676	30/57	14/200	177/419	169/229	14/230
Al_2O_3	(%)	2.64	2.95	2.79	2.40	2.88	2.44	2.86	3.07	2.46	2.86	2.98	3.03
Fe_2O_3	(%)	0.98	1.25	1.20	1.21	1.23	0.86	1.25	1.35	0.89	1.22	1.34	1.43
MgO	(%)	0.74	0.74	0.81	0.80	0.83	0.56	0.81	0.85	0.69	0.82	1.00	1.02
CaO	(%)	6.99	6.73	7.41	6.28	7.39	7.16	7.21	7.16	6.50	7.28	7.59	7.89
Na_2O	(%)	15.50	15.07	14.87	18.03	15.24	14.96	15.32	15.56	17.75	14.83	15.52	14.55
K_2O	(%)	0.85	1.00	1.13	0.78	1.43	0.54	1.38	1.40	0.77	1.25	1.80	1.29
TiO_2	(%)	0.12	0.15	0.14	0.22	0.15	0.06	0.15	0.16	0.12	0.14	0.16	0.16
P_2O_5	(%)	0.41	3.06	0.49	0.12	0.53	0.39	0.53	0.60	0.42	0.48	0.56	0.57
MnO	(%)	0.42	0.33	0.45	1.00	0.46	0.21	0.45	0.38	0.70	0.47	0.58	0.47
Pb	(%)	0.77	0.65	0.76	0.17	0.70	0.39	0.77	0.71	1.22	0.71	0.68	0.64
Sb	(%)	0.19	0.15	0.18	0.15	0.16	1.24	0.17	0.14	0.55	0.16	0.16	0.18
Ba	(ppm)	290	303	319	470	328	236	328	307	410	332	475	896
Ce	(ppm)	20	21	23	19	22	18	20	21	19	24	23	25
Co	(ppm)	20	14	17	11	17	317	17	16	15	16	17	18
Cr	(ppm)	52	53	54	57	53	48	54	61	55	55	55	60
Cu	(ppm)	970	9040	962	279	1094	993	1164	1400	1144	958	1131	1065
La	(ppm)	8	10	8	7	7	6	7	13	9	9	8	8
Li	(ppm)	16	22	16	10	19	3	18	15	9	17	25	24
Nb	(ppm)	0	0	0	1	1	0	1	0	1	1	1	2
Ni	(ppm)	31	37	32	31	33	57	33	37	38	33	35	39
Sc	(ppm)	2	2	2	3	2	1	2	2	2	2	2	2
Sr	(ppm)	415	393	412	462	420	392	423	402	435	403	437	438
V	(ppm)	18	19	20	29	21	10	21	21	24	21	23	22
Y	(ppm)	10	10	11	10	11	9	11	10	9	10	11	12
Zn	(ppm)	74	157	73	44	81	35	83	102	70	82	79	157
Zr	(ppm)	60	70	65	99	70	10	67	61	60	43	49	71
SiO_2	(%)	70.19	66.90	69.57	68.69	68.78	70.98	68.88	68.37	67.70	69.58	67.39	68.49
Colour		LB	G	LB	LG	LB	B	LB	G	LG	LB	LB	LG
Type		17	16	14	16	13	15	16	13	11	13	17	15
Decoration		-	4	-	20	-	-	20	24	-	12	-	11

Sherd No		169/3073	22/3	30/374	11/171	177/487	177/593	99/194	24/623	26/351	184/74	31/1392	26/143
Al_2O_3	(%)	2.75	2.74	2.93	2.75	2.77	2.87	2.50	2.86	2.93	2.46	2.94	2.45
Fe_2O_3	(%)	1.11	0.87	1.03	0.98	1.09	1.36	1.00	1.17	1.29	0.89	1.16	0.96
MgO	(%)	0.87	0.70	0.89	0.91	0.91	0.97	0.95	0.82	0.85	0.70	0.88	0.80
CaO	(%)	7.51	7.26	7.45	6.99	7.51	7.48	7.08	7.38	7.55	6.60	7.67	6.63
Na_2O	(%)	13.90	15.34	16.02	16.04	20.28	13.79	16.34	15.47	15.61	17.42	15.90	17.91
K_2O	(%)	1.49	0.96	0.91	0.86	0.50	1.22	0.97	1.03	1.05	0.63	0.91	0.44
TiO_2	(%)	0.14	0.11	0.13	0.13	0.14	0.15	0.15	0.14	0.14	0.12	0.15	0.12
P_2O_5	(%)	0.72	0.24	0.28	0.63	1.53	0.54	0.37	0.61	0.62	0.35	0.50	1.35
MnO	(%)	0.44	0.37	0.40	0.42	0.68	0.45	0.74	0.45	0.48	0.52	0.45	0.60
Pb	(%)	0.58	0.33	0.25	0.71	0.08	0.72	0.48	0.71	0.91	0.75	0.46	1.15
Sb	(%)	0.15	0.12	0.13	0.24	0.42	0.16	0.14	0.16	0.17	0.39	0.17	0.61
Ba	(ppm)	318	304	309	309	340	849	359	330	326	283	352	300
Ce	(ppm)	25	22	21	20	22	24	21	21	22	20	20	19
Co	(ppm)	16	11	11	14	24	17	14	16	17	12	17	21
Cr	(ppm)	53	57	51	54	59	57	62	52	54	55	51	52
Cu	(ppm)	1595	514	544	1586	4398	1010	797	1409	1338	889	1001	3884
La	(ppm)	6	7	6	7	8	8	8	8	7	7	7	7
Li	(ppm)	17	12	16	15	24	23	11	16	20	23	18	21
Nb	(ppm)	2	0	0	0	0	2	0	0	1	0	1	0
Ni	(ppm)	33	29	29	33	49	37	39	33	37	32	43	43
Sc	(ppm)	2	2	2	2	2	2	2	2	2	2	2	2
Sr	(ppm)	390	408	438	424	520	415	445	421	425	422	442	459
V	(ppm)	21	18	18	19	24	21	23	20	21	19	20	21
Y	(ppm)	10	10	10	10	10	11	10	10	10	9	11	9
Zn	(ppm)	91	48	49	81	151	149	75	85	86	57	74	133
Zr	(ppm)	65	40	56	47	58	67	50	58	67	47	72	51
SiO_2	(%)	70.08	70.81	69.42	69.08	63.52	70.02	69.09	68.95	68.16	68.98	68.60	66.48
Colour		LB	R	B/Y	LB	LB	LB	LB	LB	LB	LG	LB	LG
Type		13	16	15	16	15	16	17	16	12	11	17	14
Decoration			-	11	11	13	30	20	-	4	-	-	-

Sherd No		169/ 314b	169/ 825	24/ 480	24/ 601	169/ 3347	177/ 281	11/ 164	14/ 238	31/ 495	14/ 232	14/ 283	24/ 583
Al_2O_3	(%)	2.30	2.84	2.75	2.03	2.71	3.69	2.74	2.35	2.44	2.87	3.45	2.76
Fe_2O_3	(%)	0.88	1.13	1.08	0.83	1.23	1.81	1.09	0.77	1.23	1.25	1.49	0.95
MgO	(%)	0.69	0.74	0.79	0.57	0.87	0.87	0.86	0.70	0.89	0.84	1.12	0.77
CaO	(%)	6.55	6.77	7.40	5.40	6.91	7.23	7.28	6.60	6.57	7.35	7.75	7.33
Na_2O	(%)	18.28	15.29	15.44	10.94	16.30	13.02	14.03	17.44	16.88	14.47	13.25	14.76
K_2O	(%)	0.48	0.81	0.71	0.93	1.29	1.37	1.26	0.43	0.79	1.36	1.21	1.17
TiO_2	(%)	0.15	0.16	0.13	0.11	0.15	0.23	0.14	0.12	0.13	0.15	0.18	0.13
P_2O_5	(%)	0.12	0.43	0.42	0.33	1.05	0.38	0.42	0.10	1.13	0.54	0.54	0.37
MnO	(%)	0.65	0.44	0.48	0.34	0.60	0.35	0.55	0.59	0.69	0.46	0.45	0.40
Pb	(%)	0.14	0.61	0.47	0.29	0.90	0.56	0.80	0.12	1.41	0.96	0.56	0.44
Sb	(%)	0.20	0.16	0.16	0.07	0.25	0.17	0.12	0.21	0.62	0.16	0.12	0.15
Ba	(ppm)	312	300	303	229	340	358	321	298	367	335	450	343
Ce	(ppm)	20	24	24	19	24	27	23	19	19	22	27	20
Co	(ppm)	11	18	16	13	20	12	19	10	20	17	15	14
Cr	(ppm)	59	60	60	53	51	50	49	46	47	46	54	46
Cu	(ppm)	263	890	836	656	2544	495	767	203	2903	1061	659	707
La	(ppm)	7	7	7	7	5	7	4	3	4	4	5	4
Li	(ppm)	25	21	17	11	15	28	23	15	7	18	33	14
Nb	(ppm)	1	1	1	0	1	1	1	0	1	1	1	1
Ni	(ppm)	33	32	33	28	37	36	35	28	40	35	36	32
Sc	(ppm)	2	2	2	2	2	3	2	2	2	2	2	2
Sr	(ppm)	444	387	416	298	431	366	431	440	470	412	459	410
V	(ppm)	22	21	21	16	23	25	23	20	22	21	24	18
Y	(ppm)	9	11	11	8	11	15	10	9	9	11	12	10
Zn	(ppm)	40	69	68	55	123	58	82	33	119	82	81	66
Zr	(ppm)	68	60	49	52	70	127	65	62	59	64	81	57
SiO_2	(%)	69.43	70.43	69.98	78.02	67.37	70.16	70.52	70.45	66.81	69.38	69.69	70.60
Colour		LG	LB	LB	LB	LG	G	LB	LG	LG	LB	LG	LB
Type		13	11	17	16	12	13	13	13	13	12	16	17
Decoration			-	-	-	24	-	-	12	12	-	12	7

Sherd No		15/ 390	14/ 283	99/ 56	15/ 430	11/ 160	15/ 427	31/ 137	24/ 24	31/ 381	169/ 2840	169/ 440	15/ 400
Al₂O₃	(%)	2.40	3.45	3.22	2.46	3.03	2.49	2.94	2.69	2.99	2.88	2.74	2.90
Fe₂O₃	(%)	0.89	1.12	1.49	0.92	1.28	0.94	1.13	0.97	1.35	1.38	1.06	1.26
MgO	(%)	0.75	0.91	0.95	0.68	0.98	0.82	0.78	0.70	0.83	1.08	0.77	0.82
CaO	(%)	6.33	8.68	7.81	6.86	8.09	6.87	7.13	6.87	7.33	7.25	7.21	7.21
Na₂O	(%)	17.51	19.18	12.76	15.80	13.19	16.72	15.35	15.19	14.07	14.68	14.39	15.23
K₂O	(%)	0.45	0.42	1.33	0.76	1.65	0.72	0.74	1.14	1.11	0.60	1.20	1.20
TiO₂	(%)	0.18	0.16	0.18	0.13	0.17	0.15	0.14	0.12	0.15	0.16	0.13	0.14
P₂O₅	(%)	0.04	0.37	0.52	0.16	0.47	0.21	0.45	0.30	0.48	1.18	0.42	0.49
MnO	(%)	0.91	0.44	0.40	0.77	0.51	0.94	0.39	0.37	0.44	0.57	0.42	0.46
Pb	(%)	0.09	0.56	0.22	0.15	0.61	0.22	0.90	0.40	0.78	1.60	0.56	0.89
Sb	(%)	0.15	0.12	0.12	0.18	0.12	0.08	0.14	0.19	0.16	0.39	0.16	0.18
Ba	(ppm)	434	348	385	334	381	364	314	296	331	361	307	335
Ce	(ppm)	19	22	25	19	23	17	18	18	22	22	20	20
Co	(ppm)	10	13	15	11	17	14	16	12	16	26	17	21
Cr	(ppm)	51	53	49	46	49	49	44	41	45	51	43	43
Cu	(ppm)	80	809	779	303	746	536	921	530	916	2807	847	1022
La	(ppm)	4	4	5	4	4	4	4	4	4	4	4	4
Li	(ppm)	12	29	24	10	28	7	16	14	20	11	15	18
Nb	(ppm)	1	0	2	0	1	0	0	0	1	1	0	0
Ni	(ppm)	30	35	34	29	35	31	29	29	33	39	31	33
Sc	(ppm)	2	2	3	2	2	2	2	2	2	2	2	2
Sr	(ppm)	444	533	399	435	444	462	426	401	407	442	402	424
V	(ppm)	26	21	23	22	23	23	18	17	21	25	19	20
Y	(ppm)	10	12	12	9	11	9	11	10	11	11	10	11
Zn	(ppm)	34	76	85	44	83	48	68	56	90	117	71	79
Zr	(ppm)	89	74	106	66	75	74	70	63	78	81	69	71
SiO₂	(%)	70.18	64.39	70.81	71.00	69.71	69.68	69.71	70.91	70.11	67.83	70.75	69.01
Colour		LG	LG	LB	LG	LB	LG	LB	LB	LB	G	LB	LB
Type		17	16	11	13	16	12	16	11	16	11	14	14
Decoration			-	7	-	-	13	-	20	-	24	-	20

Sherd No		11/ 153	31/ 1253	24/ 487	177/ 299	11/ 182	31/ 381	31/ 1604	169/ 1834	31/ 1081	177/ 498	11/ 168	169/ 309
Al_2O_3	(%)	2.64	3.04	2.33	2.59	2.84	2.78	3.43	2.12	2.76	2.59	2.50	2.43
Fe_2O_3	(%)	1.12	1.17	0.89	1.34	0.97	1.15	1.68	0.60	1.15	1.39	0.88	1.09
MgO	(%)	0.79	0.79	0.70	0.80	0.75	0.79	0.84	0.56	0.79	0.80	0.73	0.77
CaO	(%)	6.93	6.81	6.62	7.64	7.05	7.18	6.89	5.83	7.22	7.57	6.54	6.36
Na_2O	(%)	15.94	13.86	15.77	13.82	15.38	14.53	12.69	17.41	14.42	13.90	15.51	16.54
K_2O	(%)	1.02	0.73	0.68	0.62	0.70	1.26	1.86	0.70	0.69	0.60	0.65	0.67
TiO_2	(%)	0.14	0.15	0.12	0.12	0.13	0.14	0.21	0.11	0.13	0.12	0.13	0.19
P_2O_5	(%)	0.62	0.46	0.17	0.73	0.40	0.58	0.26	0.08	0.59	0.75	0.48	0.16
MnO	(%)	0.56	0.29	0.59	0.58	0.38	0.44	0.33	0.50	0.42	0.58	0.59	0.85
Pb	(%)	0.92	0.40	0.19	1.74	0.45	0.78	0.09	0.09	0.88	1.85	0.43	0.21
Sb	(%)	0.24	0.12	0.18	0.14	0.15	0.16	0.16	0.18	0.19	0.13	0.25	0.15
Ba	(ppm)	321	293	316	332	290	304	350	333	300	337	294	420
Ce	(ppm)	18	22	19	22	17	19	27	16	20	21	19	18
Co	(ppm)	21	12	11	18	14	15	10	9	19	17	12	11
Cr	(ppm)	45	44	43	47	39	41	46	41	43	51	45	53
Cu	(ppm)	1502	907	319	1432	819	1184	228	110	1243	1570	1177	338
La	(ppm)	5	4	4	3	4	4	6	4	4	4	4	4
Li	(ppm)	17	18	11	11	13	16	28	6	16	11	9	10
Nb	(ppm)	0	1	1	1	0	0	2	0	1	1	0	1
Ni	(ppm)	34	29	30	35	28	30	31	27	31	35	31	29
Sc	(ppm)	2	2	2	2	2	2	2	2	2	2	2	2
Sr	(ppm)	440	374	418	409	415	416	357	371	408	406	419	430
V	(ppm)	21	19	21	21	18	19	24	16	19	21	21	27
Y	(ppm)	9	11	8	10	10	10	13	7	9	9	9	9
Zn	(ppm)	114	72	43	151	61	82	74	22	87	147	84	43
Zr	(ppm)	65	84	66	52	61	68	137	54	70	56	67	94
SiO_2	(%)	68.82	71.99	71.63	69.63	70.62	69.99	71.43	71.72	70.53	69.45	71.09	70.43
Colour		LB	LB	LG	LB	LB	LB	LB	LG	LB	LB	LG	LG
Type		17	17	11	16	14	16	16	11	16	13	14	12
Decoration			-	-	8	20	-	24	6	-	20	34	

Sherd No		7/ 31	177/ 846	99/ 112	26/ 120	169/ 2272	177/ 517	169/ 186	31/ 1878	169/ 2593	26/ 672	7/ 32	24/ 632
Al_2O_3	(%)	2.90	2.78	3.86	2.94	2.71	3.18	2.97	2.32	2.74	2.76	3.14	2.49
Fe_2O_3	(%)	1.06	1.11	1.70	1.13	1.34	1.16	1.31	0.80	1.13	1.22	0.57	0.85
MgO	(%)	0.82	0.79	0.71	0.83	0.81	0.73	0.98	0.66	0.80	0.80	0.60	0.57
CaO	(%)	7.27	7.34	6.90	7.39	7.26	5.99	7.74	6.48	7.26	7.29	7.44	6.83
Na_2O	(%)	15.54	14.82	12.29	15.11	15.01	15.16	13.90	16.43	14.53	14.16	13.48	15.17
K_2O	(%)	1.35	1.27	1.46	1.43	1.33	1.03	1.70	0.70	1.27	1.26	0.56	0.56
TiO_2	(%)	0.14	0.13	0.24	0.15	0.14	0.18	0.16	0.14	0.14	0.15	0.08	0.06
P_2O_5	(%)	0.46	0.42	0.24	0.53	1.72	2.73	0.53	0.09	0.47	0.51	0.02	0.30
MnO	(%)	0.40	0.45	0.34	0.40	0.53	0.23	0.54	0.58	0.45	0.44	0.02	0.21
Pb	(%)	0.45	0.59	0.21	0.48	0.73	0.54	0.69	0.14	0.62	0.85	0.05	0.38
Sb	(%)	0.13	0.14	0.15	0.16	0.19	0.11	0.12	0.20	0.17	0.15	0.02	1.27
Ba	(ppm)	318	290	291	329	334	279	421	282	289	287	252	247
Ce	(ppm)	19	21	31	20	21	19	24	19	22	23	18	14
Co	(ppm)	14	18	12	17	20	17	18	11	21	17	8	312
Cr	(ppm)	47	41	51	46	45	46	39	41	39	52	33	37
Cu	(ppm)	1015	882	330	1082	4327	7395	1000	181	944	1057	48	780
La	(ppm)	4	4	7	4	4	4	4	3	4	5	3	3
Li	(ppm)	16	16	29	17	44	14	23	10	15	17	8	3
Nb	(ppm)	0	0	2	1	1	1	1	1	1	0	0	0
Ni	(ppm)	31	33	33	31	41	35	35	29	33	35	23	53
Sc	(ppm)	2	2	3	2	2	3	2	2	2	2	2	1
Sr	(ppm)	437	426	345	420	445	362	419	416	413	408	393	399
V	(ppm)	19	20	28	20	21	19	23	21	20	21	9	8
Y	(ppm)	10	10	16	11	10	10	11	9	10	11	9	8
Zn	(ppm)	72	75	49	79	301	175	78	34	81	81	11	27
Zr	(ppm)	67	50	136	62	67	73	65	69	61	46	36	28
SiO_2	(%)	69.27	69.97	71.76	69.24	67.66	68.11	69.14	71.35	70.22	70.20	73.93	71.12
Colour		LB	LB	LB	LB	LB	G	LB	LG	LB	LB	B/Y	B
Type		11	17	16	12	11	12	13	13	11	14	15	15
Decoration		-	-	24	-	-	7	-	-	-	-	5	-

Sherd No		169/ 2328	169/ 801	99/ 135	14/ 265	24/ 590	31/ 1794	169/ 1959	177/ 108	11/ 146	169/ 875	24/ 509	169/ 2243
Al_2O_3	(%)	2.53	2.83	3.93	3-07	2.87	2.93	2.59	2.42	2.99	2.89	2.54	2.67
Fe_2O_3	(%)	1.00	1.21	1.82	1.34	1.18	1.17	0.96	0.90	1.24	1.05	1.21	1.29
MgO	(%)	0.78	0.83	0.87	1.15	0.85	0.84	0.77	0.72	0.82	0.86	0.68	0.81
CaO	(%)	6.38	7.19	6.67	8.34	7.43	7.38	6.72	6.32	6.60	7.24	6.46	7.02
Na_2O	(%)	17.00	14.63	12.11	13.61	14.35	14.67	16.05	16.28	15.16	15.20	16.56	14.64
K_2O	(%)	0.90	1.42	2.15	1.94	1.38	1.37	0.90	0.70	1.38	1.39	0.80	1.27
TiO_2	(%)	0.13	0.14	0.25	0.16	0.14	0.14	0.15	0.15	0.16	0.13	0.12	0.13
P_2O_5	(%)	0.68	0.54	0.36	0.86	0.38	0.53	0.32	0.27	0.71	0.46	0.78	1.72
MnO	(%)	0.63	0.46	0.33	0.42	0.52	0.45	0.69	0.77	0.35	0.41	0.44	0.53
Pb	(%)	0.73	0.98	0.09	0.66	0.45	0.58	0.39	0.27	0.00	0.56	0.31	0.70
Sb	(%)	0.29	0.15	0.13	0.13	0.12	0.16	0.18	0.19	0.00	0.15	0.59	0.18
Ba	(ppm)	314	320	363	423	337	322	359	336	312	300	261	302
Ce	(ppm)	16	19	29	20	21	19	18	18	19	19	18	19
Co	(ppm)	15	18	12	14	17	17	12	14	17	15	237	19
Cr	(ppm)	42	46	50	47	46	43	47	42	48	39	40	40
Cu	(ppm)	1875	1192	517	1744	772	1057	696	607	1662	897	2028	4284
La	(ppm)	4	4	7	4	4	4	4	4	4	4	3	4
Li	(ppm)	10	21	26	18	25	16	11	9	16	17	9	44
Nb	(ppm)	0	0	2	1	1	0	0	1	0	0	0	0
Ni	(ppm)	30	30	32	32	41	35	29	30	30	28	55	37
Sc	(ppm)	2	2	3	2	2	2	2	2	2	2	2	2
Sr	(ppm)	454	423	349	415	435	423	444	427	391	422	421	430
V	(ppm)	21	20	27	22	22	20	23	23	20	19	17	21
Y	(ppm)	9	10	16	11	10	10	9	8	10	11	10	9
Zn	(ppm)	80	100	58	79	95	76	62	49	88	64	76	286
Zr	(ppm)	52	44	160	53	68	62	45	75	71	68	65	59
SiO_2	(%)	68.66	69.40	71.12	68.03	70.14	69.57	70.10	70.85	70.32	69.47	69.19	68.48
Colour		LG	LB	LB	DO	LB	LB	LG	LG	LB	LB	B	LB
Type		11	12	11	15	11	11	11	14	13	13	11	11
Decoration		12	-	-	30	-	-	-	-	4	-	-	4

Sherd No		31/ 1462	15/ 446	11/ 173	169/ 1622	99/ 162	24/ 508	24/ 626	24/ 579	169/ 1314	14/ 228	14/ 228	99/ 53
Al₂O₃	(%)	2.74	4.26	2.76	2.89	2.35	2.86	2.66	3.03	2.49	2.88	2.78	2.04
Fe₂O₃	(%)	1.19	2.10	1.09	1.09	0.80	1.15	0.85	1.12	0.99	0.93	0.92	0.57
MgO	(%)	0.76	0.96	0.81	0.84	0.65	0.82	0.73	0.85	0.79	0.71	0.69	0.56
CaO	(%)	7.21	3.13	7.16	7.54	6.38	6.99	7.18	7.35	6.43	6.36	6.51	6.22
Na₂O	(%)	14.54	15.30	14.25	14.67	16.25	15.67	15.06	14.97	17.40	15.50	14.52	16.53
K₂O	(%)	1.19	0.67	1.23	1.34	0.79	1.35	0.95	1.45	0.53	0.99	0.92	0.43
TiO₂	(%)	0.13	0.56	0.13	0.14	0.13	0.14	0.10	0.14	0.14	0.14	0.13	0.09
P₂O₅	(%)	0.34	0.11	0.52	0.44	0.17	0.46	0.24	0.47	0.72	0.43	0.43	0.05
MnO	(%)	0.54	0.05	0.43	0.45	0.56	0.44	0.42	0.42	0.64	0.28	0.28	0.26
Pb	(%)	0.47	0.06	0.92	0.47	0.17	0.59	0.16	0.64	0.74	0.98	0.98	0.11
Sb	(%)	0.14	0.02	0.18	0.14	0.22	0.16	0.12	0.31	0.12	0.16	0.16	0.29
Ba	(ppm)	304	228	277	298	259	307	254	309	316	252	230	203
Ce	(ppm)	20	24	20	21	16	17	18	19	17	17	20	18
Co	(ppm)	14	10	15	15	11	17	17	15	16	15	16	8
Cr	(ppm)	39	69	39	40	39	36	37	37	43	41	40	38
Cu	(ppm)	620	18	1081	816	381	1004	542	973	2002	1048	976	122
La	(ppm)	4	6	4	4	4	5	3	4	4	4	4	3
Li	(ppm)	16	9	13	15	10	18	16	17	15	11	11	16
Nb	(ppm)	1	3	0	1	0	0	0	0	0	0	0	0
Ni	(ppm)	32	26	32	30	28	31	28	29	32	26	28	24
Sc	(ppm)	2	6	2	2	2	2	2	2	2	2	2	2
Sr	(ppm)	416	213	408	424	423	430	429	420	451	383	362	396
V	(ppm)	21	46	20	20	19	19	17	19	20	18	18	13
Y	(ppm)	10	12	9	10	8	10	9	11	8	8	8	7
Zn	(ppm)	68	25	79	68	43	75	54	81	81	57	58	29
Zr	(ppm)	62	213	51	80	69	75	46	73	67	63	54	51
SiO₂	(%)	70.59	72.69	70.32	69.81	71.40	69.17	71.38	69.05	68.70	70.45	71.50	72.76
Colour		LB	B/Y	LB	LB	LG	LB	LB	LG	LB	LG	LG	C
Type		12	15	11	17	11	11	11	16	14	15	15	17
Decoration		-	-	-	-	-	-	-	20	-	11	11	-

Sherd No		11/158	13/70	14/289	8/11	24/569	169/3175	11/181	15/428	24/514	177/514	15/414	169/841
Al$_2$O$_3$	(%)	2.21	2.48	2.84	2.48	2.74	2.89	2.87	2.46	2.86	2.48	2.97	2.95
Fe$_2$O$_3$	(%)	1.62	0.95	1.01	0.96	0.94	0.90	0.39	0.91	1.13	0.96	1.18	1.21
MgO	(%)	1.98	0.74	0.76	0.73	0.74	0.60	0.48	0.69	0.82	0.74	0.77	0.82
CaO	(%)	8.58	6.58	6.82	6.50	6.60	6.69	6.82	6.72	7.28	6.29	6.32	6.89
Na$_2$O	(%)	12.22	17.35	15.78	17.38	16.81	14.21	14.66	16.08	14.97	17.22	15.99	14.92
K$_2$O	(%)	0.84	0.33	1.22	0.39	1.01	1.09	0.51	0.76	1.38	0.89	1.11	1.21
TiO$_2$	(%)	0.13	0.15	0.14	0.15	0.12	0.11	0.08	0.13	0.14	0.14	0.16	0.17
P$_2$O$_5$	(%)	4.35	0.27	0.39	0.34	0.37	0.57	0.00	0.15	0.47	0.19	0.60	0.40
MnO	(%)	0.37	0.70	0.40	0.62	0.42	0.21	0.02	0.75	0.43	0.63	0.33	0.50
Pb	(%)	4.97	0.25	0.47	0.00	0.68	0.23	0.05	0.16	0.53	0.41	0.65	0.42
Sb	(%)	0.18	0.21	0.15	0.00	0.16	0.09	0.02	0.19	0.17	0.22	0.19	0.14
Ba	(ppm)	288	345	298	356	288	302	242	339	334	345	290	331
Ce	(ppm)	20	17	17	17	14	16	14	18	18	15	17	19
Co	(ppm)	18	11	14	11	18	9	7	10	17	11	20	16
Cr	(ppm)	55	44	44	42	44	41	38	43	44	45	49	50
Cu	(ppm)	9740	589	818	822	922	1477	13	293	968	410	1512	732
La	(ppm)	2	4	4	4	4	4	3	4	4	4	4	4
Li	(ppm)	10	20	14	16	i7	36	5	9	17	10	14	14
Nb	(ppm)	1	0	0	0	0	0	0	0	0	0	0	0
Ni	(ppm)	42	29	27	29	27	24	16	28	29	27	29	29
Sc	(ppm)	2	2	2	2	2	2	1	2	2	2	2	2
Sr	(ppm)	596	446	413	444	444	398	372	429	424	436	395	407
V	(ppm)	24	21	19	20	18	14	7	21	19	20	19	22
Y	(ppm)	7	10	10	10	10	8	8	9	10	9	9	9
Zn	(ppm)	200	53	69	70	64	53	6	41	72	49	86	68
Zr	(ppm)	22	71	60	68	46	47	42	69	68	59	69	67
SiO$_2$	(%)	61.45	69.82	69.84	70.26	69.22	72.17	74.02	70.87	69.62	69.69	69.48	70.19
Colour		R	LG	LB	LG	G	LG	LB	LG	LB	LG	LB	LB
Type		16	14	17	16	16	13	11	12	16	13	15	11
Decoration		4	-	-	4	-	-	-	-	20	-	20	-

Sherd No		14/ 287	177/ 443	30/ 17	14/ 204	24/ 473	169/ 1009	24/ 527	99/ 32	14/ 208	184/ 16	169/ 5	15/ 393
Al$_2$O$_3$	(%)	3.19	2.86	2.37	2.37	2.99	2.82	2.35	2.97	2.75	3.90	3.04	2.61
Fe$_2$O$_3$	(%)	1.43	1.15	1.07	0.97	1.16	1.14	0.54	1.15	1.05	1.79	1.32	1.10
MgO	(%)	1.08	0.82	0.75	0.81	0.79	0.75	0.51	0.84	0.80	1.61	0.86	0.73
CaO	(%)	7.77	7.12	6.64	6.30	6.90	6.62	6.57	7.48	7.23	9.19	7.39	7.10
Na$_2$O	(%)	12.87	15.72	15.45	16.31	14.28	14.74	14.63	15.62	14.00	10.83	15.95	13.86
K$_2$O	(%)	2.93	1.31	0.59	0.85	1.29	1.09	0.66	1.34	1.22	3.77	1.47	1.19
TiO$_2$	(%)	0.19	0.13	0.19	0.11	0.15	0.15	0.08	0.15	0.13	0.26	0.15	0.13
P$_2$O$_5$	(%)	0.48	0.41	0.18	1.09	0.64	0.44	0.13	0.52	0.40	0.64	0.56	0.34
MnO	(%)	0.52	0.47	1.01	0.62	0.31	0.44	0.44	0.45	0.44	0.53	0.47	0.41
Pb	(%)	0.62	0.48	0.26	0.00	1.44	0.41	0.08	0.50	0.47	0.56	1.02	0.49
Sb	(%)	0.10	0.18	0.15	0.00	0.15	0.14	0.08	0.17	0.15	0.08	0.17	0.21
Ba	(ppm)	435	339	375	347	306	315	231	334	305	638	361	280
Ce	(ppm)	21	17	19	15	18	18	16	20	21	29	19	23
Co	(ppm)	15	15	11	21	18	18	13	17	15	19	18	14
Cr	(ppm)	50	41	52	48	48	51	45	51	53	58	54	50
Cu	(ppm)	744	814	408	2918	1462	955	168	1087	772	790	1255	608
La	(ppm)	5	4	4	4	4	4	3	5	5	7	5	4
Li	(ppm)	28	18	5	7	14	15	4	57	17	56	19	85
Nb	(ppm)	0	0	1	0	0	0	0	0	0	3	0	1
Ni	(ppm)	35	32	30	38	29	29	28	33	32	43	34	34
Sc	(ppm)	2	2	2	2	2	2	1	2	2	3	2	2
Sr	(ppm)	443	443	439	447	377	385	364	434	396	465	446	378
V	(ppm)	24	19	29	22	19	20	14	20	19	30	21	20
Y	(ppm)	11	10	9	8	9	9	8	11	10	15	11	10
Zn	(ppm)	76	63	36	115	84	77	24	69	69	71	82	58
Zr	(ppm)	69	64	88	54	61	59	34	68	45	102	71	61
SiO$_2$	(%)	68.62	69.16	71.19	70.17	69.65	71.06	73.83	68.59	71.18	66.61	67.36	71.67
Colour		LB	LB	LG	LB	LB	LB	LB	LB	LB	LB	LB	LB
Type		13	15	12	13	17	12	15	14	11	16	17	13
Decoration		12	-	-	30	-	-	-	-	-	12	-	-

Sherd No		24/ 444	24/ 631	99/ 127	15/ 420	14/ 288	24/ 437	177/ 839	177/ 649	24/ 703	14/ 218	19/ 2	169/ 412
Al_2O_3	(%)	2.78	2.97	3.12	2.90	2.85	2.92	2.12	2.85	2.74	2.98	2.89	3-00
Fe_2O_3	(%)	0-99	1.24	1.38	1.07	1.19	1.26	0.80	0.99	1.21	1.23	1.23	1.23
MgO	(%)	0.72	1.04	0.92	0.83	0.82	0.84	0.58	0.72	0.79	0.81	0.83	0.83
CaO	(%)	6.90	7.32	7.37	7.34	7.20	7.37	6.19	7.13	7.44	6.76	7.39	6.86
Na_2O	(%)	16.79	15.98	15.65	15.66	15.17	14.49	14.46	13.16	13.41	14.93	13.88	14.68
K_2O	(%)	1.19	1.66	1.64	1.37	1.27	1.42	0.78	1.04	1.30	1.36	1.40	1.26
TiO_2	(%)	0.13	0.15	0.16	0.14	0.14	0.15	0.11	0.12	0.14	0.16	0.15	0.18
P_2O_5	(%)	0.30	0.82	0.57	0.52	0.71	0.54	0.16	0.33	0.48	0.76	0.51	0.40
MnO	(%)	0.39	0.50	0.47	0.43	0.47	0.44	0.35	0.28	0.46	0.37	0.46	0.50
Pb	(%)	0.40	0.87	0.74	0.53	0.77	0.67	0.16	0.17	0.77	0.70	0.64	0.41
Sb	(%)	0.21	0.24	0.16	0.15	0.17	0.17	0.28	0.09	0.16	0.22	0.16	0.14
Ba	(ppm)	311	374	379	332	327	339	227	271	319	319	341	341
Ce	(ppm)	17	18	20	18	18	19	19	20	21	17	19	18
Co	(ppm)	13	32	16	16	17	15	10	10	16	23	16	16
Cr	(ppm)	46	52	50	48	48	51	53	46	51	54	50	52
Cu	(ppm)	582	1871	1171	1167	1666	1051	311	669	815	1906	1017	762
La	(ppm)	5	5	5	4	5	5	4	4	4	5	4	4
Li	(ppm)	15	20	123	17	62	196	303	86	38	39	52	25
Nb	(ppm)	0	0	1	0	0	0	0	0	1	0	0	0
Ni	(ppm)	30	37	37	32	37	40	47	27	34	31	32	29
Sc	(ppm)	2	2	2	2	2	2	2	2	2	2	2	2
Sr	(ppm)	434	462	440	443	432	415	368	387	397	411	421	417
V	(ppm)	18	22	22	19	19	20	17	17	20	20	20	23
Y	(ppm)	10	11	11	10	10	10	8	9	10	10	10	10
Zn	(ppm)	50	100	77	69	89	75	48	57	66	90	78	64
Zr	(ppm)	59	43	83	66	74	74	50	56	79	71	78	75
SiO_2	(%)	69.04	66.91	67.58	68.84	68.96	69.50	73.86	72.95	70.91	69.42	70.25	70.33
Colour		LB	LB	LB	LB	LB	LB	LG	LB	LB	LB	LB	LB
Type		11	17	17	13	16	13	13	12	14	16	13	11
Decoration		-	-	-	-	20	4	-	20	20	11	-	-

Sherd No		24/ 502	169/ 2097	24/ 615	177/ 619	177/ 816	177/ 408	24/ 464	169/ 111	36/ 308	39/ 117	24/ 426	36/ 205
Al₂O₃	(%)	3.85	2.85	2.82	2.91	2.75	2.89	3.04	2.64	3.03	3.27	3.40	2.56
Fe₂O₃	(%)	1.88	1.21	1.16	0.92	1.06	1.27	1.22	1.19	1.24	1.62	1.61	0.92
MgO	(%)	1.11	0.88	0.81	0.71	0.84	0.87	1.23	0.80	0.96	1.06	0.96	0.73
CaO	(%)	9.05	7.42	7.12	7.08	7.02	7.50	8.95	7.34	7.81	8.86	8.06	7.13
Na₂O	(%)	11.28	13.90	14.54	14.90	15.01	13.56	12.37	13.15	14.34	13.92	13.87	17.26
K₂O	(%)	2.70	1.39	1.32	0.64	0.70	1.50	1.59	1.20	1.13	1.83	2.29	0.85
TiO₂	(%)	0.25	0.15	0.14	0.12	0.13	0.15	0.15	0.14	0.14	0.19	0.18	0.12
P₂O₅	(%)	1.60	0.40	0.46	0.19	0.57	0.50	0.54	0.44	0.36	0.59	0.36	0.25
MnO	(%)	0.42	0.56	0.43	0.32	0.46	0.45	0.44	0.50	0.44	0.50	0.43	0.49
Pb	(%)	0.67	0.72	0.74	0.09	0.85	0.79	0.40	0.66	0.45	0.93	0.33	0.43
Sb	(%)	0.13	0.12	0.17	0.11	0.24	0.16	0.14	0.16	0.16	0.19	0.18	0.30
Ba	(ppm)	401	345	320	272	326	337	423	315	349	364	367	277
Ce	(ppm)	28	18	17	17	17	20	23	22	22	25	26	18
Co	(ppm)	18	16	16	10	25	17	16	21	13	17	13	12
Cr	(ppm)	55	48	47	44	47	46	49	48	52	51	51	45
Cu	(ppm)	3734	752	982	378	1392	940	700	835	649	1022	578	814
La	(ppm)	6	4	4	4	4	4	4	4	7	8	10	6
Li	(ppm)	43	37	44	10	18	33	20	36	22	21	25	12
Nb	(ppm)	2	1	0	0	0	0	1	1	4	4	4	2
Ni	(ppm)	48	32	31	26	34	35	36	35	30	36	34	29
Sc	(ppm)	3	2	2	2	2	2	2	2	0	0	0	0
Sr	(ppm)	387	453	422	423	430	410	397	393	444	425	414	431
V	(ppm)	27	23	19	16	19	20	21	21	23	25	26	20
Y	(ppm)	15	10	10	9	9	10	11	9	11	12	13	9
Zn	(ppm)	162	73	77	38	92	83	75	71	79	82	82	64
Zr	(ppm)	152	83	72	55	70	79	63	57	72	93	112	52
SiO₂	(%)	66.55	70.21	70.08	71.88	70.12	70.16	69.75	71.59	69.76	66.82	68.15	68.78
Colour		R	LB	LB	B/Y	LB	LB	LB	LB	LB	G	LB	LG
Type		16	16	13	15	14	12	15	12	13	15	14	13
Decoration		4	11	12	20	20	30	6	-	12	24	-	-

Sherd No		36/ 253	36/ 250	169/ 3058	36/ 231	36/ 221	36/ 218	38/ 105	36/ 216	36/ 330	36/ 203	HAM 112	36/ 210
Al_2O_3	(%)	2.97	2.47	3.39	2.31	2.86	2.77	2.87	2.91	3.01	2.99	2.44	2.65
Fe_2O_3	(%)	1.24	0.82	1.88	0.78	1.16	1.63	1.15	1.27	1.45	1.40	1.27	1.01
MgO	(%)	0.84	0.70	1.08	0.64	0.86	0.90	0.86	0.92	0.90	0.89	0.69	0.71
CaO	(%)	7.85	6.98	9.03	6.89	7.77	7.56	7.70	7.93	8.33	8.48	6.77	7.19
Na_2O	(%)	16.32	17.66	12.46	17.22	15.09	16.01	15.48	16.01	14.86	15.16	17.95	16.93
K_2O	(%)	1.05	0.71	1.39	0.78	0.98	1.01	1.12	1.09	1.05	1.11	0.63	0.86
TiO_2	(%)	0.14	0.12	0.20	0.10	0.15	0.16	0.14	0.15	0.16	0.16	0.10	0.12
P_2O_5	(%)	0.39	0.13	0.64	0.12	0.47	0.90	0.53	0.44	0.48	0.52	0.37	0.45
MnO	(%)	0.48	0.60	0.50	0.46	0.46	0.61	0.44	0.50	0.49	0.51	0.47	0.41
Pb	(%)	0.83	0.27	1.05	0.20	0.59	2.53	0.82	0.73	0.84	0.80	0.36	0.38
Sb	(%)	0.22	0.26	0.20	0.32	0.22	0.20	0.29	0.25	0.20	0.23	1.18	0.34
Ba	(ppm)	313	299	409	258	305	288	299	374	334	335	259	259
Ce	(ppm)	20	17	28	17	22	21	21	22	23	24	19	20
Co	(ppm)	15	11	18	9	18	27	17	18	18	18	359	13
Cr	(ppm)	47	42	56	43	45	50	50	59	50	52	42	40
Cu	(ppm)	1095	362	877	350	1379	3508	1458	1063	1018	1111	1298	1446
La	(ppm)	7	6	8	6	7	6	6	7	7	6	6	6
Li	(ppm)	18	10	24	13	16	15	15	20	21	19	7	16
Nb	(ppm)	3	3	5	2	3	4	4	4	4	4	3	3
Ni	(ppm)	33	27	39	27	32	65	33	34	34	34	70	31
Sc	(ppm)	0	0	0	0	0	0	2	2	2	3	2	2
Sr	(ppm)	438	445	408	427	430	466	432	452	440	447	430	419
V	(ppm)	23	20	25	17	21	25	22	24	24	24	18	20
Y	(ppm)	11	9	14	9	11	10	11	11	12	12	9	9
Zn	(ppm)	85	40	102	41	80	419	100	79	88	87	73	72
Zr	(ppm)	78	56	97	58	70	71	69	80	58	87	51	66
SiO_2	(%)	67.45	69.15	67.97	70.05	69.15	65.22	68.35	67.58	68.02	67.52	67.51	68.71
Colour		LB	LB	G	LB	LB	LB	LB	LB	G	LB	B	LB
Type		16	13	15	11	11	16	16	16	13	17	15	13
Decoration		20	12	30	-	-	30	34	20	12	-	30	-

Sherd No		HAM 101	36/ 273	36/ 325	36/ 197	36/ 225	36/ 326	38/ 62	36/ 223	38/ 112	36/ 329	38/ 92	36/ 302
Al_2O_3	(%)	2.46	3.47	3.10	2.87	2.41	2.59	2.82	2.68	2.80	2.76	2.90	2.50
Fe_2O_3	(%)	0.92	1.02	1.55	1.25	0.88	1.14	1.14	1.28	1.16	1.50	1.30	0.96
MgO	(%)	0.73	0.64	1.74	0.79	0.79	0.86	0.79	0.83	0.78	0.71	0.82	0.74
CaO	(%)	6.52	4.26	9.78	6.95	7.05	6.92	7.34	7.29	7.44	7.01	7.54	6.70
Na_2O	(%)	17.98	17.28	12.84	17.37	18.94	18.11	16.11	16.32	15.40	16.78	15.66	19.05
K_2O	(%)	0.87	0.64	1.61	1.02	0.67	0.67	1.06	0.90	0.89	0.73	1.19	0.83
TiO_2	(%)	0.12	0.19	0.21	0.15	0.13	0.22	0.14	0.14	0.14	0.11	0.15	0.15
P_2O_5	(%)	0.54	0.12	0.96	0.58	0.19	0.14	0.41	0.86	0.42	2.35	0.47	0.24
MnO	(%)	0.48	0.10	0.68	0.40	0.78	1.26	0.45	0.43	0.46	0.59	0.47	0.67
Pb	(%)	0.60	0.22	0.64	0.63	0.57	0.29	1.90	1.81	1.15	0.67	0.86	0.33
Sb	(%)	0.52	0.05	0.13	0.48	0.53	0.13	0.25	0.53	0.24	1.00	0.25	0.31
Ba	(ppm)	266	228	710	286	305	657	288	281	291	235	307	331
Ce	(ppm)	18	18	29	20	20	21	21	21	21	20	22	19
Co	(ppm)	19	8	18	67	13	12	16	45	16	22	17	12
Cr	(ppm)	43	46	63	43	47	57	46	50	48	49	46	46
Cu	(ppm)	1899	350	1989	1979	584	370	1014	2934	990	8501	1083	750
La	(ppm)	6	8	10	6	5	6	6	6	6	6	6	6
Li	(ppm)	11	8	24	14	8	8	17	15	16	9	17	13
Nb	(ppm)	3	3	6	4	4	5	4	4	4	3	4	4
Ni	(ppm)	32	22	39	39	32	32	32	39	31	41	34	28
Sc	(ppm)	2	3	3	2	2	3	2	2	2	2	2	2
Sr	(ppm)	428	271	421	428	498	485	418	424	418	402	429	448
V	(ppm)	20	20	28	22	25	34	21	22	22	24	23	24
Y	(ppm)	8	9	11	10	9	10	10	9	10	9	11	9
Zn	(ppm)	74	29	176	90	40	44	72	127	73	112	82	63
Zr	(ppm)	54	68	109	67	68	110	77	76	71	56	82	76
SiO_2	(%)	67.97	71.90	66.40	67.20	66.89	67.48	67.39	66.52	68.92	64.84	68.17	67.34
Colour		LG	LB	G	LB	LG	LG	LB	LG	LB	G	LB	LG
Type		14	16	15	20	12	11	13	14	13	16	16	13
Decoration		-	20	-	8	-	-	30	-	30	20	20	-

Sherd No		39/88	36/233	36/305	36/328	169/709	38/108	38/103	36/327	39/116	169/2136	38/71	24/529
Al₂O₃	(%)	3.83	2.50	3.14	2.96	2.91	2.91	2.89	2.91	2.86	3.05	2.44	2.84
Fe₂O₃	(%)	2.18	1.01	1.12	1.36	1.16	1.16	1.10	1.47	1.28	1.29	0.91	1.23
MgO	(%)	1.20	0.78	0.71	0.84	0.81	0.83	0.86	0.72	0.83	1.26	0.73	0.87
CaO	(%)	8.48	7.05	5.43	7.72	7.46	7.58	7.69	6.86	7.66	8.26	6.67	7.24
Na₂O	(%)	12.61	18.44	18.20	15.43	16.36	16.68	15.41	17.47	15.90	15.55	18.69	17.24
K₂O	(%)	2.29	0.90	0.81	1.17	1.29	0.94	1.23	0.83	1.28	1.98	0.87	1.21
TiO₂	(%)	0.23	0.14	0.20	0.16	0.14	0.14	0.14	0.11	0.14	0.16	0.15	0.17
P₂O₅	(%)	0-45	0.22	0.25	0.46	0.46	0.44	0.53	2.16	0.47	0.78	0.14	0.39
MnO	(%)	0.45	0.67	0.20	0.48	0.45	0.46	0.43	0.57	0.47	0.49	0.68	0.68
Pb	(%)	0.15	0.32	0.60	0.76	0.77	0.82	0.82	0.69	0.84	1.24	0.22	0.67
Sb	(%)	0.23	0.30	0.11	0.23	0.22	0.23	0.25	0.97	0.23	0.22	0.27	0.19
Ba	(ppm)	479	314	233	312	291	297	290	238	297	417	328	325
Ce	(ppm)	31	20	20	25	22	21	21	20	22	23	18	21
Co	(ppm)	12	13	11	16	15	17	17	21	19	18	11	15
Cr	(ppm)	51	48	53	50	52	49	45	47	52	47	47	45
Cu	(ppm)	269	585	675	988	1161	1080	1316	8343	1111	1310	349	940
La	(ppm)	11	6	8	7	6	7	6	7	6	6	6	8
Li	(ppm)	40	14	10	18	17	17	14	9	18	21	12	17
Nb	(ppm)	6	4	4	4	4	4	4	3	4	4	4	4
Ni	(ppm)	39	31	28	34	32	32	33	43	34	39	29	33
Sc	(ppm)	3	2	3	2	2	2	2	2	2	3	2	3
Sr	(ppm)	383	458	316	419	421	439	429	406	426	461	453	446
V	(ppm)	30	24	23	22	21	22	22	24	22	23	24	25
Y	(ppm)	15	9	9	11	10	10	10	9	10	11	9	10
Zn	(ppm)	61	56	52	81	82	76	101	107	76	125	39	74
Zr	(ppm)	155	66	87	80	79	71	76	56	79	79	76	88
SiO₂	(%)	67.74	67.51	69.08	68.22	67.75	67.60	68.41	64.31	67.82	65.46	68.09	67.06
Colour		LB	LG	LB	LB	LB	LB	LB	G	LB	DO	LG	LG
Type		11	11	16	11	12	16	16	13	13	15	13	13
Decoration		-	-	20	30	-	13	30	-	-	30	-	12

Sherd No		24/ 1012	24/ 465	26/ 696	HAM 8	38/ 113	169/ 889	30/ 57	31/ 1565	39/ 115	31/ 505	24/ 421	36/ 327
Al₂O₃	(%)	2.34	2.70	2.99	2.56	2.86	2.79	3.17	2.94	2.65	2.97	3.01	2.98
Fe₂O₃	(%)	0.73	1.04	1.16	0.93	1.15	1.19	1.67	1.21	0.93	1.22	1.33	1.21
MgO	(%)	0.69	0.81	0.86	0.77	0.82	0.75	0.85	0.83	0.99	0.85	0.87	0.86
CaO	(%)	6.38	7.03	7.74	7.09	7.52	7.66	7.15	7.60	7.41	7.61	7.72	8.04
Na₂O	(%)	19.88	16.60	16.24	18.07	16.12	16.36	16.33	16.64	17.83	16.17	15.84	14.95
K₂O	(%)	0.68	1.01	1.42	0.88	1.25	1.20	1.42	1.34	1.43	1.32	1.42	1.46
TiO₂	(%)	0.12	0.13	0.15	0.15	0.14	0.14	0.17	0.14	0.14	0.15	0.16	0.15
P₂O₅	(%)	0.08	0.55	0.44	0.25	0.43	0.35	0.55	0.44	0.40	0.52	0.45	0.44
MnO	(%)	0.59	0.46	0.45	0.68	0.46	0.47	0.37	0.46	0.62	0.46	0.49	0.39
Pb	(%)	0.19	0.93	0.53	0.32	0.85	0.50	0.75	0.75	0.25	0.81	0.80	0.69
Sb	(%)	0.29	0.32	0.22	0.29	0.25	0.26	0.20	0.21	0.28	0.23	0.23	0.97
Ba	(ppm)	273	277	321	336	303	312	310	319	335	348	368	304
Ce	(ppm)	17	20	21	20	21	23	21	21	20	21	22	23
Co	(ppm)	9	21	17	12	17	16	18	17	12	18	16	16
Cr	(ppm)	41	46	47	46	47	44	48	46	45	51	52	50
Cu	(ppm)	178	1601	1017	637	1047	742	1446	1037	882	1350	958	900
La	(ppm)	6	6	7	6	7	8	7	7	8	7	7	6
Li	(ppm)	13	16	19	12	16	21	16	18	18	18	20	16
Nb	(ppm)	3	4	4	4	4	5	4	4	3	4	4	4
Ni	(ppm)	26	33	33	29	33	35	32	32	30	38	36	33
Sc	(ppm)	2	2	2	2	2	2	3	2	2	2	2	2
Sr	(ppm)	441	431	443	453	427	439	407	436	440	430	433	423
V	(ppm)	19	20	22	23	21	21	23	22	21	22	23	22
Y	(ppm)	8	9	11	10	10	10	10	10	10	11	11	11
Zn	(ppm)	37	90	83	68	79	62	100	79	71	94	83	69
Zr	(ppm)	62	66	78	75	73	73	80	72	77	101	108	82
SiO₂	(%)	67.92	68.16	67.59	67.84	67.94	68.15	67.12	67.23	66.87	67.44	67.47	67.66
Colour		LG	LB	LB	LG	LB	G	G	LB	LG	LB	LB	G
Type		13	11	12	12	16	15	13	16	14	15	14	13
Decoration		-	6	-	-	12	30	24	24	-	4	-	-

Sherd No		26/ 770	169/ 335	169/ 1152	169/ 2066	24/ 598	169/ 770	24/ 462	24/ 526	30/ 112	169/ 2020	169/ 3325	169/ 41
Al_2O_3	(%)	3.28	2.49	3.00	2.54	2.86	3.59	2.96	3.29	3.09	3.09	2.94	3.04
Fe_2O_3	(%)	1.47	1.04	1.29	1.19	1.23	1.76	1.06	1.37	1.13	1.28	1.31	1.24
MgO	(%)	1.23	0.76	0.86	0.88	0.82	0.85	0.75	0.88	0.79	0.88	0.84	0.83
CaO	(%)	8.22	7.23	7.38	6.68	7.46	7.43	7.11	7.54	7.28	7.52	7.46	7.49
Na_2O	(%)	12.99	16.53	16.52	18.36	15.70	13.40	17.54	14.81	16.43	16.43	16.13	15.99
K_2O	(%)	1.77	0.91	1.41	0.78	1.29	1.58	1.21	1.68	1.20	1.40	1.35	1.31
TiO_2	(%)	o.lg	0.14	0.14	0.18	0.14	0.22	0.14	0.17	0.13	0.15	0.15	0.16
P_2O_5	(%)	0.75	0.24	0.44	0.72	0.49	0.47	0.30	0.41	0.29	0.46	0.75	0.47
MnO	(%)	0.52	0.69	0.46	0.88	0.46	0.41	0.40	0.33	0.36	0.45	0.47	0.45
Pb	(%)	1.16	0.48	0.95	0.74	0.89	0.72	0.46	0.26	0.99	0.53	0.98	0.82
Sb	(%)	0.28	0.26	0.23	0.36	0.23	0.20	0.27	0.18	0.17	0.24	0.24	0.21
Ba	(ppm)	380	301	348	398	315	334	331	344	325	350	328	322
Ce	(ppm)	26	20	21	20	21	27	20	24	21	23	21	21
Co	(ppm)	32	13	19	14	17	16	14	12	11	18	18	17
Cr	(ppm)	57	51	51	55	48	55	48	53	48	50	49	49
Cu	(ppm)	1365	569	991	2404	1200	892	612	843	547	1034	2122	1064
La	(ppm)	9	6	8	7	7	10	7	9	7	7	7	7
Li	(ppm)	18	11	20	9	17	24	17	23	19	19	19	18
Nb	(ppm)	4	3	4	4	4	5	3	4	4	4	4	4
Ni	(ppm)	42	32	35	34	33	35	33	33	31	36	35	32
Sc	(ppm)	3	2	2	3	2	3	2	3	2	2	2	2
Sr	(ppm)	428	453	432	460	426	389	432	416	444	433	437	428
V	(ppm)	26	24	21	28	21	27	20	23	20	23	22	22
Y	(ppm)	13	10	11	10	10	14	10	12	10	11	10	11
Zn	(ppm)	116	51	87	97	81	74	62	64	49	84	177	83
Zr	(ppm)	130	72	103	101	88	147	99	114	93	106	88	89
SiO_2	(%)	67.88	69.07	67.10	66.33	68.20	69.16	67.63	68.88	67.98	67.35	67.05	67.77
Colour		R	LG	LB	LG	LB	G	LB	LB	8/Y	LB	LB	LB
Type		15	13	11	13	12	15	11	11	15	16	14	12
Decoration		12	12	12	-	20	30	-	4	30	24	-	-

Sherd No		30/ 194	24/ 510	26/ 335	HAM 8	31/ 171	169/ 2801	24/ 443	30/ 419	169/ 553	24/ 585	31/ 516	169/ 1483
Al₂O₃	(%)	2.82	2.58	3.00	2.49	3.08	2.42	2.34	2.76	2.77	2.98	3.40	2.51
Fe₂O₃	(%)	1.09	1.32	1.31	1.08	1.36	0.97	0.76	1.06	1.24	1.35	1.53	0.99
MgO	(%)	0.95	0.75	0.81	0.77	0.88	0.84	0.71	0.81	0.81	0.88	1.19	0.77
CaO	(%)	7.17	6.74	6.77	6.67	7.85	6.67	6.63	7.51	7.68	7.70	9.48	6.92
Na₂O	(%)	17.47	18.04	16.58	17.62	15.27	18.45	18.47	14.18	14.30	15.62	12.58	18.25
K₂O	(%)	1.12	0.72	1.15	0.61	1.55	0.86	0.62	1.20	1.21	1.44	2.52	0.89
TiO₂	(%)	0.14	0.13	0.16	0.20	0.16	0.12	0.11	0.14	0.14	0.16	0.20	0.16
P₂O₅	(%)	0.29	1.08	0.54	0.08	0.51	0.72	0.06	0.49	0.48	0.56	0.62	0.18
MnO	(%)	0.51	0.49	0.37	0.98	0.45	0.58	0.66	0.44	0.46	0.49	0.56	0.73
Pb	(%)	0.46	1.09	0.09	0.18	0.80	0.55	0.19	2.47	0.83	0.75	0.61	0.24
Sb	(%)	0.23	1.06	0.27	0.21	0.21	0.72	0.25	0.21	0.22	0.25	0.12	0.25
Ba	(ppm)	337	303	300	472	333	299	295	280	303	359	556	350
Ce	(ppm)	20	19	20	21	23	20	19	24	23	23	28	20
Co	(ppm)	14	255	20	11	15	18	10	17	lJ	18	17	11
Cr	(ppm)	54	51	55	52	49	44	47	50	47	50	51	49
Cu	(ppm)	655	3563	1504	193	1011	2295	145	1006	993	1222	823	381
La	(ppm)	8	6	7	7	7	6	6	6	6	7	8	6
Li	(ppm)	16	9	15	8	20	9	17	17	16	20	32	13
Nb	(ppm)	3	3	4	4	4	3	3	4	4	4	5	3
Ni	(ppm)	34	73	33	32	33	35	32	33	35	33	38	31
Sc	(ppm)	2	2	3	3	3	2	2	2	2	2	3	2
Sr	(ppm)	430	430	406	435	414	439	429	391	411	428	432	456
V	(ppm)	23	20	22	30	23	22	20	21	21	23	26	24
Y	(ppm)	11	9	10	10	11	9	9	10	10	11	13	10
Zn	(ppm)	65	111	91	34	83	89	39	83	90	88	90	59
Zr	(ppm)	100	83	88	100	93	63	77	74	75	80	90	82
SiO₂	(%)	67.57	65.51	68.69	68.97	67.67	66.76	69.08	68.53	69.65	67.58	66.97	67.96
Colour		LG	B	LB	LG	LB	LG	LG	LB	LB	LB	LB	LG
Type		12	15	13	12	13	13	13	13	12	14	13	14
Decoration		-	30	-	-	-	12	-	30	-	-	12	-

Sherd No		24/ 580	24/ 555	39/ 114	169/ 2820	24/ 597	24/ 546	31/ 17	169/ 826	HAM 9	26/ 540	169/ 66	169/ 683
Al$_2$O$_3$	(%)	2.94	2.50	3.10	3.00	3.02	2.75	2.77	2.29	2.42	2.63	2.92	2.78
Fe$_2$O$_3$	(%)	0.92	1.27	1.43	1.40	1.40	1.57	1.12	0.80	0.91	1.11	1.25	1.10
MgO	(%)	0.78	0.93	0.89	1.13	0.84	0.90	0.83	0.69	0.73	0.82	0.87	0.83
CaO	(%)	7.40	6.88	7.92	7.26	7.59	6.30	7.25	6.37	6.95	6.83	7.48	7.02
Na$_2$O	(%)	16.64	18.21	15.05	16.48	14.35	17.68	17.03	18.04	16.96	18.39	16.82	17.99
K$_2$O	(%)	1.05	0.80	1.51	1.37	1.45	0.63	1.15	0.67	0.83	0.98	1.41	1.21
TiO$_2$	(%)	0.12	0.12	0.17	0.17	0.17	0.36	0.13	0.13	0.14	0.18	0.16	0.14
P$_2$O$_5$	(%)	0.30	1.43	0.54	1.11	0.55	0.21	0.59	0.10	0.24	0.62	0.44	0.49
MnO	(%)	0.33	0.46	0.48	0.58	0.44	1.37	0.50	0.66	0.66	0.79	0.53	0.57
Pb	(%)	0.26	1.31	0.89	1.70	0.85	0.27	0.92	0.19	0.32	0.44	0.73	0.65
Sb	(%)	0.15	0.89	0.23	0.58	0.23	0.09	0.39	0.26	0.27	0.23	0.23	0.35
Ba	(ppm)	293	268	359	356	324	774	312	322	329	411	357	315
Ce	(ppm)	19	19	23	21	25	21	19	18	20	16	18	18
Co	(ppm)	12	98	16	25	17	12	32	10	12	14	19	18
Cr	(ppm)	49	47	52	46	56	71	45	50	52	62	51	47
Cu	(ppm)	814	4708	1142	3211	1304	591	1705	254	613	2091	1055	1519
La	(ppm)	6	7	7	8	10	8	7	7	6	7	8	7
Li	(ppm)	24	8	22	12	19	9	16	9	11	25	19	27
Nb	(ppm)	3	4	4	4	4	6	3	3	4	3	3	3
Ni	(ppm)	28	46	34	40	36	33	35	27	32	30	31	32
Sc	(ppm)	2	2	3	3	3	4	2	2	2	2	2	2
Sr	(ppm)	445	477	415	461	405	454	454	431	437	460	454	455
V	(ppm)	19	21	24	26	23	43	21	21	23	25	23	22
Y	(ppm)	9	9	11	11	11	12	10	9	9	9	11	9
Zn	(ppm)	54	129	90	127	114	53	98	36	64	135	70	108
Zr	(ppm)	67	79	90	87	94	173	70	69	72	82	82	61
SiO$_2$	(%)	68.93	64.61	67.56	64.78	68.87	67.64	67.04	69.67	69.40	66.64	66.94	66.61
Colour		LB	LB	LB	LG	LB	G	LB	LG	LG	LG	LB	LG
Type		11	15	12	11	11	15	14	11	14	13	11	13
Decoration		-	11	-	-	30	30	6	-	-	-	-	20

Sherd No		HAM E149b	39/ 112	36/ 206	HAM E149a	36/ 220	36/ 223	39/ 113
Al$_2$O$_3$	(%)	2.47	3.02	3.03	2.86	2.64	2.49	2.89
Fe$_2$O$_3$	(%)	0.93	1.34	1.35	1.22	0.94	0.92	1.25
MgO	(%)	0.80	0.85	0.87	0.83	0.71	0.72	0.85
CaO	(%)	6.74	7.45	7.60	7.62	7.15	6.78	7.40
Na$_2$O	(%)	18.43	15.97	16.00	16.15	16.81	18.14	15.74
K$_2$O	%)	0.81	0.96	1.01	1.06	0.84	0.76	1.39
TiO$_2$	(%)	0.14	0.16	0.16	0.15	0.12	0.15	0.15
P$_2$O$_5$	(%)	0.22	0.45	0.44	0.47	0.39	0.20	0.45
MnO	(%)	0.67	0.45	0.47	0.47	0.50	0.60	0.46
Pb	(%)	0.37	1.05	0.82	0.79	0.53	0.34	1.13
Sb	(%)	0.27	0.23	0.22	0.21	0.20	0.32	0.21
Ba	(ppm)	323	351	357	333	308	332	325
Ce	(ppm)	16	19	20	19	18	17	20
Co	(ppm)	11	16	15	18	14	12	17
Cr	(ppm)	48	46	49	47	45	49	46
Cu	(ppm)	652	1080	1021	1220	1146	541	1121
La	(ppm)	7	8	8	8	7	7	7
Li	(ppm)	15	23	20	18	25	14	20
Nb	(ppm)	3	4	4	3	3	3	4
Ni	(ppm)	28	32	32	31	29	29	31
Sc	(ppm)	2	2	2	2	2	2	2
Sr	(ppm)	464	429	428	443	428	438	431
V	(ppm)	23	22	23	21	19	22	22
Y	(ppm)	9	11	11	10	9	9	10
Zn	(ppm)	56	88	81	87	177	55	83
Zr	(ppm)	63	81	80	53	49	73	77
SiO$_2$	(%)	67.98	67.85	67.81	67.94	68.94	68.42	67.86
Colour		LG	LB	LB	LB	LB	LG	LB
Type		16	16	11	13	14	14	13
Decoration		39	20	-	12	-	-	12

Appendix Three. Electron microprobe analysis of the Hamwic glass *by Julian Henderson*

Analyses of two opaque yellow and a single opaque white glass, which formed spiral decoration on reticella rods decorating Anglo-Saxon vessel glass, were carried out using an electron microprobe system. Each sample was mounted in plastic and polished through a series of pastes down to .25μ diamond paste.

The quantitative analyses indicate that tin is the opacifier used to produce both the colours and opacity in all three glasses, with no antimony detected. In the case of the opaque yellow glass the opacifier is probably in the form of lead-tin oxide ($PbSnO_3$) as identified by Rooksby (1964), and in the opaque white glass crystalline tin oxide (SnO_2) probably imparts the opacity and the white colour.

The level of PbO in the opaque yellow glass is well in excess of the stochiometric ratio needed for the formation of $PbSnO_3$ and may have helped to impart extra workability to the opaque yellow glass when being formed into the rod. The lead oxide content in the opaque yellow glass is not as high as found in some earlier glasses from the Sewerby Anglian cemetery, East Yorkshire (Biek *et al* 1986, Table VII) or later opaque yellow glasses from medieval York (Henderson and Warren 1986, Table 10, nos 7 and 8), though comparable levels have been detected from Viking Ribe (Henderson and Warren 1983, Table 1, nos 59 and 61).

It is perhaps surprising to detect 8.99% PbO in the analysis of the opaque white glass, since this would not contribute to glass opacification. The lead would however have helped to dissolve tin oxide in the glass in the first instance. Tin-opacified opaque white glass tends not to contain such high levels of lead oxide.

The analyses below are a mean of three separate analyses on the same piece of glass (in weight %). A Cambridge microscan 2000 was operated at 20kV and 4 x 10^{-3} amps with a defocussed electron beam of 4μm in diameter. A ZAF correction program was employed to produce quantitative chemical analyses.

Find number	SOU 169	SOU 14	SOU 14
	Item no 2981	Item no 255	Item no 217
Colour	Opaque yellow	Opaque white	Opaque yellow
Na_2O	8.0	11.9	8.2
MgO	0.3	0.8	0.2
Al_2O_3	2.5	2.4	2.1
SiO_2	33.2	62.8	31.8
P_2O_5	0.14	0.12	ND
S	0.28	0.24	0.15
K_2O	0.94	1.04	0.36
CaO	3.56	6.05	2.32
TiO_2	0.1	0.09	0.08
MnO	0.2	0.67	0.1
Fe_2O_3	0.75	0.79	0.4
CoO	ND	ND	ND
NiO	ND	ND	ND
CuO	0.1	ND	ND
ZnO	ND	ND	ND
SnO_2	6.8	5.1	6.7
Sb_2O_5	ND	ND	ND
PbO	44.87	8.99	48.35
ND = Not detected			

Catalogue of Hamwic glass items *by J R Hunter and M P Heyworth*

The glass fragments are listed in numerical sequence by site, together with the stratigraphical context in which they were found. The following categories have been identified within the assemblage:

1   Palm cup/funnel beaker vessel series

     a   Tubular rims
     b   Tubular rims without cavity
     c   Rounded rims
     d   Bases

2   Other vessel types
3   Decorated, non-diagnostic fragments
4   Window fragments
5   Beads
6   Wasters
7   Undiagnostic vessel body fragments
8   Non-durable fragments

In all instances measurements are maximum measurements and intended essentially for recognition purposes. Where three measurements are given, the third relates to the maximum thickness of the vessel wall on the individual fragment. Where more than one fragment was recorded the dimensions of the largest fragment are given. Additional fragments entered under a single item entry are assumed to belong to the same vessel. Colour definition is simplified as much as possible, the majority of fragments being of light blue or light green glass. These colours were used as standards for the relative definition of other fragments. All colours are translucent unless otherwise stated.

SOU 7

Item no 28
F20 Level IV; 21 x 11mm; L.Green (see Plate 1 and Fig 16)
Decorated, non-diagnostic. Band of four reticella rods each containing alternate opaque white and opaque yellow spirals. Possibly from bowl form.

Item no 29
F20 Level IV; 16 x 14mm; L.Blue
Decorated, non-diagnostic. Evidence of applied arcaded trail.

Item no 30
F55 Layer i; 16 x 13mm; L.Blue (see Fig 8)
Funnel series. Rounded rim. Rim thickness 3mm. Slightly outsplayed. Decorated with opaque yellow marvered trails.

Item no 31
F54 Layer ii; 25 x 17mm; L.Blue
Funnel series. Tubular rim. Rim thickness 4.5mm. Estimated diameter 110mm. Slightly outsplayed.

Item no 32
F52 Layer IV; 35 x 21mm; Yellow/Brown
Other vessel type. Body fragment from small jar with evidence of fluted decoration. Probably same vessel as Item no 33.

Item no 33
F55 Layer i; 29 x 21mm; Yellow/Brown (see Plate 4 and Fig 14)
Other vessel type. Rim of small jar. Rim thickness 4.5mms. Estimated diameter 60mm. Rim folded inwards and flattened on inside.

SOU 8

Item no 7
F6; 5 x 3mm; Blue
Decorated, non-diagnostic. Horizontal opaque white marvered trails.

Item no 8
F25; 28 x 8mm; L.Blue
Funnel series. Tubular rim. Rim thickness 5mm. Estimated diameter 100mm. Slightly outsplayed.

Item no 9
F27; 20 x 11mm; L.Blue
Funnel series. Rounded rim. Rim thickness 2mm. Estimated diameter 90mm. Slightly outsplayed and inturned.

Item no 10
F82; 12 x 6mm; L.Blue
Decorated, non-diagnostic. Termination of applied trail. Three associated body fragments.

Item no 11
F27 iii; 30 x 23mm ; L.Green (see Plate 5)
Decorated, non-diagnostic. Red/Brown streaking.

SOU 10

Item no 1
F9; 18 x 8 x 2mm; Green

SOU 11

Item no 139
Unstratified; 21 x 18 x 3mm; L.Blue

Item no 140
F8;14 x 14mm; L.Blue
Funnel series. Rounded rim. Rim thickness 3mm. Slightly outsplayed.

Item no 141
F8; 13 x 9mm; L.Blue
Funnel series. Rounded rim. Rim thickness 2mm. Estimated diameter 140mm. Slightly outsplayed and inturned.

Item no 142
F8; 16 x 12mm; L.Blue
Decorated, non-diagnostic. Two associated fragments. Some dark streaking in metal. Evidence of applied trailing on one sherd.

Item no 143
F8; 13 x 9mm; L.Blue
Decorated, non-diagnostic. Evidence of opaque white marvered trails.

Item no 144
F49; 12 x 5 x 1mm; L.Blue
Two other fragments.

Item no 145
F49; 11 x 8mm L.Blue
Funnel series. Tubular rim. Rim thickness 4mm. Slightly outsplayed.

Item no 146
F49; 44 x 17mm; L.Blue (see Fig 8)
Funnel series. Rounded rim. Rim thickness 2.5mm. Estimated diameter 150mm. Slightly outsplayed with rim inturned almost to form right angle. Darker streaking in metal.

Item no 147
F49; 12 x 11mm; L.Blue (see Fig 16)
Decorated, non-diagnostic. Reticella rod containing opaque yellow spirals.

Item no 148
F48; 15 x 10 x 1mm; L.Blue

Item no 149
Unstratified; 26 x 12mm; L.Blue (see Fig 5)
Funnel series. Tubular rim. Rim thickness 3.5mm. Estimated diameter 120mm. Slightly outsplayed and flattened on inside. Two associated body fragments.

Item no 150
F72; 13 x 10 x 1mm; L.Green

Item no 151
F48; 10 x 2 x 1mm; L.Green

Item no 152
F15; 15 x 9mm; L.Blue
Decorated, non-diagnostic. Evidence of applied trailing. Dark streaking in metal.

Item no 153
F15; 27 x 24 x 1mm ; L.Blue
One other body fragment.

Item no 154
F12; 35 x 30mm; L.Green (see Plate 7 and Fig 12)
Funnel series. Base fragment. Showing pontil mark of diameter 22mm. Large pontil wad visible as decorative base area trimmed at edge by possible grozing. Large early form.

Item no 155
F62; 10 x 8 x 1mm; L.Blue

Item no 156
F66; 13 x 7 x 1mm; L.Blue

Item no 157
F45; 24 x 19 x 1mm; L.Blue

Item no 158
F45; 32 x 20mm; Opaque dark/light Red (see
Plate 8)
Decorated, non-diagnostic. Two fragments.
Some weathering. Striated.

Item no 159
F19; 13 x 10 x 1mm; L.Green

Item no 160
F62; 18 x 13mm; L.Blue (see Fig 16)
Decorated, non-diagnostic. Vertical reticella
rods, one containing opaque white spirals,
the other opaque yellow spirals.

Item no 161
F45; 19 x 9 x 1mm; L.Blue

Item no 162
F45; 13 x 12 x 1mm; L.Blue

Item no 163
F45; 27 x 19mm; Opaque dark/light Red (see
Plate 8)
Decorated, non-diagnostic. Striated.

Item no 164
F45; 27 x 15mm; L.Blue
Funnel series. Rounded rim. Rim thickness
2.5mm. Estimated diameter 120mm. Slightly
outsplayed and inturned. Decorated with
reticella rod containing opaque white spiral
applied to inside of rim.

Item no 165
F78; 9 x 7mm; L.Green
Funnel series. Tubular rim. Fragment of fold
only. Rim thickness 5.5mm.

Item no 166
F62; 12 x 9mm; L.Blue (see Fig 8)
Funnel series. Rounded rim. Rim thickness
2mm. Slightly outsplayed and inturned.
Decorated with reticella rod containing
opaque white spirals applied to top of rim.

Item no 167
F62; 11 x 10mm; L.Blue
Funnel series. Tubular rim. Rim thickness
4.5mm. Slightly outsplayed.

Item no 168
F62; 20 x 20mm; L.Green
Funnel series. Base fragment. Showing pontil
wad and mark. Diameter of mark 11mm.
Later form.

Item no 169
F62; 8 x 5 x 1mm; L.Blue

Item no 170
F62; 13 x 13 x 1mm ; L.Blue

Item no 171
F62; 19 x 16mm; L.Blue (see Plate 1 and
Fig 16)
Decorated, non-diagnostic. Reticella rods
containing alternate single opaque yellow
spirals and double opaque white spirals each.

Item no 172
F78; 14 x 11mm; L.Blue
Funnel series. Tubular rim. Two fragments.
Rim thickness 5mm. Estimated diameter
100mm. Slightly outsplayed. One body
fragment.

Item no 173
F62; 31 x 12mm; L.Blue
Funnel series. Tubular rim. Rim thickness
4mm. Estimated diameter 120mm. Slightly
outsplayed. One body fragment.

Item no 174
F47; 6 x 2 x 1mm; L.Blue
One other body fragment.

Item no 175
F25; 18 x 8 x 1mm; L.Green

Item no 176
F25; 10 x 8mm; Blue
Decorated, non-diagnostic. One other
associated fragment.

Item no 177
F62; 36 x 21mm; L.Green
Funnel series. Rounded rim. Rim thickness
2mm. Estimated diameter 100mm. Slightly
outsplayed and inturned.

Item no 178
F62; 11 x 10 x 1mm; L.Blue

Item no 179
F62; 8 x 8mm; L.Blue
Decorated, non-diagnostic. One other
associated fragment. Evidence of applied
trailing.

Item no 180
F62; 42 x 17 x 2mm; L.Blue

Item no 181
F62; 26 x 24mm; L.Blue
Funnel series. Tubular rim thickness 6.5mm.
Estimated diameter 140mm. Slightly
outsplayed.

Item no 182
F90; 29 x 14mm; L.Blue
Funnel series. From near base of vessel. Two
associated fragments.

Item no 183
F66; 11 x 10mm; L.Blue
Funnel series. Tubular rim. Rim thickness
3mm. Slightly outsplayed and flattened on
inside.

Item no 184
F66; 11 x 11mm; L.Blue
Funnel series. Tubular rim. Rim thickness
3.5mm. Slightly outsplayed.

Item no 185
F66; 12 x 11mm; L.Blue
Funnel series. Tubular rim. Slightly
outsplayed.

Item no 186
F66; 21 x 6 x 1mm; L.Blue

Item no 187
F62; 12 x 7 x 1mm; L.Blue
Two other body fragments.

Item no 188
F62; 17 x 5mm; L.Blue
Decorated, non-diagnostic. Horizontal
opaque yellow marvered trails.

Item no 189
F66; 17 x 12mm; Blue
Other vessel type. Tubular rim. Rim
thickness 5mms. Rim folded outwards and
probably belongs to small bowl or jar.

Item no 190
F66; 16 x 14mm; L.Blue
Decorated, non-diagnostic. Applied arcaded
trail. Some darker streaking within trail.

Item no 191
F66; 11 x 10 x 1mm; L.Blue

SOU 13

Item no 63
Unstratified; 14 x 13mm; L.Blue
Decorated, non-diagnostic. Slight traces of
applied trail.

Item no 64
F15;19 x 10 x 1mm; L.Blue

Item no 65
Surface; 15 x 9 x 2mm; L.Blue

Item no 66
F11; 45 x 29 x 4mm; L.Blue (see Fig 17)
Window fragment. Uneven. Two edges
grozed, one flame rounded. Probably
produced by cylinder method. Dark streaking
within metal.

Item no 67
F11; 44 x 33 x 4mm; L.Blue (see Fig 17)
Window fragment. Uneven. One edge
grozed, one flame rounded. Probably
produced by cylinder method. Dark streaking
within metal.

Item no 68
F29; 11 x 5 x 1mm; L.Blue

Item no 70
Surface; 15 x 14mm ; L.Green
Funnel series. Base fragment. Showing traces
of pontil mark and wad.

SOU 14

Item no 197
F6 Surface; L.Green
Bead. Circular of diameter 7mm and

maximum width 4mm. Diameter of perforation 3mm.

Item no 198
F19; 8 x 6mm; L.Green
Decorated, non-diagnostic. Decorated with applied (flattened) reticella rod with opaque white spirals.

Item no 199
F2; 26 x 15mm; Dark Green
Decorated, non-diagnostic.

Item no 200
F30; 42 x 10mm; L.Green
Funnel series. Tubular rim. Rim thickness 4mm. Estimated diameter 100mm. Smoothed on inside and slightly outsplayed.

Item no 201
F26; 16 x 16 x 1mm; Stratified; 14 x 9mm; L.Blue
Funnel series. From near base.

Item no 203
F29; 11 x 5 x 1mm; L.Blue

Item no 204
F29; 17 x 15mm; L.Blue
Funnel series. Rounded rim. Rim thickness 2.5mm. Slightly outsplayed. Decorated with broad marvered horizontal opaque yellow trail on outside of rim.

Item no 205
F34; 17 x 11mm; L.Green
Funnel series. Tubular rim. Rim thickness 4mm. Smoothed on inside and slightly outsplayed.

Item no 206
F29; 10 x 10 x 1mm; L.Green

Item no 207
F27; 16 x 7mm; L.Blue (see Fig 16)
Decorated, non-diagnostic. Decorated with applied reticella rod containing opaque white spirals.

Item no 208
F27 Surface; 21 x 17mm; L.Blue
Funnel series. Tubular rim. Rim thickness 3.5mm. Estimated diameter 100mm. Slightly outsplayed.

Item no 209
F27 Surface; 23 x 9mm; L.Blue
Funnel series. Tubular rim. Rim thickness 3.5mm. Estimated diameter 110mm. Slightly outsplayed. One associated body sherd.

Item no 210
F28 Surface; 15 x 9mm; L.Blue
Funnel series. Tubular rim. Rim thickness 3mm. Slightly outsplayed.

Item no 211
F28 Surface; 18 x 17 x 1mm; L.Blue

Item no 212
F28; 21 x 10mm; L.Blue

Funnel series. Tubular rim. Rim thickness 3.5mm. Estimated diameter 110mm. Slightly outsplayed.

Item no 213
F28 Surface; 15 x 13mm; Opaque Dark.
Decorated, non-diagnostic. Decorated with (lost) horizontal marvered trails.

Item no 214
F29; 14 x 13 x 1mm; L.Blue

Item no 215
F30 Surface; 20 x 13mm; L.Green
Funnel series. Rounded rim. Rim thickness 2.5mm. Estimated diameter 100mm. Slightly outsplayed and inturned.

Item no 216
F30; 14 x 11mm; L.Blue
Decorated, non-diagnostic. Decorated with applied reticella rod with opaque yellow spirals.

Item no 217
F30 Surface; 14 x 11mm; L.Blue
Decorated, non-diagnostic. Decorated with applied reticella rod with opaque yellow spirals.

Item no 218
F30 Surface; 22 x 16mm; L.Blue
Decorated, non-diagnostic. Decorated with (traces of) applied reticella rod with opaque yellow spirals.

Item no 219
F30 Surface; 10 x 3 x 1mm; L.Blue

Item no 220
F30 Surface; 9 x 5 x 2.5mm; L.Blue

Item no 221
F30; 13 x 12mm; L.Green
Funnel series. Rounded rim. Rim thickness 2.5mm. Estimated diameter 100mm. Slightly outsplayed and inturned.

Item no 222
F30; 12 x 8mm; Dark Opaque
Decorated, non-diagnostic. Decorated with marvered horizontal opaque yellow trails.

Item no 223
F30; 9 x 7mms; Dark Opaque Red
Decorated, non-diagnostic.

Item no 224
F30; 10 x 7 x 1mm; L.Blue

Item no 225
F30; 10 x 7mm; L.Blue
Decorated, non-diagnostic. Decorated with (traces of) applied reticella rod with opaque yellow trails.

Item no 226
F30; 15 x 6 x 1mm; L.Blue

Item no 227
F30; 11 x 5 x 1mm; L.Blue

Item no 228
F27; 25 x 15 mm; L.Green
Other vessel type. From pushed base showing junctions of applied (flattened) reticella rods with opaque yellow spirals. Bowl or jar form.

Item no 229
F28; 4 x 4 x 1mm; L.Green

Item no 230
F27; 31 x 19mm; L.Green (see Fig 14)
Other vessel type. Lower body fragment showing vertical applied reticella rods with opaque yellow spirals. Bowl or jar form. Possibly with Item no 228.

Item no 231
F28; 4 x 3 x 1mm; L.Blue

Item no 232
F82; 27 x 22mm; L.Blue
Funnel series. Tubular rim without cavity. Rim thickness 4mm. Estimated diameter 120mm. Slightly outsplayed. Decorated with applied reticella rod with opaque white spiral applied to inner edge of rim.

Item no 233
F30; 16 x 10mm; Dark Opaque
Decorated, non-diagnostic. Decorated with marvered horizontal opaque yellow marvered trails.

Item no 234
F30; 11 x 5 x 1mm; L.Blue

Item no 235
F19; 8 x 6mm; L.Blue
Decorated, non-diagnostic. Decorated with (badly) applied reticella rod with opaque yellow spirals.

Item no 236
F19; 12 x 8 x 1mm; L.Blue

Item no 237
F27 Layer 8; 20 x 15 x 1mm; L.Blue

Item no 238
F28 Layer 4; 27 x 22mm; L.Green
Funnel series. Rounded rim. Rim thickness 2.5mm. Slightly outsplayed and inturned. Decorated with applied reticella rod with opaque white spirals applied to inner edge of rim.

Item no 239
F30; 21 x 14 x 1mm; L.Green

Item no 240
F30; 16 x 11 x 1mm; L.Blue

Item no 241
F30; 19 x 10mm; L.Blue
Funnel series. Rounded rim. Rim thickness 2.5mm. Slightly outsplayed and inturned. Decorated with applied reticella rod with opaque white spirals applied to inner edge of rim.

Item no 242
F30; 13 x 11 x 1mm; Colourless

Item no 243
F30; Opaque Green (see Fig 18)
Bead. Cylindrical of diameter 7mm and length 4mm. Diameter of perforation 3mm.

Item no 244
F30; 10 x 8mm; L.Blue
Funnel series. Rounded rim. Rim thickness 2mm. Slightly outsplayed and inturned. Decorated with applied reticella rod with opaque white spirals applied to top of rim.

Item no 245
F30; 5 x 4 x 1mm; L.Blue

Item no 246
F30; 13 x 7 x 1mm; L.Green

Item no 247
F30; 8 x 6 x 1mm; L.Blue

Item no 248
F55; 11 x 8mm; L.Green
Funnel series. Tubular rim. Rim thickness 4mm. Slightly outsplayed.

Item no 249
F30; 11 x 7 x 1mm; L.Blue

Item no 250
F30; 12 x 10 x 1mm; L.Blue

Item no 251
F30; 12 x 6 x 1mm; L.Green

Item no 252
F22 Level C; 8 x 6mm; L.Blue
Other vessel type. Pronounced carination in body.

Item no 253
F30; 12 x 10 x 1mm; L.Blue

Item no 254
F30; 5 x 4 x 1mm; L.Green

Item no 255
F28 i; 16 x 6mm; L.Blue
Decorated, non-diagnostic. Decorated with applied reticella rod with opaque white spirals.

Item no 256
F28 Layer 1; 13 x 10 x 1mm; L.Green

Item no 257
F28 i; 19 x 7 x 2mm; L.Blue

Item no 258
F28 Layer 1; 13 x 9 x 1mm; L.Blue

Item no 259
F30; 21 x 11mm; L.Blue/Green (see Plate 2 and Fig 8)
Funnel series. Rounded rim. Rim thickness 3.5mm. Estimated diameter 100mm. Slightly outsplayed. Decorated with shallow flattened reticella rod with opaque white spirals

applied to outer edge of rim. Rim light blue, upper vessel green.

Item no 260
F30; 24 x 13 x 1.5mm; L.Blue

Item no 261
F30; 10 x 5mm; L.Blue
Decorated, non-diagnostic. Decorated with (flattened) reticella rod with opaque yellow spirals.

Item no 262
F30; 17 x 10 x 1.5mm; L.Green

Item no 263
F30; 9 x 7mm; Opaque Dark Red
Decorated, non-diagnostic.

Item no 264
F30; 22 x 5mm; Dark Opaque (see Fig 15)
Decorated, non-diagnostic. Decorated with marvered opaque yellow blobs (?) or small bosses.

Item no 265
F30; 39 x 19mm; Dark Opaque (see Fig 13)
Other vessel type. Rim fragment. Rim thickness 4mms. Estimated diameter 80mm. Rim folded inwards. Decorated with marvered horizontal opaque yellow trails. Probably tall beaker type.

Item no 266
F30 Layer 8; 9 x 7 x 1mm; L.Blue

Item no 267
F29 Layer 1; 10 x 8mm; L.Green (see Fig 9)
Funnel series. Rounded rim. Rim thickness 2.5mm. Slightly outsplayed. Decorated with broad marvered horizontal opaque yellow trail on outside of rim.

Item no 268
F19 Layer 1; 17 x 12 x 1mm; L.Green

Item no 269
F19 Layer 1; 10 x 9mm; L.Blue
Decorated, non-diagnostic. Decorated with opaque yellow marvered trail, possibly terminal of reticella rod.

Item no 270
F27; 23 x 10mm; L.Blue
Decorated, non-diagnostic. Decorated with applied arcaded dark opaque trail.

Item no 271
F27; 11 x 10mm; L.Green
Decorated, non-diagnostic. Decorated with (flattened) reticella rod with opaque yellow spirals.

Item no 272
F27; 15 x 13 x 1mm; L.Blue

Item no 273
F27 Layer 6; 37 x 20 x 1.5mm; L.Blue

Item no 274
F29; 8 x 8 x 1mm; L.Blue

Item no 275
F28 Layer 4; 15 x 9 x 1mm; L.Green

Item no 276
F28; 17 x 14mm; L.Green
Funnel series. Rounded rim. Rim thickness 2mm. Slightly outsplayed and inturned.

Item no 277
F28 Layer 3; 8 x 7mm; Opaque Dark Green
Decorated, non-diagnostic.

Item no 278
F28 Layer 3; 13 x 7 x 1.5mm; L.Blue

Item no 279
F34 Layer 1; 15 x 14mm; Green
Decorated, non-diagnostic. Decorated with (lost) marvered horizontal trails.

Item no 280
F19 Layer 3; 20 x 14 x 4mm; L.Blue

Item no 281
F24 Layer 2; 20 x 16mm; L.Blue
Decorated, non-diagnostic. Indications of terminal of applied trail.

Item no 282
F30 Layer 3; 11 x 7 x 1mm; L.Blue

Item no 283
F34; 21 x 12mm; L.Green
Decorated, non-diagnostic. Clouded.

Item no 284
F34; 18 x 10mm; L.Blue
Decorated, non-diagnostic. Decorated with applied reticella rod with opaque white spirals.

Item no 285
F28 Layer 1; 13 x 7 x 1mm; L.Blue

Item no 286
F29 Layer 2; 11 x 10mm; L.Blue
Decorated, non-diagnostic. Decorated with applied trail.

Item no 287
F28 Layer 2; 30 x 24mm; L.Blue (see Plate 2)
Funnel series. Rounded rim. Rim thickness 3mm. Estimated diameter 110mm. Slightly outsplayed. Decorated with applied reticella rod with opaque white spirals applied to inner edge of rim.

Item no 288
F28 Layer 2; 22 x 16mm; L.Blue
Decorated, non-diagnostic. Applied arcaded trail.

Item no 289
F30 Layer 4; 20 x 12 x 1mm; L.Blue

Item no 290
F30 Layer 4; 13 x 6mm; L.Blue
Decorated, non-diagnostic. Decorated with marvered horizontal opaque white trails.

Item no 291
F30 Layer 4a; 7 x 6 x 1mm; L.Blue

Item no 292
F30 Layer 4a; 17 x 9 x 1mm; L.Blue

Item no 293
F31; 7 x 3 x 1mms; L.Blue

Item no 294
F27 Layer 4; 15 x 15mm; L.Green
Decorated, non-diagnostic. Decorated with
marvered horizontal opaque white trails.

Item no 295
F27 Layer 4; 32 x 15mm; L.Green
Other vessel type. Body fragment decorated
with vertical applied reticella rods with
opaque yellow spirals and opaque yellow
marvered trails. Probably from bowl or jar.

Item no 296
F27 Layer 2; 10 x 3 x 1mm; L.Blue

Item no 297
F19 Layer 5; Dark Opaque (see Fig 18)
Bead. Segmented (three units) of length
15mm, maximum diameter 9mm. Diameter
of perforation 4mm. Decorated with opaque
green and opaque yellow marvered blobs.

Item no 298
F28 Layer 1; 15 x 12mm; L.Blue
Funnel series. Rounded rim. Rim thickness
2.5mm. Slightly outsplayed.

Item no 299
F30 Layer 5; 10 x 10 x 1mm; L.Blue

Item no 300
F30 Layer 5; 18 x 11mm; Dark Opaque
Decorated, non-diagnostic. Decorated with
(lost) marvered horizontal trails.

Item no 301
F30 Layer 8a; 18 x 7 x 1mm; L.Blue

Item no 302
F19; 41 x 17mm; Opaque Brown/Yellow
Other vessel type. From pushed base
showing junctions of applied (flattened)
reticella rods originally with opaque yellow
spirals. Bowl or jar form.

Item no 303
F26; 21 x 9mm; Green (see Plate 4 and
Fig 6)
Funnel series. Tubular rim without cavity.
Rim thickness 3mms. Estimated diameter
100mm. Slightly outsplayed. Decorated with
marvered horizontal opaque yellow trails.

Item no 304
F34; 16 x 10mm; Clouded Red (see Plate 1)
Decorated, non-diagnostic. Decorated with
applied reticella rod with spirals in alternate
opaque yellow and opaque white. Rod dark
opaque.

Item no 305
F101; Colourless
Bead. Circular of diameter 2mm and
thickness 1mm. Diameter of perforation
1mm. Probable spacer.

Item no 306
F101; Colourless
Bead. Circular of diameter 1.5mm amd
thickness 1mm. Diameter of perforation
1mm. Probable spacer.

Item no 307
F101; 9 x 3 x 1mm; L.Green
One associated fragment.

Item no 308
F101; 8 x 1mm; Blue
Decorated, non-diagnostic.

Item no 309
F101; 4 x 3mm; Blue
Decorated, non-diagnostic.

Item no 310
Unstratified; 27 x 15mm; L.Blue
Funnel series. Rounded rim. Rim thickness
2.5mm. Estimated diameter 130mms.
Slightly outsplayed and inturned. Decorated
with fine marvered horizontal opaque yellow
trails.

Item no 311
Unstratified; 17 x 11mm; L.Blue
Funnel series. Base fragment. Showing part
of pontil mark.

Item no 312
Unstratified; 8 x 7mm; L.Blue
Decorated, non-diagnostic. Decorated with
marvered horizontal opaque white trails.
Four associated fragments.

SOU 15

Item no 388
F2 Layer 2 ; 18 x 15 x 1mm; Colourless

Item no 389
F25 Layer ii ; 27 x 18 x 1mm; L.Blue
One other body fragment.

Item no 390
F2 Layer 2; 37 x 30 x 1mm; L.Green
One other body fragment.

Item no 391
F1 Layer 1; 20 x 13 x 1mm; L.Blue

Item no 392
F1 Layer 2; 13 x 12mm; L.Green
Decorated, non-diagnostic. Termination of
applied trail.

Item no 393
F30 Layer 1; 22 x 14mm; L.Blue
Funnel series. Rounded rim. Rim thickness
3mm. Estimated diameter 110mm. Slightly
outsplayed and inturned.

Item no 394
F27 Layer 2; 19 x 16 x 2mm; L.Green
Funnel series. Near to base.

Item no 395
F27 Layer 5; 15 x 10mm; L.Blue (see Fig 7)

Funnel series. Rounded rim. Rim thickness
2mm. Slightly outsplayed. Decorated with
horizontal fine opaque white marvered trail
inside lip.

Item no 396
F27 Layer 7; 12 x 11 x 1mm; L.Blue

Item no 397
F27 Layer 6; 15 x 14mm; L.Green
Funnel series. Rounded rim. Slightly
outsplayed.

Item no 398
F27 Layer 5; 16 x 6mm; L.Green
Funnel series. Tubular rim. Rim thickness
3mm. Slightly outsplayed and flattened on
inside.

Item no 399
F27 Layer 5; 15 x 11mm; L.Green
Funnel series. Rounded rim. Rim thickness
2.5mm. Slightly outsplayed.

Item no 400
F45 Layer 2; 22 x 14mm; L.Blue
Funnel series. Base fragment. Evidence of
pontil wad.

Item no 401
F1 Layer 4; 22 x 11 x 1mm; L.Blue

Item no 402
F1 Layer 3; 15 x 13 x 2mm; L.Blue
Funnel series. Near to base.

Item no 403
F1 Layer 5; 22 x 12 x 1mm; L.Blue

Item no 404
F49 Layer 2; 10 x 9 x 1mm; L.Green

Item no 405
F51 Layer 8; 13 x 5mm; L.Blue
Decorated, non-diagnostic. Horizontal
opaque yellow marvered trails.

Item no 406
F51 Layer 7; 9 x 6 x 1mm; L.Blue

Item no 407
F51 Layer 11; 28 x 14mm; L.Blue
Funnel series. Tubular rim. Rim thickness
5mm. Estimated diameter 130mm. Slightly
outsplayed and flattened on inside.
Decorated with applied horizontal trail.

Item no 408
S64; 12 x 12mm; L.Blue
Funnel series. Rounded rim. Rim thickness
2mm. Slightly outsplayed. Decorated with
horizontal fine opaque yellow marvered
trails.

Item no 409
F49 Layer 2; 41 x 17mm; L.Green (see
Fig 5)
Funnel series. Tubular rim. Rim thickness
4mm. Estimated diameter 100mm. Slightly
outsplayed.

Item no 410
F1 Layer 2; 15 x 8mm; Bright Green
Decorated, non-diagnostic.

Item no 411
F51 Layer 11; Opaque Green (see Fig 18)
Bead. Fragment of circular bead of estimated
diameter 25mm. Thickness 13mm. Decorated
with thick badly-made reticella-type design
of opaque yellow colour marvered around
circumference.

Item no 412
F31 Layer 3; 25 x 20mm; Yellow/Brown (see
Fig 13)
Other vessel type. Decorated with horizontal
opaque white marvered trails. Probably from
tall beaker.

Item no 413
F66 Layer 1; 13 x 9mm; L.Blue
Other vessel type. Showing pronounced
carination in body.

Item no 414
F56 Layer 1; 21 x 19mm; L.Blue (see Fig
14)
Other vessel type. Fragment of bowl or jar
showing junctions of applied trails.

Item no 415
F54 Layer 1; 18 x 8 x 1mm; L.Blue

Item no 416
S64; 16 x 8mms; L.Blue
Decorated, non-diagnostic. Dark streaking in
metal.

Item no 417
S64; 17 x 3 x 1mm; L.Green

Item no 418
F56; 15 x 12mm; L.Blue
Funnel series. Rounded rim. Rim thickness
3mm. Slightly outsplayed. Decorated with
applied reticella rod containing opaque white
spirals on lip.

Item no 419
F57 Layer 4; 17 x 7mm ; L.Blue
Funnel series. Tubular rim. Rim thickness
4.5mm. Slightly outsplayed and flattened on
inside.

Item no 420
F1 Layer 2; 25 x 18mm; L.Blue
Funnel series. Rounded rim. Rim thickness
3mm. Estimated diameter 100mm. Slightly
outsplayed.

Item no 421
F31 Layer 1; 16 x 9mm; Colourless
Decorated, non-diagnostic. Applied arcaded
trail containing darker streaking.

Item no 422
F66 Layer 2; 19 x 18 x 1mm; L.Green

Item no 423
F56 Layer 1; 12 x 9 x 1mms; L.Blue

Item no 424
F44 Layer 1; 13 x 9mm; L.Blue
Other vessel type. Pronounced carination in
body.

Item no 425
F49 Layer 2; 13 x 9mm; Colourless
Funnel series. Tubular rim. Rim thickness
3mm. Slightly outsplayed and flattened on
inside.

Item no 426
F31 Layer 5; 8 x 8mm; Dark Green
Decorated, non-diagnostic. Opaque yellow
marvered trails.

Item no 427
75 Layer 1; 18 x 9mm; L.Green
Funnel series. Tubular rim without cavity.
Rim thickness 3.5mm. Slightly outsplayed.

Item no 428
F31 Layer 5; 25 x 15mm; L.Green
Funnel series. Tubular rim without cavity.
Rim thickness 3mm. Estimated diameter
100mm. Slightly outsplayed.

Item no 429
F44 Layer 1; 17 x 13 x 1mm; L.Green

Item no 430
F1 Layer 2; 23 x 15mm; L.Green
Funnel series. Rounded rim. Rim thickness
3mm. Estimated diameter 100mm. Slightly
outsplayed.

Item no 431
F1 Layer 2; 14 x 14mm; L.Blue
Funnel series. Rounded rim. Rim thickness
2.5mm. Slightly outsplayed. Decorated with
horizontal fine opaque white marvered trail
inside lip.

Item no 432
F1 Layer 2; 13 x 8 x 1mm; L.Blue

Item no 433
F44 Layer 3; 15 x 9mm; Bright Green
Decorated, non-diagnostic.

Item no 434
F49 Layer 2; 13 x 13mm; L.Green
Funnel series. Rounded rim. Rim thickness
2mm. Estimated diameter 100mm. Slightly
outsplayed.

Item no 435
F53 Layer 1; 12 x 11 x 1mm; L.Blue

Item no 436
F1 Layer 3; 17 x 11mm; L.Blue (see Fig 13)
Other vessel type. Fragment of beaker
decorated with vertical reticella rods
containing opaque white spirals.

Item no 437
F66 Layer 5; 20 x 16mm; L.Green
Funnel series. Tubular rim. Rim thickness
3.5mm. Slightly outsplayed.

Item no 438
F49 Layer 3; 11 x 7 x 1mm; L.Blue

Item no 439
F54 Layer 5; 23 x 19 x 1mm; L.Green

Item no 440
F54 Layer 5; 9 x 8 x 1mm; L.Blue

Item no 441
F54 Layer 5; 25 x 13mm; L.Blue
Funnel series. Fragment from near base.
Evidence of termination of applied trail.

Item no 442
F77 Layer 1; 15 x 9mm; Dark Green
Decorated, non-diagnostic. Evidence of
opaque yellow marvered trails.

Item no 443
F52 Layer 1; 15 x 6 x 1mm; L.Green

Item no 444
F67 Layer 1; 13 x 12mm; L.Blue (see
Fig 16)
Decorated, non-diagnostic. Applied reticella
rods containing opaque white spirals.

Item no 445
F54 Layer 7; 12 x 10 x 2mm; L.Green

Item no 446
F52 Layer 1; 30 x 14mm; Yellow/Brown (see
Fig 14)
Other vessel type. Rim fragment of bowl or
jar. Rim thickness 5mms. Estimated diameter
140mms. Rim outfolded.

Item no 447
F52 Layer 1; 17 x 9 x 2mm; L.Green

Item no 448
F53 Layer 1; 14 x 12 x 2mm; L.Blue

Item no 449
F44 Layer 3; 16 x 7 x 1mm; L.Blue

Item no 450
F1 Layer 3; 12 x 8 x 1mm; L.Blue

Item no 451
F53 Layer 1; 11 x 10 x 1mm; L.Green

Item no 452
F54 Layer 7; 14 x 9 x 3mm; L.Blue Burnt
fragment.

Item no 453
Area C; Opaque Blue (see Fig 18)
Bead. Hexagonal. Diameter 4mm. Thickness
2mm. Diameter of perforation 1-2mm.

Item no 454
F1 Layer 4; 12 x 7mm; L.Blue
Funnel series. Tubular rim. Rim thickness
2.5mm. Slightly outsplayed.

Item no 455
F1 Layer 4 ; 16 x 10mm; L.Blue
Funnel series. Tubular rim. Rim thickness
4mm. Flattened on inside.

Item no 456
F54 Layer 8; 20 x 10mm; Dark Green
Decorated, non-diagnostic. Opaque yellow
marvered trails.

Item no 457
F54 Layer 7; 9 x 6mm; L.Blue
Decorated, non-diagnostic. Evidence of
applied trail.

Item no 458
F54 Layer 7; 11 x 8 x 1mm; L.Blue

Item no 459
F50 Layer 1; 21 x 8mm; L.Blue
Decorated, non-diagnostic. Opaque yellow
marvered trails.

Item no 460
F49 Layer 3; 33 x 17mm; Red (see Plate 8
and Fig 13)
Other vessel type. Fragment decorated with
sporadic horizontal opaque yellow marvered
trails. Probably tall beaker.

Item no 461
F49 Layer 2; 11 x 8 x 2mm; L.Blue

Item no 462
F50 Layer 3; 26 x 20mm; Dark Opaque (see
Fig 15)
Other vessel type. Pushed base of flask or jar
showing termination of reticella rods
containing opaque yellow spirals.

Item no 463
F50 Layer 3; 10 x 6 x 1mm; Colourless

Item no 464
F50 Layer 3; 10 x 9 x 1mm; L.Green

SOU 17

Item no 29
F9 Layer 2; 19 x 7 x 1.5mm; L.Blue

Item no 30
F9 Layer 2; 14 x 13mm; Dark Opaque
Decorated, non-diagnostic. Horizontal
opaque yellow marvered trail.

Item no 31
F14 Layer 1; 8 x 8 x 1mm; L.Green
Two other fragments.

SOU 18

Item no 17
F12 Layer 1; 16 x 14mm; L.Green
Decorated, non-diagnostic. Evidence of
surface decoration, possibly by abrasion or
more likely by lost marvering.

SOU 19

Item no 1
F1 Layer 7; 27 x 11mm; L.Blue
Funnel series. Tubular rim. Rim thickness
3mm. Estimated diameter 100mm. Slightly
outsplayed and flattened on inside.

Item no 2
F1 Layer 1; 22 x 20mm; L.Blue
Funnel series. Rounded rim. Rim thickness
3mm. Estimated diameter 100mm. Slightly
outsplayed and inturned.

SOU 22

Item no 1
F43/114; 24 x 14mm; Dark Green
Decorated, non-diagnostic.

Item no 2
F79 Surface; 13 x 9mm; L.Blue
Decorated, non-diagnostic. Probably from
tubular rim. Evidence of applied trail.

Item no 3
F430 Layer 3; 23 x 6mm; Red/Brown
Decorated, non-diagnostic. Applied reticella
rod containing opaque yellow spirals. Rod
colourless.

Item no 4
F114 Layer 3; Opaque Blue
Bead. Spherical of diameter 3 mm. Diameter
of perforation 1 mm.

SOU 23

Item no 11
Context 6806; 20 x 12 x 2mm; L.Blue

Item no 12
Context 6839; x 10 x 7mm; L.Blue
Decorated, non-diagnostic. Dark green
streaking within metal.

Item no 13
Context 6849; 10 x 9 x 1mm; L.Blue

Item no 14
Context 6862; 22 x 11mm; L.Blue
Funnel series. Tubular rim. Rim thickness
4mm. Estimated diameter 110mms.
Smoothed on inside and slightly outsplayed.

Item no 15
Context 6817; 21 x 17mm; L.Green (see
Fig 11)
Funnel series. Base fragment. Showing pontil
mark and wad. Base diameter 16 mm. Mark
diameter 11mm.

Item no 16
Context 6863; 9 x 4 x 1mm; L.Blue

Item no 17
Context 6839; 18 x 9mm; L.Blue
Other vessel type. Pronounced carination in
body.

Item no 18
Context 6844; 15 x 8mm; L.Green (see
Fig 6)
Funnel series. Tubular rim without cavity.
Rim thickness 2.5mm. Slightly outsplayed.
Rim surmounted by reticella rod containing
opaque white spirals.

Item no 19
Context 6859; 5 x 4 x 1mm; L.Blue

Item no 20
Context 7013; 21 x 11 x 1mm; L.Blue
Splayed form.

Item no 22
Context 6844; 11 x 7 x 1mm; L.Blue

Item no 23
Context 6844; 9 x 9mm; L.Blue
Other vessel type. Pronounced carination in
body. Three other fragments.

Item no 24
Context 6844; 9 x 6mm; L.Green
Other vessel type. Pronounced carination in
body.

Item no 25
F13 Layer 3; 18 x 9 x 1mm; L.Blue

Item no 26
Context 6839; 12 x 4 x 1mm; L.Blue

Item no 27
Context 6840; 12 x 6mm; Opaque Red
Decorated, non-diagnostic.

Item no 28
Context 6817; 12 x 4mm; L.Blue
Other vessel type. Pronounced carination in
body.

Item no 29
Context 6860; 21 x 10mm; Dark Red/Brown
Other vessel type. Rounded rim, slightly
outsplayed. Probably from tall beaker.
Decorated with horizontal opaque yellow
marvered trails below rim.

Item no 30
Spit 3; 7 x 3 x 1mm; L.Green

Item no 32
F13 Layer 1; 19 x 8mm; L.Blue
Funnel series. Tubular rim. Rim thickness
5mm. Estimated diameter 120mm. Slightly
outsplayed.

Item no 33
Context 6818; 21 x 9 x 2mm; L.Blue

Item no 34
Context 6817; 17 x 6 x 1mm; L.Green

Item no 35
Context 6840; 22 x 10mm; L.Blue
Decorated, non-diagnostic. Evidence of
applied trailing.

Item no 36
Context 6840; 19 x 12mm; L.Blue
Decorated, non-diagnostic. Evidence of
applied trailing.

Item no 37
Context 6817; 19 x 9 x 2mm; L.Blue

Item no 157
F11 Layer 6; 10 x 4mm; L.Green
Decorated, non-diagnostic. Applied arcaded
trail.

SOU 24

Item no 159
F2122 C8298; 20 x 10mm; L.Blue
Funnel series. Tubular rim. Rim thickness
3mm. Estimated diameter 120mm. Slightly
outsplayed.

Item no 420
F4005 Layer 5; 13 x 9mm; Opaque clouded
Red (see Plate 5)
Decorated, non-diagnostic.

Item no 421
F7023 Layer 1; 12 x 6 x 1.5mm; L.Blue

Item no 421
F2119 Layer 5; 17 x 14mm; L.Blue (see Fig
11)
Funnel series. Base fragment. Showing pontil
mark and wad. Base diameter 16mm. Mark
diameter 9mm.

Item no 423
F2147; 15 x 4mm; L.Green
Decorated, non-diagnostic. Horizontal
opaque white marvered trails.

Item no 424
F2001; 10 x 7 x 2mm; L.Green

Item no 425
F7037; 8 x 4 x 2mm; L.Green

Item no 426
F1018 Layer 17; 31 x 20mm; L.Blue (see
Plate 7 and Fig 11)
Funnel series. Base fragment. Showing pontil
mark and wad. Base diameter 25mm. Mark
diameter 14mm.

Item no 427
F4009 Layer 3; L.Blue (see Fig 18)
Bead. Circular of diameter 9mm, thickness
3mm. Diameter of perforation 4mm.
Irregular unmarvered opaque yellow scrabble
around circumference.

Item no 428
F2133 Layer 3; 19 x 18mm; L.Blue
Other vessel type. Pushed base with dark
streaking within metal. Flask or jar form.

Item no 429
F2133 Layer 4; 19 x 3 x 2mm; L.Blue

Item no 430
F1046 Layer 1; 18 x 6 x 1mm; L.Blue

Item no 431
F2003; 26 x 13 x 2mms; L.Blue
Splayed form.

Item no 432
F3055 Layer 1; 15 x 15mm; L.Blue
Funnel series. Rounded rim. Rim thickness
2mm. Estimated diameter 120mm. Slightly
outsplayed and inturned.

Item no 433
F2183; 9 x 8mm; Blue

Decorated, non-diagnostic. Horizontal
opaque yellow marvered trails.

Item no 434
F1093 Layer 1; 19 x 14mm; L.Blue
Funnel series. Rounded rim. Rim thickness
1mm. Slightly outsplayed and inturned.

Item no 435
F1093 Layer 1; 17 x 14mm; L.Blue
Decorated, non-diagnostic. Twisted
decoration.

Item no 436
F1093 Layer 3; 32 x 24mm; L.Green (see
Fig 7)
Funnel series. Rounded rim. Rim thickness
2mm. Estimated diameter 100mm. Slightly
outsplayed and inturned. Some dark
streaking within metal.

Item no 437
F3060 Layer 1; 21 x 16mm; L.Blue
Funnel series. Rounded rim. Rim thickness
2.5mm. Estimated diameter 100mm. Slightly
outsplayed and inturned. Some dark
streaking within metal. One associated body
fragment.

Item no 438
F7089; 8 x 7 x 1.5mm; L.Green

Item no 439
F1093 Layer 3; 8 x 4 x 3mm; L.Blue

Item no 440
F3020 Layer 14; 10 x 9 x 5mm; L.Blue

Item no 441
F2158 Surface; 6 x 5 x 1mm; L.Blue

Item no 442
F6145 Layer 1; 25 x 10mm; L.Blue
Funnel series. Tubular rim. Rim thickness
4mms. Estimated diameter 100mm.
Smoothed on inside, slightly outsplayed.

Item no 443
F1093 Layer 3; 48 x 25mm; L.Green (see
Fig 7)
Funnel series. Rounded rim. Rim thickness
2.5mm. Estimated diameter 120mm. Slightly
outsplayed.

Item no 444
F2119 Layer 3; 45 x 13mm; L.Blue
Funnel series. Tubular rim. Rim thickness
3mm. Estimated diameter 90mm. Smoothed
on inside and slightly outsplayed.

Item no 445
F2119 Layer 3; 28 x 19mm; L.Blue
Decorated, non-diagnostic. Red streaking.
Heat frosted.

Item no 446
F2133 Layer 3; 15 x 10mm; L.Blue
Other vessel type. Pronounced carination in
body.

Item no 447
F2133 Layer 3; 27 x 21mm; L.Blue (see
Plate 4)
Decorated, non-diagnostic. Striated dark/light
red colouring within metal.

Item no 448
F3027; 21 x 12 x 1mm; L.Blue

Item no 449
F2133 Layer 3; 22 x 18mm; L.Blue
Other vessel type. Pronounced carination in
body. One associated fragment.

Item no 450
F4006 Layer 5; 10 x 9 x 1mm; L.Blue

Item no 451
F4009 Layer 5; 16 x 10 x 1.5mm; Colourless

Item no 452
F1093 Layer 1; 29 x 4mm; L.Blue (see Fig
16)
Decorated, non-diagnostic. Applied arcaded
trail 4mm wide.

Item no 453
F2159 Layer 12; 17 x 16 x 1mm; L.Green
Heat distorted. Some iridescence. One
associated fragment.

Item no 454
F7018 Layer 19; 16 x 13 x 1mm; L.Blue

Item no 455
F7142; 19 x 12 x 2.5mm; L.Blue
Lower body.

Item no 456
F7007 Layer 3; 28 x 15mm; L.Blue
Funnel series. Tubular rim. Rim thickness
5mm. Estimated diameter 120mm. Slightly
outsplayed.

Item no 457
F7019 Layer 1; 35 x 15 x 2mm; L.Blue
Lower body.

Item no 458
F2183 C8087; 15 x 9 x 1mm; L.Blue
One associated body fragment.

Item no 459
F7010 Layer 7; 13 x 8 x 1mm; L.Blue

Item no 460
Trench 5 Surface; 19 x 11mm; L.Blue
Waster. Melted globule.

Item no 461
F2119 Layer 6; 8 x 4 x 1mm; L.Blue
One associated fragment.

Item no 462
F2119 Layer 3; 65 x 13mm; L.Blue (see
Plate 3 and Fig 4)
Funnel series. Tubular rim. Rim thickness
3.5mm. Estimated diameter 90mm.
Smoothed on inside, slightly outsplayed.

Item no 463
F3020 Layer 6; 24 x 12mm; L.Blue

Funnel series. Tubular rim. Rim thickness 3mm. Estimated diameter 120mms. Smoothed on inside, slightly outsplayed.

Item no 464
F7019 Layer 3; 52 x 20mm; L.Blue (see Fig 13)
Other vessel type. Twisted decoration. Probable tall beaker.

Item no 465
F2066 Layer 1; 140 x 29mm; L.Blue (see Fig 4)
Funnel series. Tubular rim. Rim thickness 5mm. Estimated diameter 95mm. Smoothed on inside, slightly outsplayed. Showing twisted body decoration.

Item no 466
F2119 Layer 2; 50 x 13mm; L.Blue (see Plate 3 and Fig 5)
Funnel series. Tubular rim. Rim thickness 3mm. Estimated diameter 90mm. Smoothed on inside, slightly outsplayed.

Item no 467
F2151 C8403; 12 x 10mm; L.Blue
Decorated, non-diagnostic. Applied trail 1mm wide.

Item no 468
F2159 Layer 12; 48 x 20 x 1mm; L.Green
Splayed. Heat distorted. One associated fragment.

Item no 469
F2159 Layer 12; 55 x 27mm; L.Green
Funnel series. Rounded rim. Rim thickness 2mm. Estimated diameter 120mm. Slightly outsplayed, inturned. Heat distorted. One associated rim fragment.

Item no 470
F3001 Layer 4; 31 x 16 x 2mm; L.Blue
Splayed form.

Item no 471
F7022; 11 x 10mm; Dark Blue
Decorated, non-diagnostic.

Item no 472
F2001 Layer 1; 19 x 7 x 1mm; L.Blue

Item no 473
F7086 Layer 2; 24 x 20 x 2mm; L.Blue

Item no 474
F2119 Layer 2; 20 x 15mm; L.Blue
Other vessel type. Pronounced carination in body.

Item no 475
F7023 Layer 1; 17 x 14mm; L.Green
Funnel series. Rounded rim. Rim thickness 2mm. Estimated diameter 100mm. Slightly outsplayed.

Item no 476
F4004 Layer 1; 9 x 7 x 1mm; L.Blue

Item no 477
F7019 Layer 3; 23 x 22mm; L.Blue

Decorated, non-diagnostic. Twisted decoration.

Item no 478
F3020; 17 x 10 x 3mm; L.Green
Lower body. Heat frosted.

Item no 479
F7010 Layer 1; 17 x 13mm; L.Blue
Decorated, non-diagnostic. Dark streaking within metal.

Item no 480
F7007 Layer 3; 28 x 21 x 2mm; L.Blue
Lower body. Splayed form.

Item no 481
F4009 Layer 3; 18 x 16mm; Clouded Red (see Plate 5 and Fig 16)
Decorated, non-diagnostic. Horizontal opaque yellow marvered trails.

Item no 482
F7018 Layer 6; 15 x 9 x 1mm; L.Blue

Item no 483
F4005 Layer 2; 11 x 7 x 1mm; L.Blue

Item no 484
F5013 Layer 9; 8 x 3 x 1mm; L.Blue

Item no 485
F5013 Layer 9; 10 x 9mm; Bright Green
Decorated, non-diagnostic. One associated fragment.

Item no 486
F4006 Layer 8; 14 x 9mm; Dark Red
Decorated, non-diagnostic. Horizontal opaque yellow marvered trails.

Item no 487
F4005; 66 x 8mm; L.Green (see Plate 3 and Fig 5)
Funnel series. Tubular rim. Rim thickness 3.5mm. Estimated diameter 90mm. Smoothed on inside. Slightly outsplayed. Broken edge shows possible grozing.

Item no 488
F3020 Layer 14; 7 x 5mm; Green
Angular chip.

Item no 489
F7018 Layer 19; 15 x 9 x 1mm; L.Blue

Item no 490
F2159 Layer 12; 27 x 15 x 1mm; L.Green
Heat distorted. Some iridescence.

Item no 491
F6054 Layer 7; 28 x 16mm; L.Blue
Other vessel type. Pronounced carination in body.

Item no 492
Surface; L.Green (see Fig 18)
Bead. Hexagonal with tapered ends of length 8.5mm, maximum diameter 6.5mm. Diameter of perforation 1mm.

Item no 493
F7010 Layer 4; 15 x 4 x 3mm; L.Blue
Lower body.

Item no 494
F7037; 16 x 11mm; L.Blue
Decorated, non-diagnostic. Horizontal opaque yellow marvered trails.

Item no 495
F3020 Layer 4; 14 x 10 x 1mm; L.Blue

Item no 498
F5013 Layer 10; 16 x 8 x 1mm; L.Blue
One associated fragment.

Item no 499
F2119; 14 x 13 x 1.5mm; L.Blue

Item no 500
F6098 Layer 12; 12 x 8mm; L.Blue
Funnel series. Tubular rim without cavity. Rim thickness 3mm. Decorated with marvered horizontal opaque yellow trails on exterior.

Item no 501
F2159 Layer 12; 18 x 10mm; L.Blue (see Plate 2 and Fig 7)
Funnel series. Rounded rim. Rim thickness 2mm. Estimated diameter 120mm. Inturned. Rim surmounted by applied reticella rod containing opaque white spirals.

Item no 502
F4009 Layer 3; 23 x 20mm; Opaque dark/light Red
Decorated, non-diagnostic. Striated.

Item no 503
F2119 Layer 2; 14 x 4 x 1mm; L.Blue

Item no 504
F6054 Layer 8; 10 x 8mm; Colourless
Other vessel type. Pronounced carination in body.

Item no 505
F5013 Layer 9; 16 x 14mm; L.Blue
Decorated, non-diagnostic. Evidence of former marvered trails. One associated body fragment.

Item no 506
F4018 Layer 3; 22 x 12 x 2mm; L.Blue

Item no 507
Surface; 22 x 8mm; L.Blue
Funnel series. Tubular rim. Rim thickness 4mm. Estimated diameter 100mm. Slightly outsplayed.

Item no 508
F7017; 38 x 12mm; L.Blue
Funnel series. Tubular rim. Rim thickness 5mm. Estimated diameter 100mm. Smoothed on inside and slightly outsplayed.

Item no 509
F2006 C7772; 20 x 10mm; Blue (see Plate 4 and Fig 5)

Funnel series. Tubular rim. Rim thickness 5mm. Estimated diameter 120mm. Slightly outsplayed.

Item no 510
F3020 Layer 4; 23 x 22mm; Blue (see Plate 5 and Fig 13)
Other vessel type. Flat with hole of diameter 8mm surrounded by concentric opaque yellow marvered trails 4mm apart. Base of (?) lamp. Function uncertain.

Item no 511
F2119 Layer 2; 15 x 14 x 1mm; L.Blue
Lower body.

Item no 512
F3024 Layer 4; 43 x 21mm; L.Blue
Funnel series. Tubular rim. Rim thickness 3.5mm. Estimated diameter 100mm. Smoothed on inside and slightly outsplayed.

Item no 513
F4009 Layer 3; 30 x 19mm; L.Blue
Decorated, non-diagnostic. Applied arcaded trail 6mm wide.

Item no 514
F1018 Layer 6; 8 x 8 x 1 mm; Colourless (see Fig 16)

Item no 515
F2159 Layer 12; 26 x 24 x 1mm; L.Green
Splayed. Heat distorted. Some iridescence.

Item no 516
F2159 Layer 12; 31 x 10 x 1mm; L.Green
Heat distorted.

Item no 517
F3020 Layer 4; 20 x 13mm; L.Blue
Funnel series. Tubular rim. Rim thickness 2.5mm. Estimated diameter 140mm. Smoothed on inside and slightly outsplayed.

Item no 518
F2147 C8367; 2 x 2mm; Opaque Green
Waster. Possible droplet.

Item no 519
F2133 C7767; 16 x 12mm; L.Blue
Decorated, non-diagnostic. Indications of applied trail.

Item no 520
F2147; 28 x 16mm; L.Green
Funnel series. Rounded rim. Rim thickness 2.5mm. Estimated diameter 90mm. Slightly outsplayed and inturned.

Item no 521
F7023 Layer 1; 17 x 12 x 2mm; L.Blue

Item no 522
F7037; 7 x 6 x 1.5mm; L.Blue

Item no 523
F2159 Layer 13; 15 x 13 x 1mm; L.Blue

Item no 524
F4009 Layer 3; 25 x 15mm; Colourless (see Fig 13)

Other vessel type. Pronounced carination in body.

Item no 525
F7023 Layer 1; 13 x 11mm; L.Blue
Funnel series. Tubular rim without cavity. Rim thickness 3.5mm. Slightly outsplayed.

Item no 526
F2119; 26 x 12mm; L.Blue (see Plate 4 and Fig 4)
Funnel series. Tubular rim. Rim thickness 6mm. Estimated diameter 100mm. Containing some dark red streaking.

Item no 527
F7022 Layer 3; 40 x 24mm; L.Blue
Other vessel type. Flat base of flask or jar. Roman.

Item no 528
F6142 Layer 1; 36 x 21 x 1mm; L.Blue

Item no 529
F4060; 27 x 14mm; L.Green (see Fig 7)
Funnel series. Rounded rim. Rim thickness 2mm. Estimated diameter 100mm. Slightly outsplayed and inturned. Rim surmounted by applied reticella rod containing opaque white spirals.

Item no 530
F7009 Layer 4; 7 x 1 x 1mm; L.Green

Item no 531
F3001 Layer 3; 4 x 3 x 1mm; L.Blue

Item no 532
F4004 Layer 2; 4 x 2 x 1mm; Colourless

Item no 533
F3058 Layer 1; 7 x 6 x 1mm; L.Green

Item no 534
F2133 Layer 3; 11 x 7 x 1mm; L.Green

Item no 535
F4009 Layer 5; 11 x 11 x 1.5mm; L.Blue

Item no 536
F3068 Layer 1; 21 x 13 x 2mm; L.Blue

Item no 537
F4006 Layer 17; 19 x 12 x 1mm; L.Blue

Item no 538
F4011; 14 x 14 x 2mm; L.Blue

Item no 539
F4009 Layer 7; 11 x 10 x 1mm; L.Blue

Item no 540
F5136; 23 x 9mm; L.Blue
Decorated, non-diagnostic. Applied arcaded trail 3.5mm wide.

Item no 541
F2119 Layer 3; 11 x 4mm; L.Blue
Funnel series. Tubular rim. Rim thickness 4mm. Smoothed on inside and slightly outsplayed. One associated body fragment.

Item no 542
F2119 Layer 10; 10 x 6 x 1mm; L.Blue

Item no 543
F6161; 6 x 3 x 1mm; L.Blue

Item no 544
F5136; 10 x 7 x 2mm; L.Blue

Item no 545
F5013 Layer 9; 19 x 7mm; L.Blue
Funnel series. Rounded rim. Rim thickness 2.5mm. Slightly outsplayed and inturned.

Item no 546
F1046 Layer 1; 30 x 20mm; Green (see Plate 8)
Other vessel type. Rim fragment. Rim folded inwards and smoothed on inside. Rim thickness 4.5mm. Estimated diameter 85mm. Decorated with horizontal opaque white marvered trails which also cover outer part of rim. Tall beaker.

Item no 547
F7007 Layer 3; 35 x 18 x 1mm; L.Blue (see Plate 5)
Splayed form.

Item no 548
F3085; 18 x 7 x 1mm; L.Blue

Item no 549
F1093 Layer 3; 14 x 13mm; L.Blue
Funnel series. Tubular rim without cavity. Rim thickness 3mm. Slightly outsplayed.

Item no 550
F7151; 13 x 5mm; L.Blue
Decorated, non-diagnostic. Red streaking within metal.

Item no 551
F2148 Layer 2; 24 x 10mm; L.Blue
Other vessel type. Pronounced carination in body.

Item no 552
F4011; 13 x 4mm; L.Green (see Plate 1)
Decorated, non-diagnostic. Applied reticella rod containing opaque yellow spirals.

Item no 553
F1046 Layer 1; 9 x 4 x 1.5mm; L.Blue

Item no 554
F7019 Layer 3; 15 x 12mm; L.Blue (see Plate 5)
Decorated, non-diagnostic. Dark streaking within metal.

Item no 555
F7064 Layer 1; 38 x 29mm; L.Blue (see Plate 1)
Other vessel type. Red streaking within metal. Applied reticella rod containing opaque yellow spirals. Rounded form, probably bowl.

Item no 556
F4004 Layer 1; 8 x 5 x 1mm; L.Blue

Item no 557
F2199 Layer 10; 20 x 14 x 2mm; L.Blue
One other body fragment.

Item no 558
F4011 Layer 5; 7 x 6 x 1mm; Colourless

Item no 559
F3020 Layer 3; 13 x 13mm; Opaque Green
Decorated, non-diagnostic. Horizontal
opaque yellow marvered trails.

Item no 560
F4005 Layer 6; 7 x 4 x 1mm; L.Green

Item no 561
F2133 Layer 3; 16 x 8 x 1mm; Green/Yellow
Decorated, non-diagnostic. Horizontal
opaque yellow marvered trails.

Item no 562
F1002 Layer 6; 17 x 16mm; L.Blue
Decorated, non-diagnostic. Red streaking and
applied trail 4mm wide.

Item no 563
F2119 Layer 18; 10 x 9mm; Blue
Decorated, non-diagnostic.

Item no 564
F7018 Layer 1; 9 x 2 x 1mm; L.Blue

Item no 565
F2159 Layer 12; 50 x 21mm; L.Green
Funnel series. Rounded rim. Rim thickness
2mm. Estimated diameter 120mm. Slightly
outsplayed, inturned. Heat distorted.

Item no 566
F1108 Layer 2; 15 x 6 x 1.5mm; L.Blue

Item no 567
F3017; 17 x 9 x 2mm; L.Green

Item no 568
F2166 Layer 2; 10 x 4mm; L.Green
Funnel series. Rounded rim. Rim thickness
2.5mm. Slightly outsplayed.

Item no 569
F6145 Layer 4; 25 x 22 x 2mm; Bright
Green
Decorated, non-diagnostic. Lower body.

Item no 570
F1115 C7568; 19 x 10mm; L.Blue (see
Fig 14)
Decorated, non-diagnostic. Applied arcaded
trail 10mm wide. Dark streaking within
metal.

Item no 571
F3060 Layer 2; 15 x 12 x 1mm; L.Blue

Item no 572
F2159 Layer 12; 25 x 21 x 1mm; L.Green
Splayed. Heat distorted. Some iridescence.

Item no 573
F3085; 22 x 15mm; Brown/Yellow
Decorated, non-diagnostic.

Item no 575
F4051 Layer 2; 18 x 10 x 1mm; L.Blue

Item no 576
F2159 Layer 1; 14 x 13 x 2mm; L.Green
Possible window glass. Possible grozing on
one long edge. Weathered on one surface.

Item no 577
F7106; 35 x 7mm; L.Blue
Funnel series. Tubular rim. Rim thickness
6mm. Estimated diameter 100mm.

Item no 578
F3132 Layer 10; 6 x 4 x 1.5mm; L.Blue
One associated body fragment.

Item no 579
Trench 1 Surface; 16 x 11mm; L.Green
Decorated, non-diagnostic. Termination of
applied trail.

Item no 580
F7152; 38 x 22mm; L.Blue (see Plate 3 and
Fig 4)
Funnel series. Tubular rim. Rim thickness
4.5mm. Estimated diameter 100mm. Slightly
outsplayed.

Item no 581
F2163 Layer 3; 16 x 11mm; L.Blue
Decorated, non-diagnostic. Dark streaking
within metal.

Item no 582
F3017; 10 x 7mm; Blue (see Plate 5)
Decorated, non-diagnostic. Horizontal
opaque yellow marvered trails.

Item no 583
F6129 Layer 6; 34 x 33 x 2mm; L.Blue
Splayed form.

Item no 584
F3001 Layer 3; 12 x 3 x 1mm; L.Blue

Item no 585
F7062; 20 x 7mm; L.Blue (see Fig 11)
Funnel series. Base fragment. Showing part
of pontil mark and wad. Base diameter
20mm.

Item no 586
F1093 Layer 3; 22 x 15 x 1mm; L.Blue
One other body fragment.

Item no 587
F3001 Layer 24; 4 x 4 x 1mm; L.Green

Item no 589
F7037; 13 x 10mm; Colourless
Decorated, non-diagnostic. Applied arcaded
trail 2mm wide, coloured dark opaque.

Item no 590
F2119 Layer 3; 49 x 11mm; L.Blue (see
Fig 5)
Funnel series. Tubular rim. Rim thickness
5mm. Estimated diameter 110mm. Slightly
outsplayed.

Item no 591
F4004 Layer 2; 4 x 2 x 1mm; Colourless

Item no 592
F1108 Layer 2; 9 x 7mm; Opaque Brown
Waster. Partial trail.

Item no 593
F2159 Layer 12; 21 x 10 x 1mm; L.Green
Heat distorted. Some iridescence.

Item no 595
F7086; 12 x 8mm; L.Blue
Funnel series. Tubular rim with cavity. Rim
thickness 3.5mm. Smoothed on inside and
slightly outsplayed.

Item no 596
F7093 Layer 1; 23 x 15 x 1mm; L.Blue

Item no 597
F1093 Layer 1; 19 x 18mm; L.Blue
Funnel series. Tubular rim. Rim thickness
3mm. Estimated diameter 120mm. Smoothed
on inside, slightly outsplayed. Decorated
with marvered horizontal opaque yellow
trails on exterior.

Item no 598
F1095 Layer 1; 14 x 13mm; L.Blue
Funnel series. Tubular rim without cavity.
Rim thickness 3mm. Slightly outsplayed.
Evidence of applied trailing. One associated
body fragment containing dark red streaking
within metal.

Item no 599
F1092; 17 x 10mm; L.Blue
Funnel series. Base fragment. Showing part
of pontil mark.

Item no 600
F3068 Layer 2; 13 x 12 x 1mm; L.Green
Upper body fragment.

Item no 601
F1095 Layer 2; 19 x 19mm; L.Blue
Decorated, non-diagnostic. Red streaking
within metal and applied horizontal trail
1mm wide. One associated body fragment.

Item no 602
F2077 Layer 1; 16 x 7mm; Blue
Decorated, non-diagnostic.

Item no 603
F7037; 15 x 14mm; L.Green
Funnel series. Tubular rim. Rim thickness
3mm. Slightly outsplayed.

Item no 604
F3001 Layer 3; 20 x 10 x 1mm; L.Blue

Item no 605
F7001 Layer 4; 4 x 4mm; L.Blue
Decorated, non-diagnostic. Sliver with traces
of applied trail.

Item no 607
F4060 Layer 8; 16 x 13mm; L.Blue

Funnel series. Tubular rim. Rim thickness 4mm. Estimated diameter 120mms. Smoothed on inside and slightly outsplayed.

Item no 608
F2159 Layer 12; 15 x 5mm L.Green
Funnel series. Rounded rim. Rim thickness 2mm. Slightly outsplayed.

Item no 609
F6098 Layer 1; 3 x 3mm; Opaque Blue
Decorated, non-diagnostic. Irregular chip. Salt weathered?

Item no 610
F2122 Layer 1; 9 x 5 x 1mm; L.Blue

Item no 611
F7018 Layer 14; 21 x 11mm; L.Blue
Decorated, non-diagnostic. Twisted decoration.

Item no 612
F2133 Layer 3; 16 x 15 x 1mm; L.Blue
One other body fragment.

Item no 613
F2159 Layer 12; 23 x 15 x 1mm; L.Green
Heat distorted. Some iridescence.

Item no 614
F5136; 14 x 10mm; L.Blue
Decorated, non-diagnostic. Horizontal opaque yellow marvered trails.

Item no 615
F2133 Layer 3; 12 x 11mm; L.Blue
Funnel series. Rounded rim. Rim thickness 2.5mm. Slightly outsplayed, inturned. Rim surmounted by applied reticella rod containing opaque white spirals. Three associated body fragments.

Item no 617
F2159 Layer 12; 15 x 6 x 1mm; L.Green
Heat distorted. Some iridescence.

Item no 618
F7062; 20 x 15 x 2mm; Blue
Possible window fragment. Possible cut edge. Evidence of glossy and matt opposing flat surfaces.

Item no 619
F3020 Layer 3; 12 x 4 x 1mm; L.Blue

Item no 620
F2119 Layer 3; 8 x 7 x 2mm; Brown/Yellow
Possible window fragment. Possible grozing on two edges. Geometric shape ?

Item no 621
F5133; 20 x 12 x 2mm; L.Blue
One associated body fragment.

Item no 623
F1093 Layer 1; 33 x 20mm; L.Blue
Decorated, non-diagnostic. Dark streaking within metal.

Item no 624
F2159 Layer 12; 20 x 10mm; L.Green
Funnel series. Rounded rim. Rim thickness 2mm. Slightly outsplayed. Heat distorted.

Item no 625
F1010 Layer 1; 9 x 7 x 1mm; Dark Green

Item no 626
F2196 C7959; 31 x 13mm; L.Blue
Funnel series. Tubular rim. Rim thickness 4.5mm. Estimated diameter 100mm. Slightly outsplayed.

Item no 627
F3068; 24 x 15mm; L.Blue
Decorated, non-diagnostic. Twisted decoration.

Item no 629
F7037; 5 x 2 x 2mm; L.Green

Item no 630
F1096 Layer 1; 19 x 10 x 1mm; L.Blue

Item no 631
F6129 Layer 6; 18 x 14 x 1mm; L.Blue
Two associated body fragments.

Item no 632
F1093 Layer 5; 30 x 19mm; Blue
Other vessel type. Tall beaker.

Item no 633
F2159 Layer 12; 41 x 20 x 1mm; L.Green
Splayed. Heat distorted.

Item no 634
F2159 Layer 12; 37 x 34mm; L.Green
Funnel series. Rounded rim. Rim thickness 2mm. Estimated diameter 120mm. Slightly outsplayed. Heat distorted. Some iridescence. Several associated fragments.

Item no 644
F3221 Layer 1; Opaque light Blue
Bead. Circular of diameter 2.5mm, thickness 1mm. Diameter of perforation 1mm.

Item no 645
F1084 Layer3; Opaque dark Blue (see Fig 18)
Bead. Cylindrical of length 10mm, diameter 8mm. Diameter of perforation 3mm. Decorated with opaque white zig-zag around centre and opaque light blue band around edges.

Item no 703
F2119 Layer 5; 44 x 18mm; L.Blue
Funnel series. From near base showing applied vertical trailing. Over forty associated fragments.

Item no 926
F6157 Layer 1; 8 x 5 x 1mm; L.Blue

Item no 993
F5155 Layer 3; 5 x 5 x 1mm; L.Blue

Item no 994
F1093 Layer 3; 17 x 11 x 1mm; L.Blue
Six other small fragments.

Item no 995
F1093 Layer 1; 9 x 8 x 1mm; L.Blue

Item no 996
F2119 Layer 10; 5 x 2 x 1mm; L.Blue

Item no 1011
F5013 Layer 9; 15 x 13 x 3mm; L.Blue
Lower body.

Item no 1012
F1093 Layer 3; 39 x 30mm; L.Green (see Fig 7)
Funnel series. Rounded rim. Rim thickness 2.5mm. Estimated diameter 120mm. Slightly outsplayed.

Item no 1013
F1093 Layer 3; 25 x 13mm; L.Blue
Decorated, non-diagnostic. Evidence of applied trailing and dark red streaking within metal.

Item no 1014
F4060; 27 x 15 x 2mm; L.Blue

SOU 26

Item no 15
4; 19 x 15mm; L.Blue
Funnel series. Rounded rim. Rim thickness 2mm. Estimated diameter 100mm. Slightly outsplayed.

Item no 23
4; 9 x 6mm; L.Green
Funnel series. Rounded rim. Rim thickness 1mm.

Item no 66
4; 12 x 8 x 2mm; Dark Green
Heat distorted fragment.

Item no 100
6; 17 x 10mm; L.Blue
Funnel series. Rounded rim. Rim thickness 2.5mm. Slightly outsplayed.

Item no 120
32; 25 x 10mm; L.Blue
Funnel series. Tubular rim without cavity. Rim thickness 5mm. Estimated diameter 110mm. Slightly outsplayed.

Item no 143
555; 23 x 9mm; L.Green
Funnel series. Base fragment. Base thickness 4mm. Base diameter 16mm. Showing part of pontil wad and mark.

Item no 155
566; 11 x 11mm; L.Blue
Decorated, non-diagnostic. Dark streaking within metal.

Item no 156
607; 14 x 8mm; L.Blue

Funnel series. Base fragment. Base thickness 4mm.

Item no 198
649; 16 x 11mm; Opaque dark/light Red (see Plate 8)
Decorated, non-diagnostic. Striated.

Item no 212
145; Blue
Bead. Circular of diameter 8mm. Diameter of perforation 3mm. Three fragments.

Item no 258
505; 15 x 7 x 1mm; L.Blue

Item no 260
23; 30 x 17mm; L.Green
Funnel series. Rounded rim. Rim thickness 3.5mm. Estimated diameter 120mm. Slightly outsplayed.

Item no 263
23; 15 x 8mm; Opaque Red
Decorated, non-diagnostic.

Item no 270
91; 17 x 4 x 1.5mm; L.Green
Funnel series. Near to base.

Item no 335
C263; 46 x 32mm; L.Blue (see Fig 8)
Funnel series. Rounded rim. Rim thickness 3.5mm. Estimated diameter 100mm. Slightly outsplayed.

Item no 351
449; 23 x 21mm; L.Blue
Funnel series. Tubular rim without cavity. Rim thickness 5mm. Estimated diameter 120mm. Slightly outsplayed.

Item no 535
F2008 Layer 2; 12 x 6 x 1mm; L.Green

Item no 540
F2009 Layer 8; 38 x 29mm; L.Green (see Fig 8)
Funnel series. Rounded rim. Rim thickness 2.5mm. Estimated diameter 100mm. Slightly outsplayed.

Item no 542
F2009 Layer 8; 28 x 20mm; Green (see Plate 5 and Fig 14)
Other vessel type. Probably from bowl or jar. Decorated with horizontal opaque yellow marvered trails. Near to base.

Item no 552
F2024 Layer 9; 23 x 19mm; L.Green
Funnel series. Rounded rim. Rim thickness 2mm. Estimated diameter 120mm. Slightly outsplayed.

Item no 562
F8007 Layer 1; 15 x 10mm; L.Blue
Funnel series. Rounded rim. Rim thickness 2mm. Slightly outsplayed.

Item no 582
F7006 Layer 1; 21 x 13 x 2.5mm; L.Green

Item no 600
F7006 Layer 1; 21 x 10mm; Opaque dark/light Red (see Plate 8)
Decorated, non-diagnostic. Applied (flattened) reticella rod containing opaque white spirals. Striated.

Item no 615
F3024 Layer 1; 14 x 10 x 1mm; L.Blue

Item no 622
F1018 Layer 1; 20 x 11 x 1.5mm; L.Green

Item no 623
F5128 Layer 3; 17 x 8 x 1.5mm; L.Blue

Item no 625
F5128 Layer 4; 15 x 8 x 1mm; L.Blue

Item no 630
F7003 Layer 1; 13 x 11mm; Green/Yellow
Decorated, non-diagnostic. Traces of opaque yellow marvered trails.

Item no 632
F7047 C943; 15 x 11 x 1mm; L.Blue

Item no 641
F7048 C944; Opaque light Green
Bead. Circular of diameter 2mm. Diameter of perforation 1mm. Thickness 1mm.

Item no 649
F3024 Layer 4; 16 x 11 x 1mm; L.Green

Item no 657
F3033 Layer 1; 29 x 15mm; L.Blue
Funnel series. Rounded rim. Rim thickness 1.5mm. Estimated diameter 120mm. Slightly outsplayed.

Item no 665
F5168 Layer 1; 21 x 8 x 1.5mm; Dark Green

Item no 672
F5022 Layer 4; 27 x 11mm; L.Blue
Funnel series. Base fragment. Base thickness 4mm. Base diameter 19mm. Showing pontil mark and wad.

Item no 693
506; 20 x 12 x 1mm; L.Blue

Item no 696
2730; 44 x 14mm; L.Blue (see Fig 6)
Funnel series. Tubular rim without cavity. Rim thickness 4.5mm. Estimated diameter 120mm. Smoothed on inside and slightly outsplayed.

Item no 753
753; 23 x 18 x 1.5mm; L.Blue

Item no 761
C2795; 13 x 11 x 1mm; L.Blue

Item no 770
950; 20 x 20 x 1.5mm; Opaque Red (see Fig 15)
Other vessel type. Probably from flask or jar. Pushed base showing junction of reticella rods containing opaque white spirals.

Item no 773
2741; 32 x 20mm; L.Green
Funnel series. Rounded rim. Rim thickness 2mm. Estimated diameter 120mm.

Item no 776
516; 15 x 13 x 2mm; L.Blue

Item no 824
F2009 Layer 8; 30 x 25mm; L.Green (see Fig 13)
Other vessel type. Pronounced carination in body. One associated fragment.

SOU 30

Item no 11
3293; 13 x 9mm; L.Blue
Decorated, non-diagnostic. Applied trail 4mm wide.

Item no 13
3332; 10 x 6 x 1mm; L.Green

Item no 17
3332; 26 x 15mm; L.Green
Funnel series. Tubular rim without cavity. Rim thickness 3mm. Estimated diameter 100mm. Slightly outsplayed and inturned.

Item no 44
3344; 28 x 13mm; L.Blue
Funnel series. Tubular rim. Rim thickness 3.5mm. Estimated diameter 100mm. Slightly outsplayed.

Item no 45
3374; 11 x 8 x 1.5mm; L.Blue

Item no 52
3571; 13 x 13 x 1mm; Colourless

Item no 57
3970; 40 x 25mm; Dark Green (see Plate 4 and Fig 8)
Funnel series. Rounded rim. Rim thickness 3mm. Estimated diameter 120mm. Decorated with applied horizontal trails and dark streaking within metal.

Item no 64
3590; 16 x 13mm; L.Green
Decorated, non-diagnostic. Horizontal (partially lost) opaque yellow marvered trails.

Item no 92
4032; 13 x 12 x 1.5mm; L.Green

Item no 112
4309; 31 x 16mm; Brown/Yellow (see Plate 8 and Fig 14)
Other vessel type. Bowl form. Rim folded outwards with cavity. Rim thickness 5mm. Estimated diameter 120mm. Decorated with horizontal opaque yellow marvered trails below rim.

Item no 113
4318; 21 x 12mm; Brown/Yellow

Other vessel type. Bowl form. Traces of opaque yellow marvered decoration.

Item no 115
4319; 17 x 11 x 2mm; L.Blue

Item no 120
4293; 19 x 12 x 1mm; L.Blue

Item no 162
3293; 11 x 5 x 1mm; L.Green

Item no 194
4348; 24 x 17mm; L.Green (see Fig 6)
Funnel series. Tubular rim without cavity. Rim thickness 3mm. Estimated diameter 100mm. Slightly outsplayed.

Item no 260
4006; 7 x 6mm; Brown/Yellow
Other vessel type. Bowl form. Decorated with horizontal opaque yellow marvered trails.

Item no 262
4293; 14 x 8 x 1mm; L.Green

Item no 269
4318; 25 x 7mm; Brown/Yellow
Other vessel type. Bowl form. Evidence of flattened reticella rod containing opaque yellow spirals.

Item no 291
3571; 13 x 10 x 1mm; L.Blue

Item no 322
4508; 8 x 4 x 1mm; L.Blue

Item no 332
3571; 14 x 12 x 1mm; L.Blue

Item no 374
4309; 18 x 11mm; Brown/Yellow (see Fig 14)
Other vessel type. Bowl form. Remains of badly executed reticella rod containing opaque yellow spirals. Four other fragments.

Item no 419
4524; 32 x 19mms L.Blue (see Plate 4 and Fig 8)
Funnel series. Rounded rim. Rim thickness 3.5mm. Estimated diameter 100mm. Slightly outsplayed and inturned. Decorated with marvered horizontal opaque yellow trail on exterior.

Item no 435
3318; Opaque Green
Bead. Cylindrical of length 11mm. Diameter 5mm. Diameter of perforation 2mm. Unmarvered.

Item no 437
3318; 10 x 8 x 1mm; L.Blue
Three other fragments.

Item no 531
3350; 11 x 6mm; L.Green
Decorated, non-diagnostic. Applied arcaded trail 2mm wide.

Item no 538
4419; 21 x 15mm; L.Blue
Flat fragment. Thickness 3.5mm. Either from flat base of vessel or window. Probably Roman.

Item no 550
3320; 14 x 12mm; L.Blue (see Fig 15)
Decorated, non-diagnostic. Small opaque yellow marvered bosses.

Item no 557
3992; 16 x 6mm; L.Blue
Decorated, non-diagnostic. Applied trail 1mm wide.

Item no 559
4518; 15 x 7 x 2mm; L.Blue
Heat crazed.

Item no 565
F1007 Layer 3; 10 x 9mm; D.Green
Decorated, non-diagnostic. Decorated with marvered opaque yellow trail.

Item no 567
F2001 Layer 3; 11 x 4 x 1mm; L.Blue

Item no 575
F1104 Layer 4; 11 x 4 x 2mm; L.Blue

Item no 576
F1007 Layer 2; 7 x 4 x 1mm; L.Green

Item no 578
F1012 Layer 2; 6 x 5 x 1mm; Brown/Yellow
Decorated, non-diagnostic.

Item no 579
F1001 Layer 11; 15 x 3 x 1mm; L.Blue

Item no 584
F3354; 7 x 4 x 2mm; L.Blue

Item no 587
F1007 Layer 1; 11 x 5 x 1mm; L.Green

SOU 31

Item no 7
4613; 19 x 13 x 1mm; L.Green
One other fragment.

Item no 17
4615; 22 x 18mm; L.Blue (see Fig 11)
Funnel series. Base fragment. Base thickness 3mm. Twisted body decoration.

Item no 30
4631; 17 x 14 x 1mm; L.Blue

Item no 39
4624; 21 x 13mm; L.Blue
Decorated, non-diagnostic. Applied arcaded trail 4mm wide.

Item no 43
4611; 11 x 9mm; L.Blue
Funnel series. Tubular rim. Rim thickness 2.5mm. Slightly outsplayed.

Item no 79
4648; 30 x 8mm; L.Blue
Funnel series. Tubular rim. Rim thickness 4mm. Estimated diameter 120mm.

Item no 83
4648; 14 x 10 mm; L.Blue
Funnel series. Rounded rim. Rim thickness 2mm. Estimated diameter 120mm. Slightly outsplayed. Rim surmounted by applied arcaded reticella rod containing opaque white spirals.

Item no 102
4803; 23 x 14 x 1.5mm; L.Blue

Item no 110
4688; 12 x 12 x 2mm; L.Blue
Two other fragments.

Item no 137
4611; 15 x 12mm; L.Blue
Decorated, non-diagnostic. Applied arcaded trail.

Item no 148
4864; 11 x 10mm; L.Blue
Funnel series. Tubular rim. Rim thickness 4.5mm. Slightly outsplayed. One associated body fragment.

Item no 167
4694; 13 x 6 x 1mm; L.Blue

Item no 171
4644; 32 x 24mm; L.Blue (see Fig 7)
Funnel series. Rounded rim. Rim thickness 2mm. Estimated diameter 100mm. Slightly outsplayed and inturned.

Item no 184
4644; 15 x 6mm; L.Blue
Funnel series. Tubular rim. Rim thickness 4.5mm. Estimated diameter 120mm. Slightly outsplayed.

Item no 256
4644; 20 x 19mm; L.Blue
Funnel series. Base fragment. Seven associated fragments, one decorated with applied arcaded trail.

Item no 280
4809; 18 x 17 1.5mm; L.Blue

Item no 282
4644; 67 x 18mm; L.Blue
Funnel series. Tubular rim. Rim thickness 4mm. Estimated diameter 110mm. Smoothed on inside and slightly outsplayed. Six associated fragments, one rim sherd, three decorated with applied trails.

Item no 298
4833; Opaque Blue
Bead. Circular of diameter 2mm. Thickness 1mm. Diameter of perforation 1mm. Probable spacer.

Item no 318
4644; 12 x 9mm; L.Blue

Decorated, non-diagnostic. Dark streaking within metal. One associated fragment.

Item no 360
4759; 19 x 5 x 1mm; Colourless

Item no 366
6641; 12 x 8 x 1mm; L.Green
One associated fragment.

Item no 368
4755; 25 x 14 x 1mm; L.Green

Item no 381
4693; 33 x 30mm; L.Blue (see Fig 16)
Decorated, non-diagnostic. Dark streaking.
Applied arcaded trail 4mm wide.

Item no 416
4688; 20 x 9mm; L.Green
Funnel series. Tubular rim without cavity.
Rim thickness 3mm. Estimated diameter
100mm. Slightly outsplayed.

Item no 420
4885; 28 x 13mm; L.Blue
Decorated, non-diagnostic. Showing
termination of applied trail.

Item no 432
?4685; 18 x 13mm; L.Blue
Funnel series. Rounded rim. Rim thickness
2mm. Estimated diameter 120mm. Slightly
outsplayed and inturned.

Item no 442
4921; 11 x 6 x 2mm; L.Blue

Item no 495
4920; 21 x 18mm; L.Green (see Fig 7)
Funnel series. Rounded rim. Rim thickness
1.5mm. Estimated diameter 120mm. Slightly
outsplayed.

Item no 505
4604; 41 x 22mm; L.Blue
Other vessel type. Pushed base with dark red
streaking. Flask/jar form.

Item no 516
4923; 28 x 24mm; L.Blue
Funnel series. Rounded rim. Rim thickness
2mm. Estimated diameter 120mm. Slightly
outsplayed. Rim surmounted by applied
reticella rod containing opaque white spirals.

Item no 533
4948; 13 x 12mm; Opaque dark/light Red
(see Plate 8 and Fig 13)
Other vessel type. Rounded rim. Rim
thickness 5mm. Slightly outsplayed.
Decorated with horizontal opaque white
marvered trails. Striated.

Item no 534
5202; 18 x 12 x 1mm; L.Blue

Item no 540
5190; 24 x 20 x 1.5mm; L.Blue

Item no 543
5233; 22 x 11 x 1mm; L.green

Item no 555
5191; 12 x 9 x 1mm; L.Blue

Item no 564
5259; 29 (see Plate 8 and Fig 6)
Funnel series. Tubular rim without cavity.
Rim thickness 4mm. Estimated diameter
120mm. Rim formed in three stages using
alternate light green and dark blue bands.

Item no 571
5237; 10 x 7 x 1mm; L.Blue

Item no 578
5249; 22 x 19mm; L.Blue
Funnel series. Tubular rim without cavity.
Rim thickness 2.5mm. Estimated diameter
100mm. Slightly outsplayed.

Item no 585
5262; 19 x 13 x 1mm; L.Blue

Item no 586
5228; 24 x 22mm; L.Blue
Decorated, non-diagnostic. Twisted
decoration.

Item no 617
5272; 48 x 27 x 1mm; L.Green
Lower body. Probable funnel form.

Item no 645
5237; 12 x 11 x 1mm; L.Green
One associated fragment.

Item no 657
5278; 10 x 5 x 1mm; L.Blue

Item no 661
5283; 28 x 15mm; Opaque dark/light Red
(see Fig 16)
Decorated, non-diagnostic. Decorated with
applied (flattened) reticella rods containing
opaque white spirals. Striated.

Item no 664
5237; 17 x 5mm; L.Blue
Funnel series. Base fragment.

Item no 665
5285; 22 x 12 x 1mm; L.Green

Item no 679
5278; 6 x 5 x 1mm; L.Blue

Item no 700
5413; 13 x 5 x 1.5mm; L.Blue

Item no 708
5298; 15 x 9mm; L.Blue
Funnel series. Rounded rim. Rim thickness
2mm.

Item no 714
5312; 20 x 16mm; L.Green
Funnel series. Rounded rim. Rim thickness
3mm. Estimated diameter 120mm. Slightly
outsplayed and inturned.

Item no 748
5435; 12 x 12 x 1mm; L.Blue

Item no 749
5447; 21 x 11 x 1.5mm; L.Blue
One associated fragment.

Item no 753
5447; 9 x 6 x 1mm; L.Blue

Item no 759
5319; 25 x 21mm; Blue
Other vessel type. Rounded vessel, probable
bowl.

Item no 777
5517; 13 x 9mm; L.Blue
Funnel series. Rounded rim. Rim thickness
2.5mm. Slightly outsplayed and inturned.
Five associated body fragments, one showing
red streaking.

Item no 778
5517; 11 x 6mm; Blue
Decorated, non-diagnostic. One associated
fragment.

Item no 801
5545; 30 x 20mm; Colourless (see Fig 15)
Other vessel type. Pushed base filled with
boss/pontil wad of brown/yellow. Probable
flask/jar form.

Item no 839
5612; 20 x 9 x 1.5mm; L.Blue

Item no 852
5449; L.Blue
Funnel series. Tubular rim. Rim thickness
5mms. Numerous shattered fragments.

Item no 881
5634; 11 x 6 x 1mm; L.Blue

Item no 892
5447; 8 x 7 x 1mm; L.Blue

Item no 966
5652; 28 x 20 x 1.5mm; L.Green
Lower body. Probable funnel form.

Item no 1013
5651; 27 x 23 x 21mm;
Waster fragment. Fired clay or stone
fragment enveloped in opaque dark vitreous
deposits and some light green vitreous
deposits.

Item no 1014
5653; 33 x 12mm; L.Blue
Decorated, non-diagnostic. Applied arcaded
trail 2 mm wide, containing dark streaking.
Probable funnel form.

Item no 1026
5540; Opaque Blue
Bead. Circular of diameter 2mm. Thickness
1mm. Diameter of perforation 1mm.
Probable spacer.

Item no 1032
5735; 22 x 10mm; L.Green
Funnel series. Tubular rim. Rim thickness
5mm. Estimated diameter 100mm. Slightly
outsplayed.

Item no 1081
5293; 28 x 18mm; L.Blue
Decorated, non-diagnostic. Applied arcaded
trail 3mm wide. Three associated fragments.

Item no 1091
5658; 13 x 5mm; L.Blue
Funnel series. Rounded rim. Rim thickness
2.5mm. Inturned.

Item no 1131
5562; 22 x 17mm; L.Blue
Funnel series. Base fragment.

Item no 1173
5261; 22 x 8 x 1mm; L.Green

Item no 1233
5582; 8 x 5 x 2mm; L.Blue

Item no 1253
5900; 39 x 36 x 1.5mm; L.Blue
Lower body. Two associated fragments.

Item no 1392
5991; 50 x 32 x 2.5mm; L.Blue
Lower body.

Item no 1462
6110; 22 x 21mm; L.Blue
Funnel series. Tubular rim without cavity.
Rim thickness 3mm. Estimated diameter
120mm. Slightly outsplayed.

Item no 1463
5294; 15 x 6 x 1mm; Blue

Item no 1484
6067; 32 x 25mm; L.Green
Funnel series. Rounded rim. Rim thickness
2mm. Estimated diameter 90mm. Slightly
outsplayed.

Item no 1485
6067; 20 x 13mm; L.Green
Funnel series. Tubular rim. Rim thickness
3mm. Estimated diameter 110mm. Slightly
outsplayed.

Item no 1509
6010; 20 x 11 x 1mm; L.Blue

Item no 1561
6067; 20 x 8 x 1mm; L.Green
Weathered surfaces. One associated
fragment.

Item no 1565
6000; 45 x 19mm; L.Blue
Decorated, non-diagnostic. Dark streaking
within metal. Applied trail pattern.

Item no 1574
6130; 41 x 13mm; L.Blue (see Fig 4)
Funnel series. Tubular rim. Rim thickness
5mm. Estimated diameter 100mm. Smoothed
on inside and slightly outsplayed.

Item no 1604
6190; 18 x 9mm; L.Blue
Decorated, non-diagnostic. Twisted
decoration. One associated fragment.

Item no 1666
6254; 21 x 17mm; L.Blue
Funnel series. Rounded rim. Rim thickness
2mm. Estimated diameter 100mm. Slightly
outsplayed.

Item no 1702
4752; 26 x 15mm; L.Blue
Decorated, non-diagnostic. Applied arcaded
trail 1.5mm wide in dark blue.

Item no 1736
6068; 22 x 11 x 2mm; L.Blue
Flat fragment. Possible grozing along curved
edge. Pitting on one flat surface. Possible
window glass.

Item no 1775
6121; 7 x 3 x 1mm; L.Blue

Item no 1794
6127; 43 x 15mm; L.Blue (see Fig 4)
Funnel series. Tubular rim. Rim thickness
4.5mm. Estimated diameter 120mm.
Smoothed on inside, slightly outsplayed.

Item no 1858
6127; 41 x 11mm; L.Green (see Fig 4)
Funnel series. Tubular rim. Rim thickness
3mm. Estimated diameter 100mm. Slightly
outsplayed.

Item no 1878
6405; 23 x 11mm; L.Green
Funnel series. Rounded rim. Rim thickness
2mm. Estimated diameter 100mm. Slightly
outsplayed and inturned. Three associated
fragments.

Item no 2310
5682; Opaque Black
Bead. Faceted tubular bead with four main
faces and chamfered corners. Diameter 7mm.
Length of faces 9mm. Diameter of
perforation 4mm.

Item no 2314
5676; 22 x 20 x 7mm; L.Blue
Possible handle.

Item no 2315
4636; 18 x 6mm; L.Green
Funnel series. Tubular rim. Rim thickness
3.5mm. Estimated diameter 120mm. Slightly
outsplayed.

Item no 2339
4699; 11 x 9mm; L.Blue
Funnel series. Rounded rim. Rim thickness
1.5mm. Slightly outsplayed. Decorated with
marvered horizontal opaque yellow trail on
exterior.

Item no 2587
4644; 19 x 10 x 1mm; L.Green

Item no 2588
5413; 10 x 9mm; Blue
Decorated, non-diagnostic.

Item no 2589
6068; 12 x 10mm; L.Green
Funnel series. Tubular rim. Rim thickness
5mm. Slightly outsplayed, containing some
opaque white streaking.

Item no 2590
6068; 20 x 7 x 1mm; L.Blue
Decorated, non-diagnostic. Some darker
streaking in metal.

Item no 2591
5447; 7 x 3 x 1mm; Blue
Decorated, non-diagnostic. Sliver.

Item no 2592
4644; 22 x 18 x 1mm; L.Green

Item no 2593
4644; 26 x 17 x 1mm; L.Green
Four associated fragments.

Item no 2594
5517; 17 x 10 x 1mm; L.Green

Item no 2595
5294; 19 x 4mm; L.Blue
Funnel series. Rounded rim. Rim thickness
2mm. Slightly outsplayed.

Item no 2627
5682; Blue
Bead. Circular of diameter 7.5mm.
Thickness 3mm. Diameter of perforation
3mm. Formed by winding.

Item no 2628
4699; 7 x 6mm; L.Blue
Decorated, non-diagnostic. Horizontal
opaque yellow marvered trails.

Item no 2632
4699; 18 x 12mm; Dark Opaque
Decorated, non-diagnostic. Remains of
reticella rod containing opaque yellow
spirals.

Item no 2633
5207; 14 x 14mm; L.Blue
Decorated, non-diagnostic. Applied arcaded
trail.

Item no 2634
5676; 15 x 9mm; L.Green
Funnel series. Tubular rim. Rim thickness
2mm. Slightly outsplayed.

Item no 2635
4636; 11 x 10mm; L.Green
Funnel series. Rounded rim. Rim thickness
2mm. Slightly outsplayed and inturned.

Item no 2636
4699; 6 x 4 x 1mm; L.Blue

Item no 2637
4699; 8 x 5 x 1mm; L.Blue

Item no 2638
5675; 13 x 6 x 1mm; L.Green

Item no 2640
4636; 10 x 5mm; L.Blue
Decorated, non-diagnostic. Horizontal opaque yellow marvered trail.

Item no 2641
4699; 10 x 9 x 1mm; L.Green

Item no 2643
5676; 10 x 10mm; L.Blue
Decorated, non-diagnostic. Opaque yellow marvered trail.

Item no 2649
4699; 12 x 5mm; Dark Opaque
Decorated, non-diagnostic. Evidence of applied opaque yellow decoration.

Item no 2650
4699; 7 x 7 x 1mm; L.Blue

Item no 2651
4698; 6 x 5 x 1mm; L.Green

Item no 2656
5682; 6 x 3 x 1mm; L.Blue

Item no 2657
5682; 3 x 2 x 1mm; L.Blue

Item no 2658
5682; 17 x 12mm; L.Blue
Decorated, non-diagnostic. Vertical applied trail of same colour as vessel. Near to base.

Item no 2661
5682; 3 x 1 x 1mm; L.Blue
One associated fragment.

Item no 2662
5675; 12 x 7 x 1mm; L.Green

Item no 2664
4699; 4 x 1 x 1mm; L.Blue
Sliver.

Item no 2687
F1039 Layer 14; 4 x 3 x 2mm; Bright Blue
Decorated, non-diagnostic. Two other angular chips.

Item no 2699
F2054 C5610; 8 x 7 x 1mm; L.Blue

Item no 2785
F2003 Layer 2; 16 x 8 x 2mm; L.Blue

Item no 2786
F2003 Layer 5; 20 x 11mm; L.Blue
Funnel series. Tubular rim. Rim thickness 4mm. Decorated with marvered horizontal opaque white trails on exterior.

Item no 2787
F2010 Layer 2; 9 x 5mm; L.Blue
Decorated, non-diagnostic. Applied trail.

Item no 2788
F2010 Layer 2; 9 x 4 x 2mm; L.Blue

Item no 2789
F4073 Layer 1; 21 x 19mm; L.Green

Funnel series. Rounded rim. Rim thickness 2mm. Slightly outsplayed. Surmounted by reticella rod with opaque yellow spirals, some white streaking.

Item no 2790
F2056 Layer 2; 7 x 5 x 2mm; L.Blue

Item no 2791
F4073 Layer 1; 19 x 19mm; L.Green
Other vessel type. Pronounced carination in body. Two associated fragments.

SOU 32

Item no 460
F2 Layer 1; 11 x 8mm; L.Blue
Funnel series. Rounded rim. Rim thickness 2mm. Slightly outsplayed and inturned.

Item no 461
P30 Layer 8; 50 x 27mm; L.Green
Funnel series. Rounded rim. Rim thickness 2mm. Estimated diameter 80mm. Slightly outsplayed.

Item no 462
P6 Layer 9; 44 x 35mm; L.Blue
Splayed form. One associated body fragment.

Item no 463
P30 and 6; 60 x 28mm; L.Green
Funnel series. Tubular rim without cavity. Rim thickness 2mm. Estimated diameter 80mm. Slightly outsplayed. One associated rim fragment and three associated body fragments.

Item no 464
P30 and 6; 45 x 35mm; L.Green
Funnel series. Base fragment. Showing pontil wad and mark. Base diameter 20mm. Mark diameter 14mm.

Item no 465
P30 and 6; 82 x 36mm; L.Green
Funnel series. Base fragment. Showing pontil mark. Base diameter 13mm. Mark diameter 10mm.

Item no 466
F20 Layer 1; 23 x 8mm; L.Blue
Decorated, non-diagnostic. Applied arcaded trail. Evidence of dark streaking.

Item no 467
Unknown; 28 x 25mm; Dark Green/Grey
Decorated, non-diagnostic.

Item no 468
F8 Layer 1; 8 x 7 x 1mm; L.Blue

Item no 470
F25 Layer 2; 10 x 6 x 1mm; L.Green

Item no 471
Pit 5 Layer 4; 17 x 7 x 1mm; L.Blue

Item no 472
Surface Layer 5; 23 x 10 x 2mm; L.Green

Item no 473
F4 Layer 4; 27 x 17mm; L.Green
Funnel series. Tubular rim without cavity. Rim thickness 3mm. Estimated diameter 100mm. Slightly outsplayed. Decorated with reticella rod containing opaque white spirals applied to top of rim.

Item no 474
F4 Layer 4; 36 x 19mm; L.Green
Funnel series. Tubular rim. Rim thickness 3mm. Estimated diameter 80mm. Slightly outsplayed.

Item no 475
Surface Layer 4; 12 x 11mm; L.Blue (see Fig 8)
Funnel series. Rounded rim. Rim thickness 2mm. Slightly outsplayed. Decorated with reticella rod containing opaque white spirals applied to rim.

Item no 476
Surface Layer 4; 17 x 11mm; L.Blue
Funnel series. Tubular rim without cavity. Rim thickness 4mm. Estimated diameter 80mm. Slightly outsplayed and inturned.

Item no 477
F4 Layer 4; 14 x 14mm; L.Blue
Funnel series. Tubular rim. Rim thickness 4mm. Slightly outsplayed. One associated body fragment.

Item no 478
F4 Layer 7; 12 x 11mm; L.Blue
Decorated, non-diagnostic. Applied trail.

Item no 479
Surface Layer 1; 17 x 12mm; L.Blue
Funnel series. Tubular rim. Rim thickness 3.5mm. Estimated diameter 80mm. Slightly outsplayed.

Item no 480
F277 Surface; 9 x 7 x 1mm; L.Blue

Item no 481
F374 Surface; 20 x 9 x 2mm; L.Blue

Item no 482
F335 Surface; 10 x 4 x 1mm; L.Blue

Item no 483
F342 Layer 2; 27 x 14mm; L.Blue
Funnel series. Tubular rim. Rim thickness 5mm. Estimated diameter 100mm. Especially pronounced fold. Slightly outsplayed and flattened on inside.

Item no 484
F342 Layer 2; 22 x 12mm; L.Blue (see Fig 11)
Funnel series. Base fragment. Evidence of pontil mark and wad. Diameter of mark 19mm. Early part of series.

Item no 485
F363 Surface; 13 x 8 x 1mm; L.Green

Item no 486
F366 Surface; 27 x 6mm; L.Blue
Funnel series. Tubular rim. Rim thickness
3mm. Estimated diameter 100mm. Slightly
outsplayed.

Item no 487
F389 Surface; 21 x 19mm; L.Green (see
Fig 13)
Other vessel type. Cut rim of thickness
1.5mm. Slightly outsplayed. Tall beaker?

Item no 488
F342 Layer 4; 9 x 5 x 1mm; L.Blue

Item no 489
F342 Layer 2; 15 x 4mm; L.Blue
Decorated, non-diagnostic. Applied trail. One
associated body fragment.

Item no 490
F391; Blue
Bead. Tubular of length 12mm and diameter
6mm. Diameter of perforation 2mm.

Item no 491
Surface; 34 x 18mm; L.Blue (see Fig 8)
Funnel series. Tubular rim without cavity.
Rim thickness 3.5mm. Estimated diameter
80mm. Slightly outsplayed.

Item no 492
F342 Surface; 30 x 17mm; Yellow/Green
Funnel series. Tubular rim without cavity.
Rim thickness 4.5mm. Estimated diameter
100mm. Slightly outsplayed and inturned.
Possible streaking in rim area.

Item no 493
F352; 9 x 5 x 1mm; L.Green

Item no 494
Surface; 16 x 13mm; L.Blue
Decorated, non-diagnostic. Applied arcaded
trail.

Item no 495
F375; 10 x 8mm; L.Blue
Funnel series. Tubular rim. Rim thickness
4mm. Slightly outsplayed and flattened on
inside.

Item no 496
F378; Surface; 30 x 13mm; Yellow
Other vessel type. Bowl or jar form. 20
associated fragments.

Item no 497
F534; 13 x 8mm; L.Blue
Funnel series. Rounded rim. Rim thickness
4mm. Slightly outsplayed and inturned.
Decorated with reticella rod containing
opaque white spirals applied to inside of rim.

Item no 498
F536; 25 x 18mm; L.Blue (see Plate 7 and
Fig 12)
Funnel series. Base fragment. Evidence of
pontil mark and wad. Diameter of mark
15mm.

Item no 499
Unstratified; 13 x 12mm; L.Green
Funnel series. Rounded rim. Rim thickness
2.5mm. Estimated diameter 100mm. Slightly
outsplayed.

Item no 500
F624/5 Surface; 12 x 7mm; L.Green
Funnel series. Tubular rim. Rim thickness
3.5mm. Slightly outsplayed.

Item no 501
F608; 21 x 14mm; L.Blue (see Fig 8)
Funnel series. Rounded rim. Rim thickness
2.5mm. Estimated diameter 80mm. Slightly
outsplayed. Decorated with reticella rod
containing opaque white spirals applied to
top of rim. Some dark streaking in metal.

Item no 502
Unstratified; 27 x 23mm; L.Blue (see Plate 1
and Fig 15)
Other vessel type. Pushed base from bowl or
jar. Showing termination of four reticella
rods containing opaque yellow spirals.

Item no 503
F553; 26 x 15mm; L.Blue (see Plate 7 and
Fig 11)
Funnel series. Base fragment. Evidence of
pontil mark of diameter 10mm. Decorated
with V-formed applied reticella rods
containing opaque yellow spirals.

Item no 504
F563; 14 x 14mm; L.Blue (see Fig 9)
Funnel series. Rounded rim. Rim thickness
2.5mm. Slightly outsplayed. Decorated with
horizontal opaque yellow marvered trails.

Item no 505
F608; 15 x 9mm; L.Blue
Waster. Angular chip with ceramic adhering
on one surface.

Item no 506
F608; 12 x 8 x 2mm; L.Blue

Item no 507
F608; 12 x 10 x 1mm; L.Green

Item no 508
F564 Top; 10 x 6 x 1mm; L.Blue

SOU 33

Item no 148
F8; 13 x 13 x 1mm; L.Blue
One associated body fragment.

Item no 149
F50; 55 x 47mm; L.Blue
Waster. Ceramic crucible fragment with light
blue vitreous deposits and thin layer of glass
coating inside.

Item no 150
F7; 28 x 17 x 1mm; Colourless

Item no 151
F14; 16 x 12mm; L.Blue

Funnel series. Rounded rim. Rim thickness
2mm. Slightly outsplayed and inturned.

Item no 152
F13; 10 x 9 x 1mm; L.Green
Heat distorted.

Item no 153
F8; 17 x 13mm; L.Blue
Decorated, non-diagnostic. Dark streaking
within metal.

Item no 154
F28; 17 x 13mm; L.Green
Funnel series. Rounded rim. Rim thickness
2mm. Slightly outsplayed and inturned.

Item no 155
F8c; 20 x 12mm; Colourless
Decorated, non-diagnostic. Opaque white
coombed marvering.

Item no 156
F28; 18 x 14mm; L.Blue
Decorated, non-diagnostic. Twisted
decoration.

Item no 157
F8c; 20 x 11mm; L.Blue
Decorated, non-diagnostic. Horizontal
opaque yellow marvered trails.

Item no 158
F35; 12 x 11 x 1mm; L.Green

Item no 159
F5; 20 x 5mm; Brown/Yellow
Decorated, non-diagnostic. Opaque yellow
marvered trails and blobs. Evidence of
applied reticella rod.

Item no 160
F8d; 29 x 19mm; L.Blue (see Fig 12)
Funnel series. Base fragment. Showing pontil
mark and wad. Mark diameter 11mm. Some
iridescence.

Item no 161
F8d; 12 x 9mm; L.Blue
Decorated, non-diagnostic. Applied reticella
rod containing opaque yellow spirals.

Item no 162
F8d; 28 x 22mm; Colourless
Decorated, non-diagnostic. Opaque white
coombed marvering. One associaed body
fragment.

Item no 163
F5; 12 x 7mm; L.Blue
Funnel series. Tubular rim. Rim thickness
4.5mm. Slightly outsplayed.

Item no 164
F55; 11 x 3mm; L.Green
Decorated, non-diagnostic. Applied reticella
rod containing opaque yellow pairs of
spirals.

Item no 165
F67; 17 x 11mm; L.Blue

Funnel series. Rounded rim. Rim thickness 2mm. Slightly outsplayed and inturned.

Item no 166
F67; 22 x 18mm; L.Blue (see Fig 7)
Funnel series. Rounded rim. Rim thickness 3mm. Estimated diameter 100mm. Slightly outsplayed and inturned. Some dark streaking in metal.

Item no 167
F67; 35 x 19mm; L.Blue
Funnel series. Tubular rim. Rim thickness 3.5mm. Estimated diameter 80mm. Smoothed on inside and slightly outsplayed.

Item no 168
F34; 44 x 27mm; L.Green
Funnel series. Tubular rim. Rim thickness 3mm. Estimated diameter 80mm. Slightly outsplayed.

Item no 169
F34; 15 x 15 x 1mm; L.Blue

SOU 34

Item no 1
Pit 146 A; 24 x 19mm; L.Blue (see Fig 7)
Funnel series. Rounded rim. Rim thickness 2.5mm. Slightly outsplayed and inturned. Decorated with applied reticella rod containing opaque white spirals on inside of rim.

Item no 3
Pit 155; 17 x 15mm; L.Green
Funnel series. Rounded rim. Rim thickness 3mm. Slightly outsplayed. Applied reticella rod containing opaque white spirals on inside lip of rim.

Item no 4
Pit 155; 28 x 27mm; L.Blue (see Fig 12)
Funnel series. Base fragment. Showing pontil mark and wad. Base diameter 18mm. Mark diameter 14mm. Some dark streaking within metal.

Item no 5
Pit 155; 38 x 23mm; L.Green (see Fig 12)
Funnel series. Base fragment. Showing part of pontil mark.

Item no 167
Pit 149; 27 x 12mm; L.Blue (see Fig 5)
Funnel series. Tubular rim. Rim thickness 4mm. Estimated diameter 100mm. Slightly outsplayed.

Item no 168
Pit 149; 19 x 18mm; L.Blue (see Fig 7)
Funnel series. Rounded rim. Rim thickness 2.5mm. Estimated diameter 100mm. Slightly outsplayed and inturned. Decorated with reticella rod containing opaque white spirals applied to rim.

Item no 169
Pit 149; 38 x 18mm; L.Green (see Fig 16)
Decorated, non-diagnostic. Opaque white

marvered trails, some in arcaded form. Evidence of carination in body.

Item no 170
Pi; L.Blue
One associated fragment.

Item no 171
Pit 120D Layer 1; 21 x 16mm; L.Green
Decorated, non-diagnostic. Evidence of applied trailing. Two associated fragments.

Item no 172
Unknown; 20 x 20 x 1mm; L.Blue
One associated fragment.

Item no 175
Surface; 27 x 16mm; L.Green
Funnel series. Rounded rim. Rim thickness 3mm. Estimated diameter 80mm. Slightly outsplayed. One associated body fragment.

Item no 176
Surface; 11 x 8 x 5mm; Opaque blue
Bead fragment. Heavily weathered.

Item no 177
Pit 145 Layer 1; 13 x 13 x 1mm; L.Green

Item no 178
Pit 144D Layer 1; 19 x 14 x 1mm; L.Blue
One other body fragment.

Item no 180
Pit 141 Layer 1; 27 x 17 x 1mm; L.Blue

Item no 181
Pit 145 Layer 1; 22 x 11 x 1mm; L.Blue
Funnel series. Near to base.

Item no 182
Pit 144C Layer 1; 19 x 8mm; L.Blue
Funnel series. Tubular rim. Rim thickness 4.5mm. Slightly outsplayed.

Item no 183
Pit 149 Layer 1; 20 x 15 x 1mm; L.Blue
One other body fragment.

Item no 184
Pit 149 Layer 1; 37 x 17mm; L.Green
Funnel series. Tubular rim without cavity. Rim thickness 2.5mm. Estimated diameter 90mm. Slightly outsplayed.

Item no 185
Pit 146A Layer 1; 17 x 9mm; L.Blue
Funnel series. Rounded rim. Rim thickness 2.5mm. Slightly outsplayed. Rim surmounted with reticella rod containing opaque white spirals.

SOU 35

Item no 35
Pit 120C; 38 x 14mm; L.Blue (see Plate 4 and Fig 5)
Funnel series. Tubular rim. Rim thickness 4.5mm. Estimated diameter 140mm. Slightly outsplayed. Decorated with horizontal

opaque yellow marvered trails also evident inside rim cavity.

Item no 38
Pit 119 Layer 6; 34 x 20 x 3mm; L.Blue
Other vessel type. Base fragment showing vertical ribbed decoration.

Item no 39
Pit 119 Layer 1; 24 x 10 x 1mm; L.Blue

Item no 40
Pit 119 Layer 1; 11 x 8mm; L.Blue
Funnel series. Tubular rim. Rim thickness 3mm. Slightly outsplayed.

Item no 41
Pit 120 Layer 1; 25 x 17mms; L.Blue
Funnel series. Rounded rim. Rim thickness 1.5mm. Slightly outsplayed and inturned. Rim surmounted with applied reticella rod containing opaque white spiral. One associated body fragment. Some surface iridescence.

Item no 42
Pit 120C Layer 3; 12 x 9mm; L.Blue
Funnel series. Rounded rim, Rim thickness 2mm. Slightly outsplayed and inturned. Rim surmounted with applied reticella rod containing opaque white spiral. One other body fragment. Some surface iridescence.

Item no 43
Pit 120C Layer 1; 13 x 5 x 1mm; L.Blue

Item no 44
Pit 128 SE Layer 3; 29 x 9 x 1mm;
Colourless

Item no 45
Pit 119 Layer 1; 24 x 13mm; L.Blue
Funnel series. Base fragment. Base thickness 3mm. Showing pontil mark of diameter 10mm.

SOU 36
(items marked by * were made available for study at a late stage and are not included in the analysis. They are included here for completeness.)

Item no 1
Pit 2 Layer 8; 20 x 11mm; Clouded Red (see Plate 5)
Decorated, non-diagnostic.

Item no 2
Pit 12 Layer 5; 25 x 18mm; Dark Green (see Fig 16)
Decorated, non-diagnostic. Applied dark opaque reticella rod containing opaque white spirals. Evidence of opaque white marvered trailing. One associated fragment.

Item no 3
Pit 15 Layer 7; 14 x 11mm; Dark Opaque
Decorated, non-diagnostic. Horizontal opaque yellow marvered trails.

Item no 4
Pit 25 Layer 1; 32 x 15mm; Colourless (see Fig 16)
Decorated, non-diagnostic. Applied arcaded reticella rod containing opaque yellow spirals.

Item no 5
Pit 10 Surface; 22 x 14mm; L.Green/Blue (see Plate 4 and Fig 9)
Funnel series. Rounded rim. Rim thickness 2mm. Estimated diameter 90mm. Slightly outsplayed. Rim formed in two stages, lower body light green, upper body and rim blue.

Item no 6
Pit 8A; 22 x 11mm; Dark Green
Decorated, non-diagnostic. Horizontal opaque yellow marvered trails.

Item no 7
Pit 18; 58 x 57mm; Blue (see Plate 6 and Fig 15)
Other vessel type. Pushed base showing pontil mark and wad. Mark diameter 16mm. Flask or jar form.

Item no 194
Pit 34 Surface; 18 x 14 x 3mm; L.Blue
Window fragment. Two possible grozed edges and one edge flame rounded. No obvious shape to quarry.

*Item no 195
Pit 30; 10 x 7mm; L.Green
Possible vessel or mount fragment showing chamfered edge/rim of thickness 2mm.

*Item no 196
Pit 29; 15 x 13mm; L.Green
Posible window fragment with grozing.

Item no 197
Pit 8; 55 x 29 x 3mm; L.Blue (see Fig 17)
Window fragment. One edge flame rounded, one edge possibly grozed.

*Item no 198
Pit 10; 30 x 25mm; L.Green(?)
Heat distorted and disFigured.

*Item no 199
P8; 20 x 15mm; L.Green
Possible window fragment with heat rounded gorzed edges.

*Item no 200
Pit 15; 22 x 12mm; Colourless/grey
Probable rectangular flat mount with all four edges cut and/or chamfered.

*Item no 201
P22; 14 x 12mm; L.Green
Probably flat and belonging to window glass.

*Item no 203
Pit 9; 33 x 20mm; L.Blue
Funnel beaker. Four fragments (one vessel). Fragments from lower body.

Item no 204
KLC Pit 2 Layer 6; 20 x 16mm; L.Green

Funnel series. Rounded rim. Rim thickness 2.5mm. Estimated diameter 120mm. Outsplayed and slightly inturned.

Item no 205
KLC Pit 2 Layer 6; 16 x 13mm; L.Green
Funnel series. Rounded rim. Rim thickness 2.5mm. Estimated diameter 100mm. Outsplayed and slightly inturned.

Item no 206
KLC Hut 2 Layer 7a; 26 x 13mm; L.Blue
Funnel series. Tubular rim. Rim thickness 2.5mm. Estimated diameter 100mm. Slightly outsplayed.

Item no 207
Pit 26; 26 x 21 x 1.5mm; Opaque
Non-durable fragment. Originally light green.

Item no 208
KLC Pit 11 Layer 2c; 23 x 16mm; L.Green
Funnel series. Base fragment. Showing part of pontil mark and wad.

Item no 209
KLC Hut 2 Layer 7b; 25 x 12mm; L.Blue
Funnel series. Tubular rim. Rim thickness 3mm. Estimated diameter 110mm. Slightly outsplayed.

Item no 210
KLC Hut 2 Layer 3; 33 x 30mm; L.Blue
Funnel series. Rounded rim. Rim thickness 2.5mm. Estimated diameter 100mm. Slightly outsplayed and inturned.

Item no 211
Pit 22 Layer 3; 26 x 13mm; L.Blue
Funnel series. Tubular rim. Rim thickness 4mm. Estimated diameter 100mm. Slightly outsplayed. Decorated with opaque yellow marvered trails.

Item no 212
Pit 22 Layer 3; 29 x 20mm; L.Blue
Funnel series. From near base of vessel.

Item no 213
Pit 22 Layer 3; 33 x 18 x 1.5mm; L.Green
One associated fragment.

Item no 214
Pit 31; 16 x 15mm; L.Blue
Funnel series. Rounded rim. Rim thickness 2.5mm. Slightly outsplayed and inturned.

Item no 215
KLC Pit 17; 8 x 2mm; L.Blue
Decorated, non-diagnostic. Decorated with reticella rod containing opaque white spirals.

Item no 216
KLC Pit 2 Layer 8; L.Blue
Decorated, non-diagnostic. Applied arcaded trail.

*Item no 217
Pit 2; 20 x 17mm; Dark Green
Possible grozing along one curved edge (?).

Item no 218
KLC Hut 2 Layer 7b; 33 x 20mm; L.Blue
Decorated, non-diagnostic. Horizontal opaque yellow marvered trails. One associated fragment.

Item no 219
KLC SQ4 Pit 7 Layer 2a; 13 x 9mm; L.Blue
Funnel series. Tubular rim. Rim thickness 2.5mms. Slightly outsplayed.

Item no 220
KLC Pit 3 Layer 11; 21 x 20mms; L.Blue
Funnel series. Base fragment. Showing part of pontil mark and wad. Mark diameter 15mm.

Item no 221
KLC Pit 6 Layer 9; 48 x 29mm; L.Blue
Funnel series. Tubular rim. Rim thickness 3mm. Estimated diameter 100mm. Slightly outsplayed. Two associated body fragments.

*Item no 222
Pit 11; 13 x 13mm; L.Blue
Funnel beaker. Fragment from upper body showing heat effects.

Item no 223
KLB Pit 22 Layer 4; 25 x 13mm; L.Green
Funnel series. Base fragment. Showing part of pontil wad and mark.

*Item no 224
Pit 8A; 10 x 8mm; Colourless.
Some iridescence.

Item no 225
KLC Pit 6; 18 x 10mm; L.Green
Funnel series. Tubular rim without cavity. Rim thickness 4mm. Estimated diameter 100mm. Slightly outsplayed and inturned.

Item no 226
KLC SQ7 Surface; 18 x 17 x 1.5mm; L.Green
Heat distorted.

Item no 227
KLC SQ2 Pit 6 Layer 1; 23 x 18 x 1.5mm; L.Green

Item no 228
KLC Pit 7 Layer 6; 30 x 19mm; L.Green
Funnel series. Tubular rim. Rim thickness 2.5mm. Estimated diameter 100mm. Slightly outsplayed.

Item no 229
KLC Pit 6 Layer 3; 25 x 20mm; L.Green
Funnel series. Tubular rim. Rim thickness 3mm. Estimated diameter 100mm. Slightly outsplayed and inturned.

Item no 230
Pit 22 Layer 3; 14 x 11 x 1mm; L.Green
One associated fragment.

Item no 231
KLC Pit 7; 44 x 11mm; L.Blue
Funnel series. Tubular rim. Rim thickness

3mm. Estimated diameter 80mm. Slightly outsplayed and inturned.

Item no 232
KLC SQ4 Pit 7 Layer 1; 20 x 11mm; L.Green
Funnel series. From near base of vessel.

Item no 233
Pit 8 Layer 8; 37 x 28mm; L.Green
Funnel series. Tubular rim. Rim thickness 3mm. Estimated diameter 100mm. Slightly outsplayed.

Item no 234
Pit 8 Layer 8; 29 x 17mm; L.Blue
Funnel series. Rounded rim. Rim thickness 2mm. Estimated diameter 60mm. Slightly outsplayed. One associated body fragment.

Item no 235
Pit 8 Layer 8; 32 x 22mm; L.Green
Funnel series. Rounded rim. Rim thickness 2.5mm. Estimated diameter 100mm. Slightly outsplayed and inturned. One associated rim fragment.

Item no 236
Pit 8 Layer 8; 15 x 11mm; L.Green/Yellow
Funnel series. Rounded rim. Rim thickness 2.5mm. Estimated diameter 60mm. Slightly outsplayed and inturned. Six associated body fragments.

Item no 237
Pit 23 Layers 1 and 2; 19 x 19mm; L.Blue
Funnel series. Rounded rim. Rim thickness 2mm. Slightly outsplayed and inturned. Some surface weathering.

Item no 238
Pit 23 Layers 1 and 2; 17 x 10 x 1mm; L.Green
Two associated body fragments.

Item no 239
Pit 18 Layer 6; 20 x 12 x 1mm; L.Green

Item no 240
KLC Pit2 Layer 2; 41 x 8mm; L.Blue
Funnel series. Tubular rim. Rim thickness 3mm. Estimated diameter 80mm. Slightly outsplayed.

Item no 241
Pit 22 Layer 1; 16 x 15mm; L.Green
Funnel series. Rounded rim. Rim thickness 2.5mm. Slightly inturned. Some weathering.

Item no 243
Pit 22 Layer 1; 30 x 11 x 1mm; L.Green
One associated body fragment.

Item no 244
KLC Hut 2 Layer 3; 29 x 14mm; Opaque dark Blue
Decorated, non-diagnostic.

Item no 246
Pit 29 Layer 4; 29 x 19mms; L.Green
Funnel series. Rounded rim. Rim thickness

3mm. Slightly outsplayed. Some surface weathering. One associated rim fragment and two body fragments.

Item no 248
Pit 10 Layer 5; 20 x 13mm; L.Green
Decorated, non-diagnostic. Horizontal opaque yellow marvered trails.

*Item no 247
Pit 29; 65 x 45mm; Green
Decorated, non-diagnostic. Probably from bowl or similar vessel with high degree of curvature.

Item no 249
Pit 10 Surface; 19 x 10mm; Green
Decorated, non-diagnostic. Dark and red streaking within metal.

Item no 250
Pit 8 Layer 8; 38 x 27mm; L.Blue
Funnel series. Rounded rim. Rim thickness 2.5mm. Estimated diameter 80mm. Outsplayed and slightly inturned. Decorated with reticella rod containing opaque white spirals applied to lip of rim.

Item no 251
Pit 29 Surface; 7 x 7mm; Red
Decorated, non-diagnostic. Streaking within metal.

Item no 252
Pit 29 Surface; 19 x 13 x 1mm; Colourless

Item no 253
Pit 31 Layer 6; 30 x 17mm; L.Blue
Decorated, non-diagnostic. Applied trail.

Item no 254
Pit 31 Layer 3; 39 x 26mm; L.Blue
Funnel series. Tubular rim. Rim thickness 3.5mm. Estimated diameter 120mm. Slightly outsplayed. One associated body fragment.

Item no 255
Pit 29 Layer 6; 21 x 16mm; L.Blue
Decorated, non-diagnostic. Applied arcaded trail.

Item no 256
KLC Unstratified; 18 x 12 x 1mm; L.Green

Item no 257
KLC Unstratified; 15 x 3 x 1mm; L.Blue

*Item no 258a
30 x 15mm; L.Blue
Funnel beaker. From lower body.

*Item no 258b
33 x 30mm; L.Green
Other vessel type. Probably from bowl.

Item no 259
Pit 38 Layer 4; 20 x 13 x 1mm; L.Blue

Item no 260
Pit 30 Layer 5; 23 x 23 x 1mm; L.Blue
Two associated body fragments.

Item no 261
Pit 30 Layer 8; 38 x 32 x 1mm; L.Green

Item no 262
KLC Pit 3 Layer 6a; 12 x 11 x 1mm; L.Blue
One associated body fragment.

Item no 263
Pit 9 Layer 6; 33 x 18 x 1.5mm; L.Blue
One associated body fragment. Splayed form.

Item no 264
Pit 36 Layer 6; 17 x 5mm; L.Blue
Decorated, non-diagnostic. Applied trail.

*Item no 265
Pit 6; 45 x 18mm; Green
Other vessel type. Probably from tall, curved vessel.

*Item 266
Pit 31; 16 x 10mm; Yellow/Brown
Near base of vessel fragment with high degree of curvature.

Item no 267
KLC Pit 2 Layer 6; 13 x 6 x 1mm; L.Green

Item no 268
KLC Pit 15 Layer 3a; 15 x 7mm; L.Blue
Decorated, non-diagnostic. Dark streaking within metal.

*Item no 269
Pit 3; 15 x 15mm; L.Green
Probable pushed base of small jar or flask. Heat distorted.

*Item no 270
25 x 20mm; Dark Green

Item no 271
KLC Pit 15 Layer 14; 32 x 11 x 1mm; L.Green

Item no 272
Pit 10 Layer 3; 19 x 6 x 1mm; L.Green

Item no 273
Pit 36 Layer 4; 33 x 20mm; L.Blue
Decorated, non-diagnostic. Horizontal applied trails.

Item no 274
Pit 38 Layer 3; 8 x 7mm; L.Blue
Decorated, non-diagnostic. Applied trail.

*Item no 275
Pit 10; 20 x 20mm; Dark Green
Vessel fragment with high degree of curvature.

Item no 276
Pit 10 Layer; 24 x 14mm; L.Green
Funnel series. Rounded rim. Rim thickness 2mm. Slightly outsplayed.

Item no 277
Pit 10 Layer 5; 22 x 19mm; L.Green
Funnel series. Rounded rim. Rim thickness 3mm. Slightly outsplayed.

Item no 278
Near Pit 36 Surface; 22 x 10mm; Opaque Blue
Bead. Part of oval mount(?) Thickness 3mms. Opaque white decoration.

*Item no 279
35 x 25mm; Green

Item no 280
Pit 22 Layer 3; 9 x 9mm; L.Blue
Decorated, non-diagnostic. Opaque yellow marvered trails.

Item no 281
Pit 22 Layer 3; 9 x 5mm; Colourless
Decorated, non-diagnostic. Opaque yellow marvered trails.

Item no 282
Pit 41 Layer 2; 21 x 9 x 2mm; L.Blue
One other body fragment.

Item no 283
KLC Pit 15 Layer 3a; Opaque light Blue
Bead. Circular of diameter 3mm and thickness 1mm. Diameter of perforation 1mm. Probable spacer.

Item no 284
Pit 6 Layer 9; 19 x 11 x 1.5mm; L.Blue

Item no 285
Near Pit 31 Surface; Opaque Blue
Bead. Tubular of length 11mm and diameter 6mm. Diameter of perforation 2mm. Possibly originally two elements (fused).

Item no 286
KLC Pit 15 Layer 12; 19 x 15 x 2mm; L.Blue

Item no 287
Pit 30 Layer 2; 49 x 24mm; L.Green
Funnel series. Rounded rim. Rim thickness 3mm. Estimated diameter 80mm. Slightly outsplayed. Some surface weathering.

Item no 288
Pit 34 Layer 1; 22 x 16 x 1mm; L.Blue

Item no 289
KLC Pit 15 Layer 10a; 10 x 10 x 1mm; Colourless
Two associated fragments.

Item no 290
KLC Pit 15 Surface; 17 x 11 x 1mm; L.Green

Item no 291
Pit 10 Layer 3; 29 x 9mm; L.Blue
Funnel series. Tubular rim. Rim thickness 3.5mm. Estimated diameter 100mm. Slightly outsplayed.

Item no 292
Pit 29 Layer 3; 11 x 7mm; Green
Funnel series. Rounded rim. Rim thickness 2mm. Slightly outsplayed and inturned. Decorated with (now lost) horizontal marvered trails.

Item no 293
Near Pit 37 Surface; 21 x 5mm; Blue
Other vessel type. Rim fragment of thickness 4mm. Possibly bowl form.

Item no 294
Pit 36 Layer 4; 18 x 8 x 1mm; L.Blue

Item no 295
KLC Hut2 Pit 18 Layer 7ai; 17 x 9 x 2mm; L.Blue

Item no 296
KLC SQ2 Pit 6 Layer 9; 15 x 10 x 1mm; L.Green
One associated body fragment.

*Item no 297a
Pit 6; 23 x 14mm; Green

*Item no 297b
Pit 6; 13 x 10mm; Colourless

*Item no 297c
Pit 6; 7 x 5mm; Brown/Green

Item no 298
KLB Pit 22 Layer 3; 10 x 9mm; L.Green
Funnel series. Rounded rim. Rim thickness 3mm. Slightly outsplayed and inturned.

Item no 299
KLB Pit 22 Layer 3; 8 x 6 x 1mm; L.Blue
Two other small fragments.

Item no 300
KLB Pit 22 Layer 3; 11 x 7 x 1mm; L.Green
Six other small fragments.

Item no 301
Pit 10 Layer 6; 21 x 11mm; L.Green (see Fig 5)
Funnel series. Tubular rim. Rim thickness 3.5mm. Slightly outsplayed. Decorated with reticella rod containing opaque white spirals applied to lip of rim.

*Item no 302
Pit 10; ; L.Green
Funnel series. Rounded rim. Rim thickness 1mm. Slightly outsplayed.

Item no 303
Pit 10 Layer 6; 32 x 10 x 1mm; L.Blue

Item no 304
Pit 31 Layer 1; 25 x 5mm; L.Green
Funnel series. Tubular rim. Rim thickness 3.5mm. Estimated diameter 80mm. Slightly outsplayed.

Item no 305
Pit 26 Surface; 31 x 19mm; L.Blue
Decorated, non-diagnostic. Horizontal applied trails.

Item no 306
Pit 32 Layer 5; 12 x 6mm; Blue
Decorated, non-diagnostic. Reticella rod containing opaque white spirals.

Item no 307
Pit 30 Layer 4; 36 x 21mm; L.Green
Funnel series. Rounded rim. Rim thickness 2mm. Estimated diameter 110mm. Slightly outsplayed and inturned.

Item no 308
Pit 33 Layer 2; 28 x 20mm; L.Blue
Funnel series. Rounded rim. Rim thickness 2mm. Slightly outsplayed and inturned. Decorated with reticella rod containing opaque white spirals applied to lip of rim.

Item no 309
Pit 33 Layer 2; 18 x 8 x 2mm; L.Blue

Item no 310
KLC Pit 15 Layer 5; Opaque colourless
Bead. Circular of diameter 2mm and thickness 1mm. Diameter of perforation 1mm. Probable spacer.

Item no 311
Pit 41 Layer 1; 19 x 19mm; L.Blue
Funnel series. Rounded rim. Rim thickness 2mm. Estimated diameter 100mms. Slightly outsplayed.

Item no 312
Pit 41 Layer 1; 16 x 14mm; L.Blue
Decorated, non-diagnostic. Two other body fragments.

Item no 313
Pit 41 Layer 2; 17 x 14mm; L.Blue
Funnel series. Tubular rim. Rim thickness 4.5mm. Estimated diameter 80mm. Slightly outsplayed.

Item no 314
Pit 41 Layer 2; 19 x 15mm; L.Blue
Decorated, non-diagnostic. Applied trail. One other body fragment.

Item no 315
Pit 43 Surface; 15 x 10mm; L.Blue
Funnel series. Rounded rim. Rim thickness 2.5mm. Slightly outsplayed and inturned.

Item no 316
Pit 43 Surface; 14 x 13mm; L.Blue
Funnel series. Rounded rim. Rim thickness 2mm. Outsplayed. Decorated with horizontal opaque yellow marvered trails.

Item no 317
Pit 43 Surface; 15 x 8mm; L.Blue (see Fig 16)
Decorated, non-diagnostic. Applied trail with opaque white overlaid trail.

Item no 318
Pit 43 Surface; Opaque Blue
Bead. Circular of diameter 2mm and thickness 1mm. Diameter of perforation 1mm. Probable spacer.

Item no 319
Pit 43 Surface; 11 x 10 x 1mm; L.Blue

Item no 320
KLC Pit 15 Layer 9; 33 x 21mm; L.Green
Funnel series. Rounded rim. Rim thickness

2.5mm. Estimated diameter 100mm. Slightly outsplayed and inturned. Heat distorted. Three associated body fragments.

Item no 321
KLC Pit 15 Layer 9; 16 x 6mm; L.Blue
Decorated, non-diagnostic. Termination of applied trail.

Item no 322
KLC Pit 15 Layer 9; 17 x 16 x 1mm; L.Green
Two associated body fragments.

Item no 323
KLC Pit 15 Layer 9; 7 x 3mm; Blue
Decorated, non-diagnostic.

Item no 324
Pit 2 Surface; 25 x 23mm; L.Green (see Fig 12)
Funnel series. Base fragment. Showing pontil mark and wad. Mark diameter 12mm.

Item no 325
KLC Hut 2 Pit 1 Layer 1; 36 x 30mm; Green (see Fig 15)
Other vessel type. Pushed base showing pontil mark and wad. Base thickness 2.5mm. Mark diameter 12mm. Small jar or flask form.

Item no 326
KLC Pit 5 Layer 4; 48 x 22mm; L.Green (see Plate 3 and Fig 5)
Funnel series. Tubular rim. Rim thickness 3.5mm. Estimated diameter 80mm. Slightly outsplayed. One associated fragment.

Item no 327
Pit 10 Layer 6; 32 x 28mm; Green (see Fig 7)
Funnel series. Rounded rim. Rim thickness 3mm. Estimated diameter 90mm. Slightly outsplayed and inturned.

Item no 328
Pit 31 Layer 4; 47 x 17mms; L.Blue (see Fig 4)
Funnel series. Tubular rim. Rim thickness 4.5mm. Estimated diameter 140mm. Smoothed on inside and slightly outsplayed. Decorated with horizontal opaque white marvered trails. One associated body fragment.

Item no 329
Pit 10 Layer 6; 45 x 35mm; Green
Decorated, non-diagnostic. Applied trail. One associated fragment.

Item no 330
Pit 41 Layer 3; 31 x 23mm; Green (see Plate 2)
Funnel series. Rounded rim. Rim thickness 2.5mm. Estimated diameter 80mm. Slightly outsplayed. Decorated with reticella rod containing opaque white spirals applied to lip of rim. Some darker streaking in metal.

Item no 331
Pit 41 Layer 3; 22 x 22mm; L.Blue (see

Plate 5 and Fig 13)
Other vessel type. Decorated with horizontal opaque white marvered trails. Probable tall beaker form.

Item no 332
Pit 6 Layer 9; 70 x 60mm; L.Green (see Fig 10)
Funnel series. Intact apart from rim, but thinness of wall and outsplayed profile suggests rounded rim type. Estimated diameter 75mm. Base of diameter 12mm.

Item no 333
Pit 30 Layer 8; 160 x 80mm; L.Green (see Plate 7 and Fig 10)
Funnel series. Substantially intact showing rounded rim. Rim diameter 3mm. Estimated diameter 80mm. Base of diameter 10mm.

Item no 334
Pit 12 Layer 5; 15 x 7mm; L. Blue (see Fig 5)
Funnel series. Tubular rim. Rim thickness 3.5mm. Slightly outsplayed.

Item no 335
Pit 6 Layer 9; 50 x 19mm; L.Green
Funnel series. Tubular rim. Rim thickness 4mm. Estimated diameter 100mm. Smoothed on inside and slightly outsplayed.

Item no 342
Pit 22 Layer 1; 16 x 12 x 1.5mm; L.Blue

Item no 362
Pit 10 Layer 6; 33 x 27mm; L.Green
Funnel series. Rounded rim. Rim thickness 2mm. Estimated diameter 100mm. Slightly outsplayed and inturned.

SOU 38

Item no 62
GSB Pit 53 Layer 3; L.Blue
Funnel series. Rounded rim. Rim thickness 2mm. Estimated diameter 90mm. Slightly outsplayed and inturned. Decorated with horizontal opaque yellow marvered trails and blobs.

Item no 63
GSB Pit 53 Layer 3; 17 x 7 x 1mm; L.Green

Item no 65
GSA Pit 60 Layer 6; 54 x 23mm; L.Blue
Funnel series. Tubular rim. Rim thickness 4mm. Estimated diameter 100mm. Slightly outsplayed. One conjoining body fragment.

Item no 66
GSA Unstratified; 26 x 19 x 1mm; Blue
Decorated, non-diagnostic. Twisted decoration.

Item no 67
GSA Pit 50 Layer 1b; 19 x 8 x 1mm; L.Green
One associated body fragment.

Item no 68
GSB Pit 59 Layer 6; 10 x 5 x 1mm; Colourless

Item no 69
GSB Pit 58 Surface; 51 x 17mm; L.Green
Funnel series. Tubular rim. Rim thickness 4mm. Estimated diameter 100mm. Smoothed on inside and slightly outsplayed.

Item no 70
GSB Pit 58 Layer 1; 14 x 11 x 1.5mm; L.Blue

Item no 71
GSA Pit 50 Layer 1; 24 x 14mm; L.Green
Funnel series. Rounded rim. Rim thickness 3mm. Slightly outsplayed and inturned.

Item no 72
GSA Pit 60 Layer 1b; 21 x 14mm; L.Blue
Funnel series. Rounded rim. Rim thickness 2mm. Estimated diameter 100mm. Slightly outsplayed and inturned. One associated body fragment.

Item no 73
GSA pit 54 Layer 1; 11 x 10mm; L.Green
Funnel series. Rounded rim. Rim thickness 2mm. Estimated diameter 80mm. Slightly outsplayed and inturned.

Item no 75
GSA Pit 58 Layer 1; 13 x 2 x 1mm; L.Green

Item no 76
GSA Pit 46 Layer 1; 14 x 9 x 1mm; L.Blue
One other body fragment.

Item no 78
GSA Pit 50; 17 x 10mm; L.Green
Other vessel type. Pronounced carination in body. One associated fragment.

Item no 79
GSB Pit 59 Layer 2; 18 x 7mm; L.Green
Funnel series. Rounded rim. Rim thickness 2mm. Slightly outsplayed and inturned. Decorated with reticella rod containing opaque white spirals applied to lip of rim.

Item no 80
GSB Pit 59 Layer 1; 13 x 10 x 1mm; L.Blue

Item no 81
GSA Pit 60 Layer 1; 14 x 8mm; Blue
Decorated, non-diagnostic. Opaque yellow marvered trails (mostly lost).

Item no 82
Pit 56 Layer 1; 14 x 10 x 1mm; L.Blue
Lower body. One other body fragment.

Item no 83
Pit 58 filling; 13 x 10 x 1mm; L.Blue
One other body fragment.

Item no 84
GSA Pit 46 Layer 1; 11 x 9mm; L.Blue
Funnel series. Tubular rim. Rim thickness 4.5mm. Slightly outsplayed.

Item no 85
GSA Pit 46 Layer 1; 12 x 8mm; L.Blue
Decorated, non-diagnostic. Opaque yellow
marvered trails. Some dark streaking within
metal. One other associated fragment.

Item no 86
GSA Pit 60 Layer 2; 18 x 5 x 1mm; L.Blue

Item no 88
GSA Pit 51 Surface; 22 x 21 x 3mm; L.Blue

Item no 89
Pit 59 Layer 1; 15 x 11 x 1mm; Colourless

Item no 90
GSA Pit 56 Layer 3; 10 x 8mm; L.Blue
Decorated, non-diagnostic. Dark streaking
within metal.

Item no 91
GSB Pit 58 Layer 1; 11 x 10mm; L.Blue
Funnel series. Rounded rim. Rim thickness
2mm. Slightly outsplayed and inturned.

Item no 92
GSA Pit 60 Layer 1; 24 x 10mm; L.Blue
Decorated, non-diagnostic. Applied arcaded
trail. Three associated body fragments.

Item no 93
GSA Pit 46 Layer 1; 14 x 8 x 1mm; L.Blue

Item no 94
GSA Pit 46 Layer 1; 13 x 10 x 2mm; L.Blue

Item no 96
Pit 58 Layer 3; 13 x 12 x 1mm; L.Blue

Item no 100
GSA Pit 58 Layer 2; 21 x 13mm; L.Green
Funnel series. Rounded rim. Rim thickness
2.5mm. Estimated diameter 80mms. Slightly
outsplayed and inturned.

Item no 101
GSA Pit 58 Layer 2; 17 x 6 x 1mm; L.Green

Item no 102
GSA Pit 58 Layer 2; 13 x 6 x 1mm; L.Blue
One other body fragment.

Item no 103
GSA Pit 60 Layer 2; 40 x 20mm; L.Blue
Decorated, non-diagnostic. Horizontal
opaque yellow marvered trails. One
associated fragment.

Item no 104
GSA Pit 60 Layer 2; 10 x 10mm; Blue
Decorated, non-diagnostic.

Item no 105
GSA Pit 48 Layer 1c; 23 x 18mm; L.Blue
(see Plate 5 and Fig 17)
Decorated, non-diagnostic. Curved opaque
yellow marvered trail. Dark streaking within
metal.

Item no 106
Pit 53 Layer 3; 27 x 15mm; L.Blue
Decorated, non-diagnostic. Arcaded reticella

rods containing opaque yellow spirals on
inner curve and opaque white spirals on
outer curve. Also opaque yellow marvered
trail.

Item no 107
GSA Pit 60 Layer 1a and 1b; 42 x 23 x
1.5mm; L.Blue (see Fig 17)
Decorated, non-diagnostic. Twisted
decoration. One associated body fragment.

Item no 108
GSB Pit 53 Layer 3; 28 x 13mm; L.Blue (see
Plate 1 and Fig 17)
Decorated, non-diagnostic. Arcaded reticella
rods containing opaque yellow spirals on
inner curve and opaque white spirals on
outer curve.

Item no 109
GSB Pit 53 Layer 3; 19 x 16mm; L.Blue (see
Fig 16)
Decorated, non-diagnostic. Horizontal
opaque yellow marvered trails.

Item no 110
GSB Pit 53 Layer 3; 12 x 7 x 1mm; L.Blue

Item no 111
GSB Pit 53 Layer 4; 19 x 12mm; L.Blue (see
Fig 5)
Funnel series. Tubular rim. Rim thickness
5.5mm. Estimated diameter 80mm. Slightly
outsplayed.

Item no 112
GSB Pit 53 Layer 4; 26 x 22mm; L.Blue (see
Fig 9)
Funnel series. Rounded rim. Rim thickness
2mm. Estimated diameter 80mm. Slightly
outsplayed and inturned. Decorated with
horizontal opaque yellow marvered trails.
One associated rim fragment.

Item no 113
GSB Pit 53 Layer 4; 25 x 10mm; L.Blue (see
Fig 17)
Decorated, non-diagnostic. Decorated with
reticella rods containing opaque white
spirals. One associated body fragment.

Item no 114
GSB Pit 53 Layer 4; 17 x 16 x 1mm; L.Blue
One other body fragment.

SOU 39
Item no 1
Pit 70; 43 x 24mm; L.Blue (see Fig 16)
Decorated, non-diagnostic. Applied arcaded
reticella rods containing opaque white
spirals.

Item no 88
CLS.B Pit 68 Layer 3; 39 x 18mm; L.Blue
Funnel series. Tubular rim. Rim thickness
6mm. Estimated diameter 120mm. Smoothed
on inside and slightly outsplayed.

Item no 89
CLS.B Pit 68 Layer 1; 16 x 15mm; L.Blue

Funnel series. Tubular rim without cavity.
Rim thickness 2.5mm. Slightly outsplayed.
One associated body fragment.

Item no 90
CLS.B Pit 70; 16 x 8 x 1mm; L.Blue

Item no 91
CLS.A Pit 67A Layer 1; 17 x 10 x 1.5mm;
L.Blue

Item no 92
Pit 70 Surface; 20 x 8mm; L.Green
Decorated, non-diagnostic. Applied trail.

Item no 93
CLS.B Pit 70 Layer 1; 14 x 8mm; L.Blue
(see Fig 15)
Decorated, non-diagnostic. Decaying
marvered opaque yellow blobs or small
bosses. Two associated fragments.

Item no 94
CLS.B Pit 70 Layer 1; 13 x 10 x 1mm;
L.Green

Item no 95
Near Pit 36 Surface; 14 x 5mm; L.Blue
Funnel series. Tubular rim. Rim thickness
3.5mm. Slightly outsplayed.

Item no 96
CLS.A Pit 64 Layer 3; 6 x 4 x 1mm; L.Blue

Item no 97
CLS.A Pit 65B Layer 1; 18 x 10mm; L.Blue
Funnel series. Rounded rim. Rim thickness
2mm. Estimated diameter 100mm. Slightly
outsplayed and inturned. Decorated with
(now lost) horizontal marvered trails.

Item no 98
CLS.B Pit 70 Unstratified; 11 x 5mm; Green
Decorated, non-diagnostic. Arcaded reticella
rod containing opaque white spirals.

Item no 99
CLS.B Pit 66a Layer 9; 15 x 12mm; L.Blue
Funnel series. Tubular rim. Rim thickness
4mm. Estimated diameter 80mm. Slightly
outsplayed.

Item no 100
Pit 70 filling; 22 x 14mm; L.Blue
Funnel series. Tubular rim. Rim thickness
4mm. Slightly outsplayed.

Item no 101
Pit 70 filling; 21 x 7mm; L.Blue
Decorated, non-diagnostic. Reticella rod
containing opaque white spirals. Two other
body fragments.

Item no 102
CLS.B Pit 71 Layer 1; 14 x 13mm; L.Green
Funnel series. Tubular rim without cavity.
Rim thickness 3mm. Estimated diameter
80mm. Slightly outsplayed.

Item no 103
Pit 70 Layer 2; 17 x 16mm; L.Blue
Other vessel type. Pronounced carination in
body.

Item no 104
CLS.B Pit 68 Layer 2; 9 x 8 x 1mm; L.Green

Item no 105
CLS.B Pit 70; 20 x 8mm; L.Blue
Funnel series. Tubular rim. Rim thickness
3mm. Estimated diameter 80mm. Smoothed
on inside and slightly outsplayed.

Item no 106
CLS.B Pit 70; 23 x 21mm; L.Blue
Funnel series. Rounded rim. Rim thickness
2mm. Estimated diameter 90mm. Slightly
outsplayed.

Item no 107
CLS.B Pit 70; 16 x 15 x 1mm; L.Blue

Item no 108
CLS Pit 66b Layer 1; 21 x 20mm; L.Blue
Funnel series. Tubular rim. Rim thickness
3.5mm. Estimated diameter 70mm. Slightly
outsplayed and inturned.

Item no 109
CLS.B Pit 70 Layer 3; 17 x 16mm; L.Blue
Other vessel type. Pronounced carination in
body. One associated fragment.

Item no 110
CLS.B Pit 70 Layer 3; 20 x 13mm; L.Blue
Three other fragments.

Item no 111
Pit 70; 27 x 25mm; L.Blue
Funnel series. Rounded rim. Rim thickness
2mm. Estimated diameter 100mm. Slightly
outsplayed.

Item no 112
Pit 70; 38 x 19mm; L.Blue
Decorated, non-diagnostic. Applied trail.
Four other body fragments.

Item no 113
CLS Unstratified; 26 x 7mm; L.Blue (see
Fig 7)
Funnel series. Rounded rim. Rim thickness
2.5mm. Estimated diameter 100mm.
Outsplayed and slightly inturned. Decorated
with reticella rod containing opaque white
spirals applied to lip of rim.

Item no 114
CLS.A Pit 64 Layer 3; 30 x 13mm; L.Blue
Funnel series. Tubular rim without cavity.
Rim thickness 3mm. Estimated diameter
100mm. Slightly outsplayed and inturned.

Item no 115
CLS.A Pit 64 Layer 3; 32 x 15mm; L.Green
(see Fig 12)
Funnel series. Base fragment. Showing part
of pontil mark and wad. Mark diameter
11mm.

Item no 116
Pit 70; 42 x 30mm; L.Blue (see Fig 8)
Funnel series. Rounded rim. Rim thickness
2.5mm. Estimated diameter 100mm. Slightly
outsplayed and inturned.

Item no 117
Pit 70; 37 x 30mm; Green (see Plate 6 and
Fig 15)
Other vessel type. Pushed base showing
termination of 7 decayed trails, possibly
reticella. Some dark streaking in metal.
Small jar or flask.

Item no 118
Pit 70; 15 x 9mm; L.Blue
Decorated, non-diagnostic. Applied arcaded
trail and dark streaking within metal. Two
associated body fragments.

Item no 119
Pit 70; 26 x 20 x 2mm; L.Green

Item no 120
Pit 70; 17 x 15 x 1mm; L.Blue
Four associated body fragments.

SOU 40

Item no 10
Pit 121 SE Layer 1; 28 x 14mm; L.Blue
Funnel series. Tubular rim. Rim thickness
4.5mm. Estimated diameter 90mm. Slightly
outsplayed.

Item no 11
Pit 121 SE Layer 2; 19 x 15 x 8mm; L.Blue
Other vessel type. Probably from base.

SOU 85

Item no 15
Bevois St Redev; 10 x 5mm; L.Blue
Funnel series. Tubular rim. Rim thickness
3.5mm. Slightly outsplayed.

SOU 99

Item no 10
Context 606; 10 x 5 x 1mm; L.Blue

Item no 21
Context 244; 24 x 19mm; L.Blue
Funnel series. From near base of vessel.
Some iridescence.

Item no 32
Context 284; 35 x 28mm; L.Blue
Funnel series. From near base of vessel.
Probably large early form.

Item no 52
Context 319; 22 x 19mm; Opaque dark/light
Red
Decorated, non-diagnostic. From near base
of vessel. Some iridescence. Striated.

Item no 53
Context 303; 25 x 14 x 1mm; Colourless
Some iridescence.

Item no 54
Context 538; 11 x 10 x 3mm; L.Blue

Item no 55
Context 547; 20 x 13mm; L.Blue

Decorated, non-diagnostic. Red clouding in
metal. Some iridescence.

Item no 56
Context 551; 23 x 13mm; L.Blue
Funnel series. Tubular rim. Rim thickness
4.5mm. Estimated diameter 110 mm. Slightly
outsplayed and flattened on inside.

Item no 67
Context 24; 19 x 16mm; Opaque dark/light
Red
Decorated, non-diagnostic. Some
iridescence. Striated.

Item no 68
Context 59; 9 x 6mm; Opaque dark/light Red
Decorated, non-diagnostic. Red clouding in
metal. Some iridescence. Striated.

Item no 69
Context 429; 14 x 7 x 1mm; L.Blue (see
Plate 5)
Some iridescence.

Item no 96
Context 556; 25 x 22mm; Bright Green (see
Plate 5)
Decorated, non-diagnostic. Decorated with
dark horizontal streaking within metal.
Pronounced funnel curvature. Four
associated fragments.

Item no 112
Context 604; 81 x 53mm; L.Blue (see
Fig 10)
Decorated, non-diagnostic. Decorated with
applied arcaded trails and dark streaking in
metal. Parts of trails hollow. Probably early
form of funnel series. One associated
fragment.

Item no 113
Context 286; 20 x 20mm; L.Blue (see Fig
13)
Other vessel type. From pushed base of jar
form. Possible perforation in vessel base.
Some iridescence.

Item no 116
Context 608; 22 x 21mm; L.Blue
Funnel series. From near base of vessel.
Some iridescence.

Item no 117
Context 519; 43 x 23mm; Opaque.
Non-durable fragment. Heavily weathered.

Item no 127
Context 281; 18 x 12 x 1mm; L.Blue
Some iridescence.

Item no 135
Context 672; 17 x 10mm; L.Blue
Funnel series. Tubular rim. Rim thickness
6.5mm. Slightly outsplayed.

Item no 136
Context 136; 16 x 10 x 1mm; L.Blue
Some iridescence.

Item no 154
Context 667; 19 x 11mm; L.Blue
Decorated, non-diagnostic. Red clouding in
metal. Some iridescence.

Item no 162
Context 222; 23 x 8mm; L.Green
Funnel series. Tubular rim. Rim thickness
3.5mm. Estimated diameter 110mm. Slightly
outsplayed and flattened on inside. Some
iridescence.

Item no 194
Context 241; 13 x 12 x 1mm; L.Blue
Some iridescence.

Item no 229
Context 672; 24 x 15mm; L.Blue
Funnel series. From near base of vessel.
Some iridescence.

Item no 230
Context 519; 24 x 12mm; Opaque
Non-durable fragment. Flat fragment (core
only). Heavily weathered.

SOU 169

Item no 5
T1 C8423; 18 x 15 x 2mms; L.Blue
Lower body.

Item no 13
T1 C8409; 19 x 16mm; L.Blue (see Plate 4
and Fig 9)
Funnel series. Rounded rim. Rim thickness
2.5mm. Estimated diameter 100mm. Slightly
outsplayed and inturned. Decorated with
marvered horizontal opaque yellow trail on
exterior.

Item no 22
T2 C8468; 13 x 10mm; L.Green
Funnel series. Rounded rim. Rim thickness
2mm. Slightly outsplayed.

Item no 26
T1 C8411; 9 x 7 x 1mm; L.Blue

Item no 27
T1 C8426; 15 x 11mm; L.Blue
Funnel series. Tubular rim. Rim thickness
4mm. Slightly outsplayed.

Item no 29
T1 C8419; 17 x 11 x 1mm; L.Blue

Item no 41
T2 8544; 36 x 16mm; L.Blue (see Fig 6)
Funnel series. Tubular rim without cavity.
Rim thickness 3.5mm. Estimated diameter
100mm. Slightly outsplayed and inturned.

Item no 66
T2 C8463; 34 x 13mm; L.Blue (see Fig 4)
Funnel series. Tubular rim. Rim thickness
3.5mm. Estimated diameter 90mm.
Smoothed on inside and slightly outsplayed.

Item no 71
T1 C8419; 9 x 4 x 1mm; L.Blue

Item no 74
T2 C8558; 27 (diameter) x 22mm; L.Blue
(see Fig 12)
Funnel series. From near base.

Item no 85
T1 C8439; 13 x 9 x 1mm; L.Blue

Item no 91
T2 C8561; 14 x 10 x 1mm; L.Blue

Item no 111
T2 C8588; 22 x 10mm; L.Blue
Funnel series. Tubular rim without cavity.
Rim thickness 4mm. Estimated diameter
120mm. Slightly outsplayed.

Item no 115
T1 C8428; 11 x 8 x 1mm; Colourless

Item no 126
TC C8669; 20 x 17 x 1.5mm; L.Blue

Item no 132
T2 C8672; 37 x 19mm; L.Blue (see Plate 5
and Fig 17)
Decorated, non-diagnostic. Applied arcaded
trail 4mm wide containing dark streaking.

Item no 133
T2 C8659; 25 x 20 x 2.5mm; L.Green
Lower body.

Item no 147
T1 C8634; 58 x 26mm; Green (see Fig 14)
Other vessel type. Fragment of folded rim.
Rim thickness 4.5mm. Estimated diameter
80mm. Smoothed on inside. Decorated with
horizontal opaque yellow marvered flashes.
Flask or jar form.

Item no 157
T2 C8548; 9 x 8 x 2.5mm; L.Blue

Item no 159
T1 C8616; 37 x 15mm; L.Green
Funnel series. Tubular rim. Rim thickness
4mms. Estimated diameter 90mm. Slightly
outsplayed.

Item no 176
T1 C8641; 26 x 17mm; Blue (see Fig 13)
Other vessel type. Decorated with opaque
white marvered trails (combed?). Rounded
vessel.

Item no 181
T2 C8600; 15 x 13 x 1.5mm; L.Blue
Lower body.

Item no 182
T2 C8600; 13 x 8 x 1mm; L.Blue

Item no 183
T2 C8600; 15 x 8mm; L.Green
Funnel series. Tubular rim. Rim thickness
3mm. Slightly outsplayed.

Item no 185
T2 C8721; 8 x 7 x 1mm; L.Blue

Item no 186
T2 C8600; 22 x 18mm; L.Blue
Funnel series. Rounded rim. Rim thickness
1.5mm. Estimated diameter 120mm. Slightly
outsplayed. Two body fragments.

Item no 187
T2 C8600; 22 x 12mm; L.Green
Funnel series. Rounded rim. Rim thickness
2.5mm. Estimated diameter 110mm. Slightly
outsplayed and inturned.

Item no 208
T2 C8706; 14 x 10 x 1mm; L.Blue
One other body fragment.

Item no 212
T1 C8641; 28 x 19 x 4mm; Opaque
Non-durable fragment. Internal
decomposition. One associated fragment.

Item no 216
T1 C8419; 22 x 8mm; L.Green
Funnel series. Tubular rim. Rim thickness
4mm. Estimated diameter 100mm. Slightly
outsplayed.

Item no 226
T2 C8847; 14 x 10 x 1mm; L.Blue
Two other body fragments.

Item no 229
Unknown; 34 x 23 x 1mm; L.Blue
Splayed form. One associated body
fragment.

Item no 230
T2 C8600; 36 x 18mm; L.Green
Funnel series. Rounded rim. Rim thickness
3.5mm. Estimated diameter 100mm. Slightly
outsplayed and inturned. One associated rim
fragment and two body sherds.

Item no 231
T2 C8695; 13 x 13 x 1mm; L.Blue

Item no 233
T2 C8736; 24 x 14 x 1mm; L.Blue

Item no 237
T1 C8641; L.Blue
Bead. Circular of diameter 9mm, and
thickness 3mm. Diameter of perforation
3mm. Dark streaking within metal.

Item no 242
T2 C8736; 19 x 14mm; L.Green
Decorated, non-diagnostic. Applied trail
containing dark streaking.

Item no 243
T1 C8619; 15 x 12mm; L.Blue
Decorated, non-diagnostic. Twisted
decoration.

Item no 255
T2 C8736; 12 x 11 x 2mm; L.Blue

Item no 299
T1 C9856; 8 x 7 x 1mm; L.Blue

Item no 309
T1 C8967; 25 x 14mm; L.Green
Funnel series. Tubular rim without cavity.
Rim thickness 4mm. Estimated diameter
110mm. Slightly outsplayed.

Item no 314
T2 C8600; 21 x 10mm; L.Blue
Funnel series. Rounded rim. Rim thickness
2mm. Estimated diameter 100mm. Slightly
outsplayed and inturned. One associated rim
fragment and two body fragments.

Item no 316
T1 C8762; 13 x 10mm; L.Blue
Decorated, non-diagnostic. Traces of opaque
yellow marvered trail.

Item no 323
T1 C9885; 12 x 10 x 1mm; Colourless

Item no 329
T1 C8641; 34 x 14 x 4mm; Opaque
Non-durable fragment. Internal
decomposition. Four associated fragments.

Item no 335
T2 9958; 31 x 10mm; L.Green
Funnel series. Rounded rim. Rim thickness
3mm. Estimated diameter 100mm. Slightly
outsplayed. Rim surmounted by applied
reticella rod containing opaque white spirals.

Item no 342
T1 C8644; 15 x 11mm; L.Green
Funnel series. Tubular rim without cavity.
Rim thickness 3mm. Estimated diameter
100mm. Slightly outsplayed.

Item no 343
T1 C9891; 9 x 6 x 1mm; L.Blue

Item no 353
T2 10061; 10 x 7mm; L.Blue
Funnel series. Tubular rim without cavity.
Rim thickness 2.5mm. Slightly outsplayed.

Item no 354
T1 C9883; 52 x 31 x 29mm;
Waster. Stone fragment showing green
vitreous deposit.

Item no 398
T1 C8862; 13 x 13mm; L.Blue (see Plate 4
and Fig 9)
Funnel series. Rounded rim. Rim thickness
2.5mm. Estimated diameter 120mm. Slightly
outsplayed and inturned. Decorated with
marvered horizontal opaque yellow trails on
exterior.

Item no 401
T2 C9960 ; 19 x 17 x 2mm; L.Blue

Item no 411
T1 1027; 11 x 3 x 1mm; L.Green

Item no 412
T2 C9907; 28 x 8mm; L.Blue
Funnel series. Tubular rim. Rim thickness
5mm. Estimated diameter 100mm. Smoothed
on inside and slightly outsplayed.

Item no 440
T2 C10177; 27 x 17mm; L.Blue (see Fig 11)
Funnel series. Base fragment. Showing pontil
mark. Base diameter 17mm. Mark diameter
14mm. Applied vertical trail.

Item no 447
T1 8419; 10 x 8 x 1.5mm; L.Blue

Item no 455
T1 C10027; 26 x 24mm; L.Blue
Other vessel type. Pronounced carination in
body.

Item no 461
T1 C10224; 17 x 5 x 1.5mm; L.Blue

Item no 465
T1 8866; 18 x 5 x 1.5mm; L.Blue

Item no 467
T1 C10230; 17 x 14 x 1mm; L.Green
Two associated body fragments.

Item no 468
T1 10230; 14 x 13mm; L.Blue (see Plate 2
and Fig 8)
Funnel series. Rounded rim. Rim thickness
1.5mm. Estimated diameter 110mm. Slightly
outsplayed and inturned. Decorated with
reticella rod containing opaque white spirals
applied to lip of rim.

Item no 473
T1 C8643; 16 x 16mm; L.Green
Funnel series. Rounded rim. Rim thickness
1.5mm. Estimated diameter 110mm. Slightly
outsplayed.

Item no 479
T2 8561; 23 x 13 x 1mm; L.Blue

Item no 484
T1 10027; 16 x 15mm; L.Blue
Funnel series. Tubular rim. Rim thickness
4mm. Smoothed on inside and slightly
outsplayed.

Item no 495
Unknown; 24 x 16mm; Dark Blue/Colourless
(see Fig 6)
Funnel series. Tubular rim without cavity.
Rim thickness 2mm. Rim formed in three
stages using alternate colourless and dark
blue bands.

Item no 496
T1 C10027; 18 x 11 x 1mm; L.Blue

Item no 499
T2 C8561; 13 x 7 x 1mm; L.Blue

Item no 500
T2 C9920; 21 x 10mm; Dark Green
Decorated, non-diagnostic.

Item no 505
T1 C9873; 10 x 9 x 1mm; L.Green
One associated fragment.

Item no 506
T2 C10274; 8 x 7 x 1mm; L.Blue

Item no 522
T2 C8457; 23 x 7 x 1mm; L.Green

Item no 525
T1 C10205; 17 x 14mm; L.Blue (see Plate 4

and Fig 5)
Funnel series. Tubular rim. Rim thickness
5mm. Slightly outsplayed. Containing some
red streaking.

Item no 535
T1 C8421; 12 x 10 x 1mm; L.Green

Item no 551
T1 C8622; 14 x 11 x 1mm; L.Blue

Item no 553
T1 C10310; 46 x 16mm; L.Blue (see Plate 3
and Fig 6)
Funnel series. Tubular rim without cavity.
Rim thickness 4mm. Estimated diameter
110mm. Slightly outsplayed.

Item no 554
T2 10361; 23 x 8mm; L.Blue
Decorated, non-diagnostic. Applied arcaded
trail 5mm wide.

Item no 556
T2 C10274; 14 x 8 x 1mm; L.Blue

Item no 569
T2 C10383; 40 x 22mm; L.Blue
Funnel series. Tubular rim. Rim thickness
4mm. Estimated diameter 110mm. Smoothed
on inside and slightly outsplayed.

Item no 581
T1 C10238; 12 x 10mm; L.Blue
Decorated, non-diagnostic. Applied arcaded
trail 6mm wide.

Item no 608
T1 C10203; 9 x 3 x 1mm; L.Blue

Item no 623
T2 C10383; 19 x 10 x 1mm; L.Blue

Item no 628
T1 C10101; 9 x 7 x 1mm; L.Blue

Item no 629
T1 C10328; 11 x 7 x 1mm; L.Blue

Item no 637
T1 10469; 22 x 12mm; L.Blue
Funnel series. Tubular rim. Rim thickness
4.5mm. Estimated diameter 120mm. Slightly
outsplayed.

Item no 638
T2 C10380; 10 x 9 x 1mm; L.Green

Item no 649
T1 C8419; 29 x 20 x 18mm;
Waster. Stone fragment showing green
vitreous deposit.

Item no 656
T2 8822; 14 x 8 x 1mm; L.Blue

Item no 664
T1 10481; 14 x 12mm; L.Green
Funnel series. Tubular rim without cavity.
Rim thickness 2mm. Slightly outsplayed.

Item no 674
T2 C10527; 14 x 9 x 1mm; L.Blue

Item no 676
T1 10486; 17 x 11mm; L.Blue
Decorated, non-diagnostic. Applied arcaded trail 4mm wide. Two other associated body fragments.

Item no 681
T1 10486; 29 x 15 x 1mm; L.Blue

Item no 682
T2 10594; 23 x 22 x 1mm; L.Blue

Item no 683
T1 10486; 31 x 26mm; L.Green
Funnel series. Rounded rim. Rim thickness 2.5mm. Estimated diameter 100mm. Slightly outsplayed. Evidence of applied trail.

Item no 695
T2 10676; 21 x 6 x 2mm; L.Green
Lower body.

Item no 709
T2 C10403; 35 x 11mm; L.Blue (see Fig 6)
Funnel series. Tubular rim without cavity. Rim thickness 3mm. Estimated diameter 110mm. Smoothed on inside.

Item no 730
T1 C8409; 14 x 10 x 1mm; L.Green

Item no 753
T1 C10237; 85 x 45mm;
Waster. Base fragment of hard fired pottery vessel, wall thickness 10mm. Green vitreous deposits and concretions on exterior.

Item no 770
T1 C10237; 30 x 18 x 3mm; Dark Green (see Plate 8 and Fig 13)
Other vessel type. Pushed base fragment with central hole of diameter 6mm surrounded by concentric opaque yellow marvered trails. Flask or jar.

Item no 788
T1 C11409; 19 x 11 x 1mm; L.Blue
Decorated, non-diagnostic. Applied trail. One other body fragment.

Item no 801
T2 10971; 19 x 16mm; L.Blue
Funnel series. Tubular rim without cavity. Rim thickness 4mm. Estimated diameter 110mm. Slightly outsplayed.

Item no 807
T1 1019; 13 x 13mm; L.Blue
Decorated, non-diagnostic. Dark streaking within metal. One associated body fragment.

Item no 813
T2 11101; 20 x 7mm; L.Green
Decorated, non-diagnostic. Termination of applied trail containing darker streaking. One associated body fragment.

Item no 814
T1 10328; 14 x 12mm; L.Green

Funnel series. Rounded rim. Rim thickness 2.5mm. Estimated diameter 110mm. Slightly outsplayed.

Item no 825
T2 8537; 26 x 12mm; L.Blue
Funnel series. Tubular rim. Rim thickness 6mm. Estimated diameter 110mm. Slightly outsplayed.

Item no 826
T1 C11017; 32 x 14mm; L.Green (see Fig 4)
Funnel series. Tubular rim. Rim thickness 3mm. Estimated diameter 90mm. Slightly outsplayed.

Item no 834
T1 11023; 7 x 2 x 1mm; L.Blue

Item no 837
T1 C8889; 85 x 45mm;
Waster. Base fragment of hard fired pottery vessel with wall thickness 9mm. Green vitreous deposit on interior. Green vitreous deposits and concretions on exterior.

Item no 839
T2 10987; 25 x 24 x 1mm; L.Blue
Splayed.

Item no 840
T2 11153; 39 x 24 x 1mm; L.Blue
Splayed.

Item no 841
T2 11156; 32 x 13mm; L.Blue
Funnel series. Tubular rim. Rim thickness 4mm. Estimated diameter 100mm. Smoothed on inside and slightly outsplayed.

Item no 858
T1 10778; 16 x 10 x 1mm; L.Blue
Item no 867
T2 C11138; 18 x 8 x 2mm; L.Green

Item no 875
T2 C11256; 25 x 15mm; L.Blue
Funnel series. Rounded rim. Rim thickness 2.5mm. Estimated diameter 100mm. Slightly outsplayed.

Item no 880
T1 11206; 17 x 13mm; L.Blue (see Plate 4 and Fig 7)
Funnel series. Rounded rim. Rim thickness 2.5mm. Estimated diameter 110mm. Slightly outsplayed and inturned. Decorated with marvered horizontal opaque yellow trails on exterior.

Item no 889
T2 11289; 43 x 36mm; Green (see Plate 6 and Fig 15)
Other vessel type. Pushed base showing pontil wad. Intermittent opaque yellow trail concentric to wad on underside of vessel. May have been intended as a dot-dash design. Small flask/jar form.

Item no 897
T1 10771; 14 x 8 x 1mm; Dark Green

Item no 934
T2 11301; 17 x 11mm; L.Blue
Decorated, non-diagnostic. Applied trail.

Item no 948
T2 C11318; 13 x 8mm; L.Blue
Funnel series. Rounded rim. Rim thickness 3mm. Slightly outsplayed.

Item no 951
T2 11156; 17 x 13 x 1mm; L.Blue

Item no 971
T2 C11339; 18 x 13mm;
Waster. Fragment of hard fired pottery showing green vitreous deposit.

Item no 981
T1 C8633; 12 x 5 x 2mm; L.Blue

Item no 990
T1 C11047; 22 x 16mm; Brown/Yellow (see Plate 5 and Fig 13)
Other vessel type. Probably from near rim of tall beaker. Decorated with horizontal opaque yellow marvered trails.

Item no 995
T1 C10464; 14 x 11 x 2mm; L.Green

Item no 1007
T1 C11409; 33 x 26mm; L.Green (see Plate 7 and Fig 11)
Funnel series. Base fragment. Showing pontil mark. Base diameter 18mm. Mark diameter 13mm.

Item no 1009
T2 11339; 20 x 15mm; L.Blue
Funnel series. Tubular rim without cavity. Rim thickness 3mm. Estimated diameter 110mm. Slightly outsplayed. One associated body fragment and one other body fragment.

Item no 1030
T1 11442; 18 x 16mm; L.Blue
Decorated, non-diagnostic. Horizontal opaque yellow marvered trails.

Item no 1033
T2 8849; 24 x 11mm; L.Blue
Funnel series. Tubular rim. Rim thickness 4mm. Estimated diameter 120mm. Smoothed on inside and slightly outsplayed.

Item no 1057
T1 C11444; 10 x 6mm; Dark Green
Decorated, non-diagnostic. Opaque yellow marvered trail.

Item no 1063
T2 11510; 18 x 14mm; L.Green (see Fig 13)
Other vessel type. Pronounced carination in body.

Item no 1124
T1 C11021; 7 x 5 x 1.5mm; L.Blue

Item no 1150
T1 C10219; 10 x 4 x 1mm; L.Blue

Item no 1152
T1 C8641; 24 x 17mm; L.Blue (see Fig 4)
Funnel series. Tubular rim. Rim thickness
3.5mm. Estimated diameter 110mm.
Smoothed on inside and slightly outsplayed.
Rim surmounted by applied reticella rod
containing opaque white spiral.

Item no 1154
T2 C8600; 9 x 7 x 1mm; L.Green

Item no 1185
T1 C8447; 14 x 13mm; L.Blue (see Plate 1
and Fig 14)
Other vessel type. Band of five applied
reticella rods containing opaque white
spirals. Probably bowl form.

Item no 1218
T1 C8867; 30 x 8mm; L.Green
Funnel series. Tubular rim. Rim thickness
3.5mm. Estimated diameter 100mm. Slightly
outsplayed.

Item no 1219
T1 C8867; 15 x 9 x 1mm; L.Green
One other associated fragment.

Item no 1228
T1 C8867; 11 x 6 x 1mm; L.Green

Item no 1230
T1 C11606; 10 x 9 x 1mm; L.Blue

Item no 1238
T1 11861; 13 x 8mm; L.Blue
Decorated, non-diagnostic. Horizontal
opaque yellow marvered trail.

Item no 1300
T3 C11954; 13 x 11mm; Green (see Fig 14)
Other vessel type. Rounded rim. Rim
thickness 3mm. Decorated with horizontal
opaque white marvered trails. Probable bowl
form.

Item no 1314
T3 C11957; 27 x 12mm; L.Blue
Funnel series. Base fragment. Showing pontil
mark.

Item no 1336
T1 12133; 9 x 7mm; L.Blue
Funnel series. Rounded rim. Rim thickness
2mm. Slightly outsplayed and inturned. Rim
surmounted by applied reticella rod
containing opaque white spiral.

Item no 1349
T1 C12140; 12 x 8mm; Dark Green
Other vessel type. Pronounced carination in
body.

Item no 1351
T1 C12102; 12 x 6mm; Blue
Decorated, non-diagnostic. Traces of
horizontal opaque white marvered trails.

Item no 1356
T1 C12111; 12 x 8mm; Brown/Yellow

Decorated, non-diagnostic. Twisted
decoration.

Item no 1359
T1 C8409; 16 x 8 x 1mm; L.Blue

Item no 1370
T1 C12111; 10 x 8 x 1mm; L.Blue

Item no 1375
T1 12157; 19 x 18mm; Green/Yellow
Decorated, non-diagnostic.

Item no 1379
T1 C8409; Opaque pink
Bead. Circular of diameter 2.5mm and width
1mm. Diameter of perforation 1mm.
Probable spacer.

Item no 1390
T1 12133; 29 x 22mm; L.Blue (see Plate 5)
Decorated, non-diagnostic. Red streaking
within metal. One associated fragment.

Item no 1402
T3 11955; 13 x 12mm; L.Blue (see Plate 2
and Fig 8)
Funnel series. Rounded rim. Rim thickness
1.5mm. Estimated diameter 120mm. Slightly
outsplayed and inturned. Rim surmounted by
applied reticella rod containing opaque white
spiral.

Item no 1410
T1 C12111; 16 x 4 x 1mm; L.Blue

Item no 1413
T1 C8419; 22 x 17 x 2.5mm; L.Blue
Lower body.

Item no 1419
T1 12133; 18 x 9 x 1mm; L.Blue

Item no 1428
T2 C11662; 55 x 44 x 32mm;
Waster. Hard fired clay or stone showing
green vitreous deposit.

Item no 1454
T2 C12094; 39 x 14 x 1mm; L.Green
Splayed.

Item no 1462
T3 C11970; 12 x 7 x 1mm. L.Blue

Item no 1468
T1 12190; 12 x 7 x 1mm; L.Green

Item no 1472
T1 C12190; 15 x 11 x 1mm; L.Green

Item no 1473
T1 C8765; 23 x 11mm; L.Blue
Funnel series. Tubular rim. Rim thickness
4mm. Estimated diameter 110mm. Slightly
outsplayed.

Item no 1474
T1 C12190; 15 x 10mm; Clouded red
Decorated, non-diagnostic. Evidence of
former marvered trails.

Item no 1483
T3 11961; 20 x 14mm; L.Green (see Fig 11)
Funnel series. Base fragment. Showing pontil
mark. Base diameter 15mm. Mark diameter
12mm.

Item no 1551
T2 Surface; 18 x 14 x 1.5mm; L.Blue

Item no 1567
T3 C11977; 14 x 7 x 1mm; L.Green

Item no 1573
T3 C11982; 20 x 8 x 1mm; L.Blue

Item no 1592
T1 11625; 16 x 13 x 1.5mm; L.Green

Item no 1601
T1 C12200; 11 x 8mm; Green/Yellow
Decorated, non-diagnostic. Horizontal
opaque yellow marvered trails.

Item no 1614
T1 11634; 19 x 8mm; L.Blue
Decorated, non-diagnostic. Horizontal
opaque yellow marvered trails.

Item no 1615
T1 C12200; 15 x 5mm; Blue
Decorated, non-diagnostic. Opaque white
marvered trails. Combed?

Item no 1622
T1 C11634; 20 x 17 x 1.5mm; L.Blue
Two associated body fragments.

Item no 1628
T1 C12200; 16 x 10mm; L.Green
Funnel series. Tubular rim without cavity.
Rim thickness 3mm. Estimated diameter
100mm. Slightly outsplayed.

Item no 1629
T3 C11986; 12 x 11 x 1mm; L.Blue

Item no 1630
T3 11976; 10 x 7 x 1mm; Colourless

Item no 1654
T1 C12200; 34 x 26mm; Blue (see Plate 5
and Fig 15)
Other vessel type. Probably from bowl form
decorated with opaque white combed
marvered trails.

Item no 1662
T1 12271; 21 x 12mm; L.Blue (see Plate 2
and Fig 8)
Funnel series. Rounded rim. Rim thickness
2mm. Estimated diameter 110mm. Slightly
outsplayed and inturned. Rim surmounted by
(imperfect) applied reticella rod containing
opaque white spirals.

Item no 1666
T1 C12271; 10 x 6mm; L.Blue
Funnel series. Tubular rim. Rim thickness
3mm. Slightly outsplayed.

Item no 1672
T1 C12271; 9 x 8mm; L.Blue

Decorated, non-diagnostic. Applied reticella rod containing opaque white spirals.

Item no 1699
Unstratified; 24 x 12mm; L.Green
Funnel series. Base fragment. Base diameter 15mm. Mark diameter 15mm.

Item no 1748
T3 C11987; 14 x 13mm; Opaque dark/light Red
Decorated, non-diagnostic. Striated with dark and white streaks.

Item no 1755
T1 12283; 5 x 2 x 1mm; L.Blue

Item no 1807
T3 11988; 10 x 8mm; Colourless
Funnel series. Tubular rim without cavity. Rim thickness 3mm. Slightly outsplayed.

Item no 1810
T3 12303; 22 x 15mm; Green
Decorated, non-diagnostic. Termination of applied trail.

Item no 1817
T3 C12335; 48 x 31 x 30mm;
Waster. Fired clay (brick like) showing green vitreous deposit on face.

Item no 1822
T3 12337; 16 x 9mm; L.Blue
Funnel series. Tubular rim. Rim thickness 5.5mm. Smoothed on inside.

Item no 1834
T3 C11961; 32 x 12mm; L.Green
Funnel series. Tubular rim. Rim thickness 4.5mm. Estimated diameter 100mm. Smoothed on inside and slightly outsplayed.

Item no 1845
T3 C12303; 31 x 16 x 1mm; L.Green
Splayed form.

Item no 1864
T3 12355; 19 x 4mm; L.Green
Funnel series. Tubular rim without cavity. Rim thickness 2.5mm. Slightly outsplayed.

Item no 1868
T3 11967; 19 x 10 x 2mm; L.Blue

Item no 1872
T3 12356; 16 x 12 x 1.5mm; L.Green

Item no 1890
T3 12349; 6 x 5 x 1.5mm; L.Green

Item no 1899
T3 11952; 16 x 12 x 2mm; Colourless
Burnt.

Item no 1906
T3 11995; 27 x 15mm; L.Green (see Fig 17)
Decorated, non-diagnostic. Applied irregular trail.

Item no 1908
T3 12356; 13 x 10mm; L.Green

Funnel series. Rounded rim. Rim thickness 2.5mm. Slightly outsplayed and inturned.

Item no 1935
T3 C12324; 20 x 19 x 2mm; L.Green
Lower body.

Item no 1936
T3 12321; 17 x 6 x 1mm; L.Green

Item no 1937
T3 12362; 16 x 13 x 1mm; L.Green

Item no 1941
T1 C10212; 11 x 8 x 1mm; L.Blue

Item no 1942
T3 C12339; 26 x 16mm; L.Green
Funnel series. Tubular rim. Rim thickness 3.5mm. Estimated diameter 100mm. Slightly outsplayed.

Item no 1956
T3 C11995; 17 x 11 x 1mm; L.Blue

Item no 1959
T1 C8413; 33 x 14mm; L.Green
Funnel series. Tubular rim. Rim thickness 3.5mm. Estimated diameter 100mm. Smoothed on inside and slightly outsplayed.

Item no 1976
T3 12386; 20 x 12 x 1mm; L.Blue

Item no 1979
T1 C10222; 17 x 11 x 1.5mm; L.Green

Item no 1981
T1 C8623; 13 x 5 x 1.5mm; L.Blue

Item no 1982
T3 C12388; 30 x 18mm; L.Blue
Funnel series. Rounded rim. Rim thickness 2mm. Slightly outsplayed. Rim surmounted by applied reticella rod containing opaque white spiral.

Item no 1989
T3 C12377; 10 x 9 x 1.5mm; L.Blue

Item no 2020
T1 C12300; 36 x 30mm; L.Blue (see Fig 17)
Decorated, non-diagnostic. Arcaded trail containing dark streaking.

Item no 2028
T3 12377; 15 x 11 x 1mm; L.Blue

Item no 2047
T3 12321; 14 x 7 x 1.5mm; L.Blue

Item no 2048
T1 12298; 20 x 8 x 1.5mm; L.Blue

Item no 2066
T3 C12378; 36 x 20mm; L.Green
Funnel series. Rounded rim. Rim thickness 2mm. Estimated diameter 100mm. Slightly outsplayed.

Item no 2093
T3 C12351; 9 x 4 x 1mm; L.Green

Item no 2094
T1 C10782; 18 x 16 x 2.5mm; L.Blue
Funnel series. From near to base of vessel.

Item no 2095
T3 C12470; 14 x 14mm; L.Green
Funnel series. Rounded rim. Rim thickness 2mm. Estimated diameter 120mm. Slightly outsplayed and inturned.

Item no 2096
T3 C12476; 13 x 4mm; Blue
Decorated, non-diagnostic. Traces of opaque yellow marvered trail.

Item no 2097
T1 C12298; 26 x 20mm; L.Blue
Decorated, non-diagnostic. Evidence of applied reticella rod containing opaque yellow spirals.

Item no 2101
T3 12475; 10 x 8 x 1mm; L.Blue

Item no 2131
T3 C12357; 17 x 17 x 1mm; L.Blue

Item no 2136
T3 C12468; 27 x 17mm; Opaque Dark (see Plate 8 and Fig 14)
Other vessel type. Rounded rim. Rim thickness 3.5mm. Estimated diameter 60mm. Decorated with horizontal opaque yellow marvered trails. Small flask or jar.

Item no 2182
T3 C12487; 17 x 15mm; L.Blue
Funnel series. Rounded rim. Rim thickness 2mm. Estimated diameter 110mm. Slightly outsplayed.

Item no 2200
T1 C10310; 33 x 17 x 1mm; L.Blue
Lower body.

Item no 2201
T3 C12515; 12 x 11 x 1mm; L.Green

Item no 2202
T1 C12200; 7 x 5 x 1mm; L.Green

Item no 2205
T3 C12346; 17 x 11mm; L.Green
Funnel series. Tubular rim. Rim thickness 4mm. Slightly outsplayed.

Item no 2209
T1 8852; 16 x 13 x 3.5mm; L.Blue
Funnel series. From near to base of vessel.

Item no 2210
T1 C10310; 20 x 6 x 1mm; L.Blue

Item no 2211
T1 8852; 11 x 10mm; L.Green
Funnel series. Tubular rim. Rim thickness 3mm. Slightly outsplayed.

Item no 2224
T3 12523; 16 x 15 x 1mm; L.Blue

Item no 2243
T3 12527; 30 x 15mm; L.Blue (see Fig 5)
Funnel series. Tubular rim. Rim thickness
3mm. Estimated diameter 100mm. Smoothed
on inside and slightly outsplayed. Containing
some dark red streaking.

Item no 2253
T3 C12528; 12 x 12 x 1mm; L.Blue

Item no 2272
T3 12528; 52 x 8mm; L.Blue
Funnel series. Tubular rim. Rim thickness
4mm. Estimated diameter 100mm. Smoothed
on inside and slightly outsplayed.

Item no 2314
T3 12351; 13 x 8 x 1mm; L.Blue

Item no 2324
T3 C12470; 31 x 12 x 1mm; L.Green

Item no 2328
T1 10467; 42 x 27mm; L.Green (see Fig 5)
Funnel series. Tubular rim. Rim thickness
3.5mm. Estimated diameter 90mm. Slightly
outsplayed. Rim surmounted by applied
reticella rod containing opaque white spirals.

Item no 2335
T3 C12387; 18 x 15 x 1mm; L.Green
Lower body.

Item no 2342
T3 C12388; 27 x 23 x 1.5mm; L.Blue

Item no 2384
T1 12743; 18 x 11mm; L.Blue
Decorated, non-diagnostic. Twisted
decoration. Red streaking within metal.

Item no 2385
T1 8875; 16 x 7 x 2mm; L.Green

Item no 2386
T1 C8419; 17 x 11 x 1mm; L.Blue

Item no 2406
T3 C12806; 17 x 15mm; L.Blue
Funnel series. Rounded rim. Rim thickness
2mm. Estimated diameter 120mm. Slightly
outsplayed.

Item no 2461
T1 C12404; 13 x 8mm; L.Blue
Funnel series. Rounded rim. Rim thickness
2.5mm. Slightly outsplayed and inturned.
Decorated with marvered horizontal opaque
yellow trail on exterior.

Item no 2466
T3 C12811; 10 x 6mm; Blue
Decorated, non-diagnostic.

Item no 2500
T1 C12301; 9 x 7mm; L.Blue
Other vessel type. Pronounced carination in
body.

Item no 2527
T3 C12840; 27 x 12 x 1mm; L.Blue

Item no 2541
T3 C12953; 15 x 6 x 1mm; L.Green

Item no 2564
T1 C8882; 10 x 9mm; Dark Green
Decorated, non-diagnostic. Dark streaking
within metal.

Item no 2577
T3 12987; 11 x 6 x 1mm; L.Blue

Item no 2582
T3 12987; 21 x 20mm; Green
Other vessel type. Rounded form, probable
bowl.

Item no 2593
T1 C10338; 23 x 16mm; L.Blue
Funnel series. Tubular rim. Rim thickness
4mm. Estimated diameter 110mm.
Smoothed on inside and slightly outsplayed.

Item no 2594
T1 C8447; 50 x 39 x 28mm;
Waster. Stone fragments showing green
vitreous deposit.

Item no 2598
T3 12339; 7 x 4 x 1mm; L.Blue

Item no 2640
T1 12401; 13 x 7mm; Dark Opaque
Decorated, non-diagnostic. Horizontal
opaque yellow marvered trail.

Item no 2654
T3 C11966; 17 x 15mm; L.Blue
Funnel series. Rounded rim. Rim thickness
1.5mm. Estimated diameter 100mm. Slightly
outsplayed.

Item no 2660
T3 C13010; 17 x 13mm; L.Blue
Funnel series. Rounded rim. Rim thickness
2.5mm. Estimated diameter 120mm. Slightly
outsplayed.

Item no 2726
T1 12888; Opaque Blue
Bead. 10 examples. Circular of diameter
2mm and thickness 1mm. Diameter of
perforation 1mm. Probable spacers.

Item no 2729
T1 C8419; Opaque Blue/Red/Green (see Fig
18)
Bead. 10 examples. Circular of diameter
2mm and thickness 1mm. Diameter of
perforation 1mm. Probable spacers. Various
colours.

Item no 2780
T1 C8419; 7 x 1 x 1mm; L.Green
Two associated body fragments.

Item no 2796
T3 C12385; 11 x 7 x 1mm; L.Blue

Item no 2801
T3 C13080; 36 x 16mm; L.Green (see Plate
2 and Fig 7)
Funnel series. Rounded rim. Rim thickness

2.5mm. Estimated diameter 110mm. Slightly
outsplayed and inturned. Rim surmounted by
applied reticella rod containing opaque white
spirals.

Item no 2814
T3 13080; 34 x 14 x 1mm; L.Blue

Item no 2820
T1 C11613; 62 x 15mm; L.Green (see Fig 4)
Funnel series. Tubular rim. Rim thickness
6mm. Estimated diameter 120mm. Smoothed
on inside and slightly outsplayed.

Item no 2822
T1 C8419; Blue
Bead. Tubular of length 3mm and diameter
3mm. Diameter of perforation 1mm.

Item no 2827
T1 C11628; 3 x 3 x 1.5mm; L.Blue

Item no 2840
T1 C11613; 31 x 14mm; Green (see Fig 4)
Funnel series. Tubular rim. Rim thickness
6.5mm. Estimated diameter 100mm. Slightly
outsplayed.

Item no 2842
T3 12370; 15 x 11mm; L.Blue
Funnel series. Tubular rim. Rim thickness
3mm. Slightly outsplayed.

Item no 2848
T3 C12828; 16 x 7mm; L.Blue
Funnel series. Tubular rim. Rim thickness
3.5mm. Smoothed on inside.

Item no 2866
T3 12000; 15 x 12mm; L.Blue
Decorated, non-diagnostic. Twisted
decoration.

Item no 2894
T3 13139; 16 x 10mm; Blue
Decorated, non-diagnostic.

Item no 2918
T1 C8778; 14 x 10mm; L.Blue
Funnel series. Rounded rim. Rim thickness
2mm. Slightly outsplayed and inturned.
Traces of marvered horizontal opaque yellow
trail on exterior.

Item no 2940
T3 13169; 10 x 9 x 1mm; L.Blue

Item no 2953
T3 C12908; 20 x 11 x 9mm; L.Green
Waster. Irregular fragment of glass.

Item no 2981
T3 12462; 7 x 5mm; L.Blue
Decorated, non-diagnostic. Applied reticella
rod containing opaque yellow spirals.

Item no 2999
T3 C13134; 28 x 15mm; Dark Brown (see
Plate 8 and Fig 17)
Decorated, non-diagnostic. Horizontal
opaque marvered trail.

Item no 3040
T1 13211; 23 x 14 x 1.5mm; L.Blue

Item no 3058
T1 10028; 26 x 13mm; Green (see Plate 4
and Fig 14)
Other vessel type. Fragment of tubular rim.
Rim folded outwards. Rim thickness 3.5mm.
Estimated diameter 110mm. Evidence of lost
horizontal marvered trail. Bowl or jar form.

Item no 3069
T1 C10028; 33 x 14mm; Green (see Fig 14)
Other vessel type. Fragment of Tubular rim.
Rim folded outwards leaving cavity. Rim
thickness 3.5mm. Estimated diameter
110mm. Evidence of lost horizontal
marvered trail. Bowl or jar form. Probably
same vessel as Item no 3058.

Item no 3073
T1 10338; 23 x 18mm; L.Blue
Funnel series. Rounded rim. Rim thickness
3mm. Estimated diameter 120mm. Slightly
outsplayed.

Item no 3086
T2 C12770; 27 x 5 x 1mm; L.Green

Item no 3087
T2 C12770; 12 x 4 x 1.5mm; L.Blue

Item no 3144
T2 12774; 15 x 7 x 1mm; L.Blue

Item no 3145
T2 12771; 11 x 8 x 1.5mm; L.Blue

Item no 3150
T3 13162; 5 x 5 x 1mm; L.Blue
Sliver. One associated fragment.

Item no 3165
T1 9882; 20 x 12mm; L.Green
Decorated, non-diagnostic. Twisted
decoration.

Item no 3170
T1 C12868; 3 x 1 x 1mm; L.Green

Item no 3171
T1 11628; 15 x 10mm; L.Blue
Decorated, non-diagnostic. Horizontal
opaque yellow marvered trails.

Item no 3175
T1 9883; 30 x 17mm; L.Green
Funnel series. Rounded rim. Rim thickness
3.5mm. Estimated diameter 100mm. Slightly
outsplayed.

Item no 3178
T3 C12305; 17 x 11 x 1.5mm; L.Green

Item no 3208
T3 C12462; 13 x 13 x 1mm; L.Blue

Item no 3279
T3 12462; 9 x 7 x 1mm; L.Blue

Item no 3325
T3 C12363; 23 x 9mm; L.Blue (see Fig 11)

Funnel series. Base fragment. Showing pontil
mark and wad. Mark diameter 13mm.

Item no 3326
T3 C12363; 20 x 14mm; L.Green
Decorated, non-diagnostic. Termination of
applied trail.

Item no 3335
T3 12362; 22 x 7mm; L.Green
Decorated, non-diagnostic. Applied arcaded
trail containing dark streaking.

Item no 3342
T3 12396; 12 x 10 x 1mm; L.Green

Item no 3343
T3 C12363; 14 x 8mm; L.Blue
Decorated, non-diagnostic. Applied trail.

Item no 3347
T3 12363; 27 x 25mm; L.Green
Funnel series. Tubular rim without cavity.
Rim thickness 3mm. Estimated diameter
90mm. Slightly outsplayed. One associated
body fragment.

Item no 3713
T1 C10015; L.Blue
Bead. Circular of diameter 3mm and
thickness 1mm. Diameter of perforation
1mm.

Item no 3776
T2 8466; 10 x 5 x 1mm; L.Green

Item no 3777
T2 8467; 11 x 8 x 1mm; L.Blue

Item no 3778
T2 8468; 18 x 15mm; L.Green
Funnel series. Rounded rim. Rim thickness
3mm. Slightly outsplayed and inturned.
Some evidence of lost marvered trailing.
Heat distorted.

Item no 3779
T2 C8468; 10 x 6 x 1mm; L.Green

Item no 3780
T2 C8468; 6 x 2 x 1mm; L.Green

Item no 3781
T2 8552; 6 x 4 x 1mm; L.Green

Item no 3782
T2 8555; 6 x 4 x 1mm; L.Blue

Item no 3783
T2 8545; 12 x 6 x 1mm; L.Blue
One other body fragment.

Item no 3784
T2 C8545; 6 x 5mm; Green
Decorated, non-diagnostic. Opaque yellow
marvered trail.

Item no 3785
T2 8557; 15 x 10 x 1mm; L.Green

Item no 3786
T2 8564; 2 x 1 x 1mm; L.Green
Some iridescence.

Item no 3787
T2 8569; 14 x 8mm; L.Green
Funnel series. Tubular rim. Rim thickness
2.5mm. Slightly outsplayed.

Item no 3788
T2 8574; 2 x 1 x 1mm; L.Green

Item no 3789
T2 8575; 6 x 5 x 1mms; L.Green
Two other body fragments.

Item no 3790
T2 8588; 7 x 1 x 1mm; Colourless

Item no 3791
T2 8679; 20 x 6 x 1mms; L.Green

Item no 3792
T1 8627; 2 x 2 x 1mm; L.Blue

Item no 3793
T2 8687; 9 x 7 x 1mm; L.Green

Item no 3794
T2 8688; 6 x 5 x 1mm; L.Blue

Item no 3795
T1 8647; 3 x 2 x 1mms; L.Green

Item no 3796
T2 8689/91; 6 x 4 x 1mm; L.Blue

Item no 3797
T2 C8736; 17 x 2 x 2mm; L.Blue
Two other body fragments.

Item no 3798
T1 8789; 2 x 1 x 1mm; Colourless

Item no 3799
T2 8835; 6 x 5 x 1mm; L.Green

Item no 3800
T2 8839; 16 x 5 x 1mm; L.Blue

Item no 3801
T2 8841; Amber
Waster. Droplets.

Item no 3802
T2 9701; 13 x 8 x 2mm; L.Green

Item no 3803
T1 8854; 12 x 8mm; Green
Decorated, non-diagnostic. Reticella rod
containing opaque yellow spirals.

Item no 3804
T1 8865; 16 x 6 x 1mm; L.Green
One other body fragment.

Item no 3805
T2 9734; 10 x 6 x 1mm; L.Blue

Item no 3806
T1 8870; 3 x 1 x 1mm; L.Green

Item no 3807
T1 11789; 8 x 5 x 1mm; L.Green

Item no 3808
T1 8876; 5 x 2 x 1mm; Colourless

Item no 3810
T1 8900; 5 x 4 x 1mm; Colourless

Item no 3811
T1 8774; 4 x 3mm; Red
Decorated, non-diagnostic.

Item no 3812
T1 9852; 5 x 2 x 1mm; L.Green

Item no 3813
T1 9854; 4 x 1 x 1mm; Opaque

Item no 3814
T2 9818; 4 x 2 x 1mm; L.Green
Some iridescence.

Item no 3815
T2 9935; 25 x 11mm; L.Green
Funnel series. Rounded rim. Rim thickness
3mm. Estimated diameter 80mm. Slightly
outsplayed and inturned.

Item no 3816
T1 9884; 11 x 3 x 2mm; Opaque White
Some burning.

Item no 3817
T1 9885; 2 x 2 x 1mm; L.Blue

Item no 3818
T2 9957; 1 x 1 x 1mm; Colourless
Waster. Droplet.

Item no 3819
T1 9868; 4 x 1 x 1mm; L.Green

Item no 3820
T1 9900; 5 x 2 x 1mm; L.Green

Item no 3821
T1 10003; 14 x 5 x 1mm; L.Blue

Item no 3822
T2 9945; 6 x 3 x 1mm; Opaque
Weathered surfaces.

Item no 3823
T1 10013; 7 x 4 x 1mm; L.Blue

Item no 3824
T1 8785; 4 x 3 x 1mm; L.Green
One other body fragment.

Item no 3825
T2 10007; 10 x 8 x 1mm; L.Green

Item no 3826
T1 C10024; 16 x 13 x 1mm; L.Blue

Item no 3827
T1 10028; 5 x 3 x 1mm; L.Blue

Item no 3828
T1 10017; 7 x 4 x 1mm; Colourless

Item no 3829
T1 9886; 4 x 2 x 1mm; L.Green

Item no 3830
T1 10025; 9 x 7mm; L.Blue
Funnel series. Rounded rim. Rim thickness
2mm. Slightly outsplayed and inturned.
Decorated with reticella rod containing
opaque white spiral applied to top of rim.

Item no 3831
T1 10008; 4 x 4 x 1mm; L.Green

Item no 3832
T1 10043; 2 x 2 x 1mm; L.Green

Item no 3833
T2 9909; 4 x 2 x 1mm; L.Green

Item no 3834
T1 10105; 5 x 2 x 1mm; L.Green

Item no 3835
T2 10155; 13 x 5 x 1mm; L.Green

Item no 3836
Unknown; 5 x 3 x 1mm; L.Green
One other body fragment.

Item no 3837
T2 10080; 11 x 9mm; L.Blue
Funnel series. Tubular rim. Rim thickness
3.5mm. Slightly outsplayed and smoothed on
inside.

Item no 3838
T1 8867; 5 x 3 x 1mm; L.Green

Item no 3839
T1 10223; 7 x 2 x 1mm; L.Green

Item no 3840
T1 10225; 17 x 5mm; Dark Opaque
Decorated, non-diagnostic.

Item no 3841
T1 10230; 3 x 3mm; L.Green
Decorated, non-diagnostic. Evidence of
opaque yellow marvered trail.

Item no 3842
T1 10237; 7 x 3 x 1mm; L.Blue

Item no 3843
T1 10250; 5 x 3 x 1mm; L.Blue

Item no 3844
T1 10248; 5 x 1 x 1mm; Colourless

Item no 3845
T1 10306; 4 x 2 x 1mm; L.Green

Item no 3846
T2 10364; 6 x 2 x 1mm; L.Blue

Item no 3847
T1 10318; 6 x 3 x 1mm; L.Green
Some iridescence.

Item no 3848
T1 10310; 6 x 3 x 1mm; L.Blue

Item no 3849
T2 10381; 3 x 1 x 1mm; L.Blue

Item no 3850
10344; 2 x 1 x 1mm; L.Blue

Item no 3851
T1 10341; 8 x 6 x 1mm; L.Blue

Item no 3852
T2 10416; 5 x 3 x 1mm; L.Blue

Item no 3853
T2 10447; 3 x 1 x 1mm; L.Green

Item no 3854
T2 10524; 2 x 1 x 1mm; L.Blue

Item no 3855
T2 10554; 4 x 3 x 1mm; L.Blue

Item no 3856
T2 10555; 11 x 7mm; L.Blue
Funnel series. Rounded rim. Rim thickness
2mm. Slightly outsplayed and inturned.

Item no 3857
T2 10558; 9 x 7 x 1mm; L.Green
One other body fragment.

Item no 3858
T2 10600; 5 x 3mm; L.Blue
Funnel series. Rounded rim. Rim thickness
2mm.

Item no 3859
T1 10594; 19 x 10 x 1mm; L.Blue
One other body fragment.

Item no 3860
T1 8892; 3 x 2 x 1mm; L.Green

Item no 3861
T1 10782; 18 x 12 x 1mm; L.Green

Item no 3862
T2 10951; 7 x 6mm; L.Green
Decorated, non-diagnostic. Reticella rod
containing opaque white spiral. Red
clouding.

Item no 3863
T2 10291; 7 x 4 x 2mm; Opaque
Some iridescence.

Item no 3866
T2 11286; 6 x 4 x 1mm; L.Blue
Three other body fragmnets.

Item no 3867
T1 11416; 4 x 1 x 1mm; L.Green

Item no 3868
11414; 8 x 2mm; Opaque Red
Decorated, non-diagnostic.

Item no 3869
T1 11442; 3 x 2 x 1mm; L.Green

Item no 3870
11615; 2 x 2 x 1mm; Colourless

One other body fragment.

Item no 3871
T1 11616; 8 x 7 x 1mm; L.Green

Item no 3872
11630; 6 x 4 x 1mm; L.Green
One other body fragment.

Item no 3873
T2 11597; 9 x 6mm; L.Green
Decorated, non-diagnostic. Opaque yellow
marvered trail.

Item no 3874
T1 11410; 6 x 5 x 1mm; L.Blue

Item no 3875
T1 11632; 4 x 2 x 1mm; L.Green

Item no 3876
T1 11753; 5 x 3 x 1mm; L.Green

Item no 3877
T2 11598; 24 x 19mm; L.Green
Funnel series. Rounded rim. Rim thickness
2mm. Slightly outsplayed.

Item no 3878
11757; 6 x 3 x 2mm; L.Green
Heat frosted.

Item no 3879
T1 11755; 19 x 3mm; L.Blue
Decorated, non-diagnostic. Horizontal
opaque yellow marvered trail.

Item no 3880
T1 11650; 6 x 4 x 1mm; L.Blue

Item no 3881
T1 11781; 7 x 4 x 1mm; L.Green

Item no 3882
T2 11286; 6 x 5 x 1mm; Opaque
Some iridescence. One other body fragment.

Item no 3883
T1 9867; 3 x 2 x 1mm; L.Blue

Item no 3884
T1 8640; 3 x 3 x 1mm; L.Green

Item no 3885
11786; 3 x 3 x 1mm; Colourless

Item no 3886
T1 10335; 3 x 1 x 1mm; L.Green

Item no 3887
T1 8626; 3 x 2 x 1mm; L.Blue

Item no 3888
T1 8776; 4 x 1 x 1mm; L.Blue

Item no 3889
T1 10768; 4 x 4 x 1mm; L.Green

Item no 3890
T1 11863; 6 x 3mm; L.Blue
Decorated, non-diagnostic. Dark streaking
within metal.

Item no 3891
T1 11867; 7 x 4 x 1mm; L.Green

Item no 3892
T1 11878; 5 x 4 x 1mm; L.Green

Item no 3893
T1 11879; 4 x 3 x 1mm; L.Blue

Item no 3894
T2 8850; 5 x 3 x 1mm; L.Blue

Item no 3895
T1 11887; 12 x 10 x 1mm; L.Green

Item no 3896
T2 12103; 8 x 8 x 1mm; L.Blue

Item no 3897
T1 12113; 5 x 4 x 1mm; L.Green

Item no 3899
T1 12140; 5 x 4 x 4mm; L.Blue

Item no 3900
T1 11436; 6 x 5 x 1mm; L.Green

Item no 3901
T1 10319; 9 x 6 x 1mm; L.Blue

Item no 3902
T1 12112; 7 x 3 x 2mm; L.Green

Item no 3903
T1 12136; 4 x 3 x 1mm; L.Green

Item no 3904
T1 12157; 16 x 15mm; Green
Other vessel type. Pronounced carination in
body.

Item no 3905
T1 12133; 6 x 4 x 1mm; L.Green

Item no 3906
T1 11644; 12 x 6 x 1mm; L.Green

Item no 3907
T1 12145; 6 x 2 x 1mm; L.Green

Item no 3908
T1 12200; 10 x 3 x 1mm; L.Green

Item no 3909
T3 12321; 6 x 4 x 2mm; L.Blue

Item no 3910
T1 12285; 8 x 7 x 1mm; L.Blue

Item no 3911
T1 12300; 18 x 8 x 2mm; L.Green

Item no 3912
T3 12357; 6 x 2 x 1mm; Colourless

Item no 3913
T3 13192; 6 x 5 x 1mm; L.Blue

Item no 3914
T3 12528; 16 x 10mm; L.Green
Funnel series. Rounded rim. Rim thickness
2.5mm. Slightly outsplayed and inturned.

Item no 3915
T3 13080; 3 x 2 x 1mm; L.Green

Item no 3916
T1 8635; 11 x 5 x 1mm; L.Green

Item no 3917
T3 C12967; 15 x 14mm; L.Green
Decorated, non-diagnostic. Applied arcaded
trail.

Item no 3918
T1 8637; 3 x 3 x 1mm; L.Green

Item no 3919
T1 11441; 4 x 4 x 1mm; L.Green

Item no 3920
T1 12734; 16 x 10 x 1mm; L.Green

Item no 3945
T1 8634; 10 x 6 x 1mm; L.Green

Item no 3946
T3 11966; 4 x 3 x 1mm; L.Green

Item no 3948
T1 10781; 5 x 4 x 1mm; L.Green

Item no 3949
T1 10117; 5 x 4 x 1mm; Opaque
Non-durable fragment. Irridescent.

Item no 3953
T1 11230; 9 x 4 x 1mm; L.Green

Item no 3960
T2 C8600; 10 x 6mm; L.Blue
Decorated, non-diagnostic. Opaque yellow
marvered trails and blobs.

Item no 3961
T1 C8967; 6 x 5 x 2mm; L.Blue

Item no 3962
T2 C8600; 31 x 22mm; L.Blue
Funnel series. Rounded rim. Rim thickness
2mm. Estimated diameter 120mm. Slightly
outsplayed. Eight body fragments.

Item no 3963
T2 C8600; 28 x 23mm; L.Green
Funnel series. Rounded rim. Rim thickness
2.5mm. Estimated diameter 100mm. Slightly
outsplayed. One associated rim fragment and
four body fragments.

Item no 3964
T3 C12303; 9 x 8 x 1mm; L.Blue

Item no 3965
T1 C8419; Opaque Black (see Fig 18)
Bead. 8 examples. Hexagonal of maximum
diameter 2mm and thickness 3mm. Diameter
of perforation 1mm. Probable spacers.

Item no 3966
T2 8545; 9 x 8 x 1mm; L.Green

Item no 3967
T2 8564; 2 x 1 x 1mm; L.Blue

Item no 3968
T2 8569; 6 x 5 x 1mm; L.Green

Item no 3969
T2 8574; 2 x 2 x 1mm; L.Green

Item no 3970
T2 8588; 4 x 2 x 1mm; Opaque
Weathered surfaces.

Item no 3971
T1 8789; 3 x 1 x 1mm; L.Green
One other body fragment.

Item no 3972
T1 8865; 2 x 1 x 1mm; Colourless

Item no 3973
T1 8900; 2 x 1 x 1mm; L.Green

Item no 3974
T1 9884; 2 x 2 x 1mm; L.Green
Some burning.

Item no 3975
T1 10028; 5 x 3 x 1mm; L.Green

Item no 3976
Unknown; 3 x 3 x 1mm; Dark Opaque

Item no 3977
T1 10223; 5 x 4 x 1mm; L.Blue

Item no 3978
T1 10225; 7 x 4 x 1mm; L.Green

Item no 3979
T1 10230; 6 x 2 x 1mm; L.Green

Item no 3980
T1 10248; 3 x 2 x 1mm; L.Green

Item no 3981
T2 10364; 5 x 3 x 1mm; L.Green

Item no 3982
10344; 1 x 1 x 1mm; Colourless

Item no 3983
T2 10447; 3 x 1 x 1mm; Opaque
Some iridescence.

Item no 3984
T2 10554; 8 x 4 x 1mm; L.Green

Item no 3985
T2 10555; 10 x 4mm; L.Green
Funnel series. Rounded rim. Rim thickness
2mm. Slightly outsplayed and inturned.

Item no 3986
T1 8892; 2 x 1 x 1mm; Colourless

Item no 3987
T1 10782; 17 x 12 x 1mm; L.Blue

Item no 3988
T2 11286; 4 x 3 x 1mm; L.Blue

Item no 3989
T1 8776; 2 x 1 x 1mm; Colourless

Item no 3990
T1 12140; 8 x 8 x 2mm; L.Green
Two other body fragments.

Item no 3991
T1 12133; 4 x 3 x 2mm; L.Blue

Item no 3992
T3 13080; 4 x 3 x 1mm; L.Blue

Item no 3993
T1 12888; Opaque Black
Bead. Hexagonal of maximum diameter
2mms and thickness 1mm. Diameter of
perforation 1mm. Probable spacer.

SOU 177

Item no 11
Context 20; 15 x 15mm; L.Green
Funnel series. Rounded rim. Rim thickness
2mm. Slightly outsplayed. Decorated with
horizontal opaque yellow marvered trails.

Item no 12
Context 20; 17 x 15mm; L.Blue
Funnel series. Rounded rim. Rim thickness
3mm. Estimated diameter 90mm. Slightly
outsplayed and inturned. Two fragments.
One associated body fragment.

Item no 18
Context 106; 14 x 7 x 1mm; L.Blue

Item no 74
Context 116; 10 x 9mm; L.Blue
Decorated, non-diagnostic. Applied trail and
opaque yellow marvered trails.

Item no 84
Context 10; 16 x 12mm; L.Blue
Funnel series. Rounded rim. Rim thickness
2.5mm. Slightly outsplayed.

Item no 87
Context 101; 20 x 7mm; L.Blue
Funnel series. Rounded rim. Rim thickness
2mm. Estimated diameter 100mm. Slightly
outsplayed and inturned. One associated
body fragment.

Item no 108
Context 1; 30 x 26mm; L.Green (see Fig 12)
Funnel series. Base fragment. Showing pontil
mark of diameter 12mms. Late form. Some
iridescence. Eight associated body sherds.

Item no 137
Context 140; 17 x 13 x 1mm; L.Blue

Item no 143
Context 44; 16 x 11mm; L.Green
Funnel series. Rounded rim. Rim thickness
2mm. Slightly outsplayed and inturned.
Some surface iridescence.

Item no 153
Context 156; 16 x 4 x 1mm; L.Green
Some iridescence.

Item no 185
Context 165; 13 x 9 x 1mm; L.Blue

Item no 191
Context 172; 30 x 20mm; Dark Green (see
Plate 4 and Fig 7)
Funnel series. Rounded rim. Rim thickness
2.5mm. Estimated diameter 80mm. Slightly
outsplayed and inturned.

Item no 203
Context 172; 23 x 12mm; L.Blue
Funnel series. Tubular rim. Rim thickness
3.5mm. Estimated diameter 100mm. Slightly
outsplayed.

Item no 243
Context 183; 15 x 14mm; Dark Green
Decorated, non-diagnostic.

Item no 248
Context 216; 12 x 6mm; L.Green
Decorated, non-diagnostic. Combed opaque
white marvered trails. Some iridescence.

Item no 281
Context 182; 29 x 22mm; Dark Green (see
Plate 4)
Funnel series. Rounded rim. Rim thickness
2.5mm. Estimated diameter 80mm. Slightly
outsplayed and inturned.

Item no 283
Context 136; 13 x 5 x 1mm; L.Blue

Item no 286
Context 167; 21 x 14mm; Dark Blue
Other vessel type. Rounded rim fragment.
Rim thickness 2mm. Possible tall vessel.

Item no 288
Context 169; 14 x 13mm; L.Blue
Decorated, non-diagnostic. Applied arcaded
trail.

Item no 299
Context 195; 14 x 10mm; L.Blue
Decorated, non-diagnostic. Applied trail.

Item no 300
Context 257; 12 x 10 x 1mm; L.Green
Some iridescence.

Item no 311
Context 147; 27 x 26mm; L.Blue
Funnel series. Rounded rim. Rim thickness
2.5mm. Estimated diameter 100mm. Slightly
outsplayed and inturned. Decorated with
applied reticella rod containing opaque white
spirals on top of rim.

Item no 327
Context 304; 17 x 12 x 1mm; L.Blue
One other fragment.

Item no 337
Context 191; 23 x 19mm; L.Blue
Funnel series. Rounded rim. Rim thickness
3mm. Estimated diameter 90mm. Slightly
outsplayed and inturned.

Item no 343
Context 102; 19 x 18mm; Dark Green
Decorated,non-diagnostic.

Item no 357
Context 102; 12 x 9mm; L.Blue
Funnel series. Rounded rim. Rim thickness
2mm. Slightly outsplayed and inturned.

Item no 359
Context 319; 11 x 7mm; Colourless
Decorated, non-diagnostic. Horizontal
opaque yellow marvered trails.

Item no 385
Context 243; 15 x 14 x 2mm; L.Blue
Some iridescence.

Item no 393
Context 102; 33 x 27mm; L.Blue
Funnel series. Rounded rim. Rim thickness
3mm. Estimated diameter 100mm. Slightly
outsplayed. Dark streaking within metal.

Item no 394
Context 328; 11 x 11mm; L.Blue
Funnel series. Rounded rim. Rim thickness
2.5mm. Slightly outsplayed. Dark streaking
within metal.

Item no 395
Context 328; 18 x 7mm; L.Green
Other vessel type. Pronounced carination in
body.

Item no 406
Context 102; Opaque Dark (see Fig 18)
Bead. Cylindrical of length 6mm. Diameter
9mm. Diameter of perforation 2mm.
Decorated with marvered opaque yellow
crossed waves.

Item no 408
Context 325; 28 x 20mm; L.Blue (see Fig 6)
Funnel series. Tubular rim without cavity.
Rim thickness 3.5mm. Estimated diameter
120mm. Slightly outsplayed and flattened on
inside. Decorated with opaque yellow
marvered blob, presumably termination of
trail. One body fragment.

Item no 409
Context 332; 35 x 24mm; L.Blue
Funnel series. Rounded rim. Rim thickness
2.5mm. Estimated diameter 100mm. Slightly
outsplayed and inturned.

Item no 418
Context 243; 14 x 13mm; L.Green
Funnel series. Rounded rim. Rim thickness
2mm. Slightly outsplayed. Heat crazed.

Item no 419
Context 362; 29 x 20mm; L.Blue
Funnel series. Rounded rim. Rim thickness
2.5mm. Estimated diameter 100mm. Slightly
outsplayed and inturned. Decorated with
reticella rod containing opaque white spirals
applied to top of rim.

Item no 421
Context 102; 19 x 12mm; L.Blue

Funnel series. Rounded rim. Rim thickness
2.5mm. Estimated diameter 90mm. Slightly
outsplayed and inturned.

Item no 432
Context 412; 9 x 6 x 1mm; L.Green

Item no 436
Context 485; 37 x 22mm; L.Blue
Decorated, non-diagnostic. Dark streaking
within metal. Some iridescence. One other
body fragment.

Item no 439
Context 439; 12 x 11 x 1mm; L.Blue
One other fragment.

Item no 443
Context 460; 20 x 20mm; L.Blue
Other vessel type. Fragment of pushed base
from small jar(?).

Item no 487
Context 449; 30 x 18 x 5mm; L.Blue (see
Fig 13)
Other vessel type. Formed as handle or rod
with one side flat and the opposing surface
convex. Decorated on convex side with
marvered(?) opaque white strip applied
longitudinally along centre. Possibly Roman.

Item no 498
Context 540; 32 x 25mm; L.Blue (see Plate 4
and Fig 9)
Funnel series. Rounded rim. Rim thickness
3mm. Estimated diameter 120mm. Slightly
outsplayed and inturned. Decorated with
horizontal opaque yellow marvered trails and
darker streaking within metal.

Item no 504
Context 519; 11 x 8 x 1mm; L.Blue
Six associated fragments.

Item no 514
Context 365; 25 x 13mm; L.Green
Funnel series. Rounded rim. Rim thickness
3mm. Estimated diameter 80mm. Slightly
outsplayed.

Item no 516
Context 545; 16 x 13 x 1mm; L.Blue

Item no 517
Context 549; 28 x 23mm; Green (see Fig 6)
Funnel series. Tubular rim without cavity.
Rim thickness 4mm. Estimated diameter
100mm. Slightly outsplayed and inturned.
Red clouding within metal.

Item no 546
Context 140; 21 x 9 x 1mm; L.Green

Item no 561
Context 307; 33 x 28 x 1mm; L.Blue

Item no 568
Context 365; 17 x 3 x 1mm; L.Blue

Item no 575
Context 343; 14 x 10 x 1mm; Colourless
Some iridescence.

Item no 581
Context 713; 12 x 6 x 1mm; L.Blue

Item no 585
Context 750; 12 x 6 x 2mm; L.Blue

Item no 593
Context 626; 36 x 21mm; L.Blue (see
Fig 17)
Decorated, non-diagnostic. Applied trail
5mm wide and partial opaque yellow
marvered trails. One associated fragment.

Item no 594
Context 724; 10 x 3 x 1mm; L.Blue

Item no 611
Context 521; 21 x 11mm; L.Green
Funnel series. Tubular rim. Rim thickness
4mm. Slightly outsplayed and flattened on
inside. Some iridescence.

Item no 619
Context 652; 38 x 12mm; Brown/Yellow
(see Plate 4 and Fig 14)
Other vessel type. Tubular rim. Rim
thickness 5mm. Estimated diameter 60mm.
Folded inwards and flattened on inside.
Evidence of applied horizontal trailing below
rim. Probably small jar. Some iridescence.

Item no 649
Context 347; 27 x 15mm; L.Blue (see Plate 4
and Fig 5)
Funnel series. Tubular rim without cavity.
Rim thickness 6mm. Estimated diameter
110mm. Rim folded inwards to form right-
angle. Decorated with applied horizontal
trails of same colour as vessel.

Item no 651
Context 811; 12 x 8 x 1mm; L.Blue

Item no 656
Context 792; 13 x 9 x 1mm; L.Green

Item no 670
Context 825; 30 x 26mm; L.Green (see Plate
7 and Fig 12)
Funnel series. Base fragment. Showing pontil
mark of diameter 15mm. Some iridescence.

Item no 696
Context 349; 9 x 7mm; L.Blue
Funnel series. Rounded rim. Rim thickness
2.5mm. Slightly outsplayed. Dark streaking
within metal.

Item no 697
Context 608; 14 x 13mm; L.Blue
Decorated, non-diagnostic. Applied trails.

Item no 742
Context 820; 12 x 9mm; L.Blue
Decorated, non-diagnostic. Red streaking
within metal.

Item no 780
Context 260; 26 x 12mm; L.Green
Funnel series. Tubular rim. Rim thickness
5.5mm. Estimated diameter 90mm. Slightly
outsplayed.

Item no 782
Context 899; 26 x 13mm; L.Blue (see Fig 16)
Decorated, non-diagnostic. Traces of reticella
rods with opaque white spirals. Some opaque
yellow marvered spread, presumably from
termination of trails.

Item no 806
Context 1017; 9 x 7mm; L.Blue
Decorated, non-diagnostic. Applied trail.
Some iridescence.

Item no 816
Context 1028; 43 x 35mm; L.Blue (see Plate
7 and Fig 11)
Funnel series. Base fragment. Showing pontil
mark of diameter 19mm. Decorated with
applied vertical trailing terminating at base.
Some iridescence.

Item no 822
Context 536; 33 x 5 x 1mm; L.Blue
Adjacent to rim.

Item no 838
Context 838; 15 x 12 x 1mm; L.Blue

Item no 839
Context 1071; 21 x 19mm; L.Green
Funnel series. Rounded rim. Rim thickness
2.5mm. Estimated diameter 80mm. Slightly
outsplayed. Some iridescence.

Item no 846
Context 846; 23 x 12 x 3.5mm; L.Blue
Some iridescence.

Item no 855
Context 445; 15 x 11mm; L.Blue
Funnel series. Tubular rim. Rim thickness
3.5mm. Slightly outsplayed. One associated
body fragment.

Item no 941
F248; 6 x 4 x 1mm; L.Blue
One other fragment.

Item no 944
F223; 8 x 3 x 1mm; L.Blue
Some iridescence.

Item no 945
F273; 6 x 4 x 1mm; L.Blue

Item no 1008
T1 F25; 9 x 4 x 2mm; L.Green
Some iridescence.

Item no 1011
T2 F362; 8 x 6 x 1mm; L.Blue
Four other small fragments.

Item no 1020
T1 F467; 29 x 14 x 1mm; L.Blue
Some iridescence.

Item no 1021
F256; 7 x 2 x 2mm; L.Blue

Item no 1022
T1 F519; 6 x 5 x 1mm; L.Blue

Item no 1024
T1 F538; 12 x 6 x 1mm; L.Blue

Item no 1027
T2 F664; 12 x 11 x 1mm; Green
Decorated, non-diagnostic. Applied
horizontal trail.

Item no 1028
T2 F667; 12 x 11 x 1mm; D.Green
Decorated, non-diagnostic. Applied trail.

Item no 1034
T1 F1091; 6 x 4 x 1mm; D.Green

Item no 1035
F556; 6 x 5 x 1mm; Bright Blue
Decorated, non-diagnostic.

SOU 184

Item no 16
T2 61; 31 x 14mm; L.Blue
Decorated, non-diagnostic. Vertically applied
reticella rod containing opaque white spirals.
Possibly tall vessel.

Item no 46
T2 79; 12 x 11mm; L.Blue
Decorated, non-diagnostic. Evidence of
applied trailing.

Item no 65
T2 62; 33 x 25 x 3.5mm; L.Blue
Window fragment. Grozed along one edge,
flame rounded on another. Some surface
weathering and frosting. Possibly re-used
Roman piece.

Item no 74
T2 81; 34 x 13mm; L.Green
Funnel series. Tubular rim. Rim thickness
2mm. Estimated diameter 100mm. Slightly
outsplayed and flattened on inside.

Item no 85
T1 234; 14 x 12mm; L.Blue
Decorated, non-diagnostic. Evidence of
applied trailing.

Item no 97
T1 234; 13 x 5 x 1mm; L.Blue

Item no 109
T2 263; 11 x 9mm; L.Blue
Funnel series. Rounded rim. Rim thickness
2mm. Slightly outsplayed and inturned.

Item no 129
T1 420; 42 x 14mms; L.Blue
Funnel series. Tubular rim. Rim thickness
4mm. Estimated diameter 90mm. Partial
cavity only. Slightly outsplayed.

Item no 136
T2 387; 12 x 3mm; Green
Decorated, non-diagnostic. Fine opaque
yellow marvered trail.

Item no 137
T1 208; 30 x 26mm; Dark Green
Decorated, non-diagnostic.

Item no 154
T2 487; 12 x 4 x 1mm; L.Blue
One associated fragment.

SOU 254

Item no unknown
Context 2574; 6 x 4 x 1mm; Opaque
Devitrified.

Item no unknown
Context 2853; 6 x 4 x 1mm; Opaque
Devitrified.

Item no unknown
Context 3055; 3 x 2 x 1mm; Colourless

Item no unknown
Context 3563; 20 x 20 x 2mm; Colour?
Window (?) fragment. Possible cut edge.
Possibly post-medieval.

Item no unknown
Context 4404; 49 x 11 x 2mm; L. Blue
Window fragment, possibly in original shape
of quarry. Slight red discolouration in one
place. Heat distorted.

Item no 113
Context unknown; opaque
Small granules of devitrified material.
Possibly non-durable glass.

Item no 262
T2 147; L. Green
Funnel series. Partial tubular rim.

Item no 297
T2 154; Dark Opaque
Decorated, non-diagnostic. Opaque yellow
marvered trail

Item no 933
Context unknown; 21 x 8mm; Opaque
yellow/opaque pink
Cylindrical bead. Central perforation of
diameter 2mm. Formed from alternate
opaque yellow and opaque pink spirals.

Item no 1109
T3 2775; L. Green

Item no 1279
Context unknown; 9 x 5 x 1mm; Colourless
Probably modern.

Item no 1314
Context unknown; 8 x 5 x 1mm; L. Blue
Some surface devitrification. Post medieval?

Item no 1315
Context unknown; 9 x 4 x 1mm; Colourless
Some surface devitrification. Post medieval?

Item no 1380
Context unknown; 25 x 19 x 2mm;
Colourless/L. Green
Exhibiting possible evidence of mould
blowing.

Item no 1397
T4 455; L. Blue
Decorated, non-diagnostic. Evidence of three
applied trails.

Item no 1876
T4 1375; L. Blue

Item no 2162
T4 747; L. Blue
Decorated, non-diagnostic. Possible evidence
of marvered trail.

Item no 2379
Context unknown; 5 x 3 x 2mm; Opaque
Devitrified, probably medieval.

Item no 2380
Context unknown; 2 x 2 x 1mm; L. Blue

Item no 2381
Context unknown; 4 x 4 x 1mm; L. Blue

Item no 2383
Context unknown; 5 x 5 x 1mm; Colourless
Possible evidence of surface marvering.
Some weathering.

Item no 2385
Context unknown; 10 x 8 x 2mm; Opaque
Heavily weathered and devitrified, also
possibly burnt. Non-durable glass.

Item no 2480
Context unknown; 1 x 1 x 1mm; L. Green?

Item no 2481
Context unknown; 2 x 2 x 1mm; Opaque?
Weathered.

Item no 2564
Context unknown; < 1 x 1 x 1mm; Opaque?

Item no 2567
Context unknown; 1 x 1 x 1mm; Opaque?
Weathered.

Item no 2568
Context unknown; 4 x 1 x 1mm; Opaque
Weathered.

Item no 2570
Context unknown; 4 x 4 x 1mm; L. Blue
One other fragment. Slight surface
weathering.

Item no 2589a
Context unknown; 5 x 4 x 1mm; L. Blue
One of ther fragment. Slight surface
weathering.

Item no 2589b
Context unknown; 5 x 3 x 1mm; Opaque
Devitrified, non-durable glass.

Item no 2590
Context unknown; 1 x 1 x 1mm; Colourless

Item no 2593
Context unknown; 2 x 2 x 1mm; L. Green
Slight surface weathering.

Item no 2607
Context unknown; 6 x 3 x 2mm; L. Blue

Item no 2608a
Context unknown; 7 x 4 x 2mm; Opaque
With associated flake. Devitrified, non-
durable glass.

Item no 2608b
Context unknown; 6 x 2 x 1mm; L. Blue
Some surface weathering.

Item no 2641
T4 934; L. Blue

Item no 2692a
Context unknown; 5 x 3 x 2mm; Opaque
Partly devitrified.

Item no 2692b
Context unknown; 3 x 3 x 2mm; Colourless
Partly devitrified.

Item no 2693
Context unknown; 4 x 4 x 1mm; Colourless

Item no 2695a
Context unknown; 5 x 3 x 1mm; L. Blue

Item no 2695b
Context unknown; 4 x 1 x 1mm; Opaque
Devritified.

Item no 2768
T4 2592; L. Blue
Decorated, non-diagnostic. Evidence of
applied trail.

Item no 2770
T4 1320; L. Blue
Decorated, non-diagnostic. Evidence of
applied trail.

Item no 2776
Context unknown; 6 x 5 x 1mm; Opaque
Surface weathering and some devitrification.

Item no 2804
T4 1316; L. Blue

Item no 2925a
T4 1306; L. Blue

Item no 2925b
T4 1317; L. Blue

Item no 2926a
T4 1297; L. Blue
Decorated, non-diagnostic. Evidence of
applied trail.

Item no 2926b
T4 1318; L. Blue
Funnel series. Tubular rim.

Item no 2926c
T4 2480; L. Blue

Item no 2927
T4 1319; L. Blue

Item no 2934a
T4 2610; L. Blue
Decorated, non-diagnostic. Possible ribbing.

Item no 2934b
T4 2611; L. Blue

Item no 2947
T4 2612; L. Green

Item no 2957
T4 2613; L. Green

Item no 2997
T4 1387; L. Blue

Item no 2998a
T4 1389; L. Blue

Item no 2998b
T4 2614; L. Blue

Item no 3038
T5 1134; L. Blue

Item no 3380
T5 1277; L. Blue

Item no 3812
T5 2382; L. Blue

Item no 3816
T5 2482; L. Green

Item no 3825
T5 2615; L. Blue

Item no 4399a
T5 1671; L. Blue
Decorated, non-diagnostic. Evidence of
mould-blown ribbing.

Item no 4399b
T5 1672; L. Blue

Item no 4399c
T5 1673; L. Blue

Item no 4399d
T5 1674; L. Blue

Item no 4399e
T5 1675; L. Green

Item no 4399f
T5 1676; Olive Green
Other vessel type. Probably fragment of
bowl form.

Item no 4399g
T5 1677; L. Blue

Item no 4401
T5 2696; L. Green

Item no 4408
T5 2483; L. Blue
Decorated, non-diagnostic. Decorated with
reticella rod containing alternate opaque
yellow and opaque white spirals.

Item no 4409a
T5 1683; L. Blue

136

Decorated, non-diagnostic. Decorated with reticella rod containing opaque white spiral.

Item no 4409b
T5 1697; L. Blue

Item no 4409c
T5 1698; L. Blue
Probably from near rim.

Item no 4409d
T5 1699; L. Blue

Item no 4417
T5 2386; L. Blue
Decorated, non-diagnostic. Decorated with opaque yellow marvered trail.

Item no 4533
T5 1691; L. Blue

SOU 349

Item no 6
Context unknown; 27 x 7 x 1mm; L. Blue
Decorated, non-diagnostic. Decorated with applied arcaded trail of diameter 5mm.

Item no 7
Context unknown; 37 x 13 x 1mm; L. Green
Funnel series. Tubular rim. Rim thickness 2mm. Estimated diameter 190mm. Rim smoothed on inside and outsplayed.

Item no 17
Context unknown; 35 x 23 x 1mm; L. Blue
Decorated, non-diagnostic. Decorated with applied arcaded trail of diameter 5mm.

Item no 36
Context unknown; 27 x 11 x 1mm; L. Green
Funnel series. Tubular rim. Rim thickness 3mm. Estimated diameter 180mm. Outsplayed.

Item no 37
Context unknown; 20 x 7 x 1mm; L. Blue
Decorated, non-diagnostic. Decorated with applied arcaded(?) trail of diameter 3mm containing dark streaking.

Item no 41
Context unknown; 12 x 9 x 2mm; L. Green

Item no 79
Context unknown; 18 x 17 x 1mm; L. Blue
Decorated, non-diagnostic. Red streaking evident.

Item no 83
Context unknown; 19 x 12 x 2mm; L. Blue
Decorated, non-diagnostic. Red streaking evident.

Item no 121
Context unknown; 18 x 10 x 1mm; L. Blue
Decorated, non-diagnostic. Decorated with opaque yellow marvered trail.

Item no 126
Context unknown; 47 x 25 x 2mm; L. Blue
Other vessel type. From near base, showing pontil mark. Decorated with applied vertical trails of thickness 5mm.

Item no 131
Context unknown; 13 x 9 x 1mm; Blue
Decorated, non-diagnostic. Dark streaking evident.

Item no 142
Context unknown; 51 x 38 x 2mm; L. Blue
Other vessel type showing pushed base and evidence of applied spiral trailing and dark streaking. Probably small flask or jar.

Item no 143
Context unknown; 21 x 6 x 4mm; Blue
Decorated, non-diagnostic. Part of extruded trail?

Item no 145
Context unknown; 18 x 6 x 1mm; L. Blue
Probably mound-blown.

Item no 146
Context unknown; 11x 6 x 1mm; L. Green

Item no 147
Context unknown; 21 x 5 x 1mm; L Blue

SOU 412

Item no 5
Context unknown; 8 x 6 x 2mm; L. Blue
Decorated, non-diagnostic. Decorated with reticella rod containing opaque yellow and opaque red spirals.

1946-1951 sites

1946-51 Item no 101b
Muller Waterman Unstratified; 11 x 9 x 1mm; L.Blue
Decorated, non-diagnostic. Dark streaking within metal.

1946-51 Item no 101a
Muller Waterman Unstratified; 36 x 31mm; L.Green
Funnel series. Base fragment. Showing pontil mark and wad. Mark diameter 11mms.

? Item no 112
Context unknown; 29 x 14mm; Blue
Other vessel type. Rim fragment. Rim thickness 5mm. Estimated diameter 120mm. Rim folded outwards leaving cavity. Slightly outsplayed. Decorated with horizontal opaque yellow marvered trails. Bowl or small jar.

Index

Page numbers in italics refer to illustrations or tables